MONAST
REDEMP
LIGUORI

THY KINGDOM COME

To
JESUS, MY KING
and
MARY, MY QUEEN

THY KINGDOM COME

A SYNTHESIS OF THE PRINCIPLES AND
PRACTICES OF THE SPIRITUAL LIFE

By
THE REV. BERNARD J. KELLY, C.S.Sp.
Director of House of Philosophy, Kimmage, Dublin

265
KE

A Selection of

THE SPIRITUAL BOOK ASSOCIATES
with the permission of

BURNS, OATES AND WASHBOURNE, LTD.

DUBLIN *and* LONDON

PERMISSU SUPERIORUM RELIGIOSORUM

Nihil obstat ... ... GEORGIUS D. SMITH, S.T.D., Ph.D.,
Censor deputatus.

Imprimatur ... ... EDWARDUS MYERS,
Vic. Cap.

Westmonasterii

Printed in the U. S. A.
THE SPIRITUAL BOOK ASSOCIATES
381 Fourth Ave., New York 16, N. Y.

CONTENTS

INTRODUCTION

THE christian life is explained in revelation by means of many comparisons, all of which have, ultimately, the same deep meaning, but are at the same time sufficiently diversified to provide our feeble minds with many alternative possibilities of understanding its sublime nature. The purpose of this present book is to take one such image—that namely of the Kingdom of heaven, in which God is King and we are subjects —and to show how it may be used by souls as the framework of their spiritual synthesis. Even a cursory reading of the Gospel tells us that the image of the kingdom was most dear to Our Blessed Lord. He realized its power of gripping minds to which human loyalties mean more than do the divine. And since human nature remains ever the same in what is really fundamental in its constitution, we may believe that were He on earth to-day He would have no occasion to forsake it in place of a clearer one. He would find, we may be sure, that nothing more than the magic of His voice would be needed to give to such words as " King " and " Kingdom " the power to inflame hearts with a spirit of love and sacrifice in the service of their God.

Certain points, such as the nature of the Gifts of the Holy Ghost and the Sacraments, which I have treated more fully elsewhere, receive here nothing more than that amount of attention which is demanded by their immediate context. Those who desire further details will find them in the books to which I refer. May it be permitted me, in conclusion, to pay merited tribute here to the memory of the late Fr. Kearney, C.S.Sp., to whom more than to anyone else I am indebted for whatever understanding I have of the idea of God's royal right to man's service. Submission to the Will of God was the theme in all his conferences ; and in our years of studentship he considered it his great duty as director to impress it upon our minds in season and out of season. To him and to all those of my confrères who have been so unstinted in their assistance and advice, my deepest thanks are due.

HOLY GHOST MISSIONARY COLLEGE, KIMMAGE, DUBLIN. *The Feast of the Annunciation,* 1943.

THY KINGDOM COME

CHAPTER I

THE KINGDOM OF THIS WORLD

" *Thou hast crowned him with glory and honour : and hast set him over the works of thy hands*" (Ps. 8, 6).

MAN has an extraordinary power of perceiving nobility and worth where they exist only in shadow and of ignoring them when they appear in substance. The reason may be that the shadows demand only his admiration, whereas the substance demands something that costs, his respect, namely. If this be the reason, one more of the puzzling problems of human psychology finds its ultimate answer in the fact of original sin. For original sin is such that it leaves the intellect more free to detect the good than the will is to follow it. Hence it is that we can admire the royal nobility of the untamed beast while we ignore the kingship of our fellow men. It costs nothing to admit that a beast is noble. No matter how noble it may be, it will be killed when its death is profitable. Its nobility is understood as shadowy and relative. But admit that a man is a king and you are in face of unpleasant obligations. If a man be a king at all, he is a real king. To admit his kingship is to admit in one's world a value which is independent of one's thought and will. It is to place a limit to what one's ambition may achieve, to place a bound which one's greed is forced to respect. And the result is what might have been anticipated : for the hundred who will admit the royalty of the brute termed by men the king of the beasts, there is scarce one who will admit the royalty of man whom God has made king of the visible creation. It is thought safe to play with make-believe, but the corner-stone of reality is seen to be hard, and it has been known to crush.

To regard a beast as a king, even of beasts, is anthropomorphic. The bearing of an animal appears noble when we interpret it as proceeding from intellect and will. In itself it lacks true nobility ; just as the stately palm is stately only because it looks like a stately human being. But this particular anthropomorphic error points to a very vital truth. To make a brute a king you need only clothe it with humanity. Any humanity will do. There is no need to seek out the humanity of a well-known hero and make it serve as substance to the shadow-royalty of the brute. The port of the lion would be kingly were it supported by nothing more than the humanity of a beggar. There must be a reason why this should be so. And like most reasons for fundamental things it is not far to seek if one has eyes to see. It is nothing less amazing than this, that every man is a king, lacking but the trappings of stately port and flashing eye to make what is so clear to God and angels visible to the kings themselves.

For, to be king over all that is lower than man, it is sufficient to be endowed with reason. When God made man He gave him reason, that he might be a king. The Psalmist is struck with admiration at the majesty of the works of God's hands. And greater than any work of God on earth is man, for God has achieved in man the miracle of a creature who is also a king. It is a little thing to have made beasts and birds and fishes, for their worth is of a day. But to have made man— that was something that only an Almighty God could have done. " What is man that Thou art mindful of him ? . . . Thou hast made him a little less than the angels, Thou hast crowned him with glory and honour : and hast set him over the works of Thy hands. Thou hast subjected all things under his feet, all sheep and oxen : moreover the beasts also of the fields. The birds of the air, and the fishes of the sea, that pass through the paths of the sea " (Ps. 8, 5–9). This kingship of man over all that is lower than himself is based on the fact that man alone of the creatures of this earth has reason. Reason is the lowest of the knowing powers which is capable of grasping the order and interrelation of things. Below reason is sense, which can only grasp and react to what is immediately present, without conscious co-ordination of present reaction to future needs. Above reason is pure intellect. And though we may, if we wish, say that the angels, by the very elevation of their natures are kings of all the material creation, and even of man, they could conceivably have been segregated by God from its life and activity, so that their kingship, if such there be, is more a title of honour than an office of necessity. But man is necessarily king of the world, because his nature—half spirit and half animal—demands that he consort with two creations, the creation of matter and the creation of spirit. In so far as he is animal he needs the lowly company of the weak things of God ; but in so far as he is spirit he cannot mix with them otherwise than as their master. The secret of man's kingship is, therefore, the demand of a soul that must perforce move among bodies. Man has need of matter ; but only that he may use it. His whole being craves for the company of the material ; but only that he may reign in its midst.

To be a king, then, in this very real sense, it is sufficient that man have reason. Reason gives him the power of proposing to himself an end to be achieved, and of grasping the way in which he may make things lesser than himself help him to the attainment of the end he has so selected. The kingly dignity lies in this capacity : the exercise of kingly power comes into being the moment he determines the use of anything. If we are so often unconscious of man's kingly nature, the reason is that we do not reflect sufficiently on the momentous implications of our simplest act of choice. Do we but sharpen a pencil to write an unimportant note we have declared our kingship over matter. We have asserted that we have the right to subject it to our needs and wishes. We are its masters, its kings. And if this be true of us who but sharpen the pencil, what is not the kingship of him who fells the forest giant and of him who bursts into the secret recesses of the earth's bosom ? Such exercises as these of a well-nigh despotic power over nature are so common as to have lost their splendour in our eyes. There is little of kingly feeling in most of our woodmen and miners. They look rather to the fact that they are the slaves of their masters than that they are the masters of the universe. And never having learned their true dignity they aspire no higher than to be cogs in a pseudo-impartial machine. Their minds are not their master's, and by their minds they are kings. Chain their minds and they are utter slaves : and the tragedy of their lives is that to chain their minds there is no need to use force, for they themselves inevitably succumb to the magic of a shining fetter.

Besides this kingship of man over matter which is the prerogative of every man, there is another kingship of man over man, which, in the very nature of things, can be the prerogative of but one in every group. Whereas the kingship of all over matter is based on the capacity of all to use matter for the end of each, the kingship of man over man is based on the need of finding one who will direct all to the end of all. Each man has his own end, attainable with the help of material things. His end being inviolable he has necessarily the right to use such things in the way and measure in which they are indispensable to him. In addition, however, to his need of material things, man has need of the help of his fellow-men His intellect being weak, he cannot arrive at an adequate control of the material necessities of life if left in isolation ; while there is still less possibility of his attaining to his full intellectual stature by the path of solitary reflection. His bodily powers are weak, also, and gain by union with those of other men, weak though they too may be. No one man could build the pyramids of Egypt, seeing that to bring a cow to the fair is a task for a man and a dog. Further, his will is weak. He has not got the grit to strike out alone on venturesome paths. He will throw up an undertaking if it become protracted. He will slither out of his whole moral panoply unless he can see someone else who wears it with success. No matter how you view the powers of any one man they stand to gain by the help of those of other men. In consequence it is a necessity of human nature that men come together in groups for the sake of common good : that is to say, to establish an order of things the end of which will be to make it possible for each to attain his individual end. That they should so come together is a necessity not merely for that abstraction, the common good, but for that which is utterly concrete, the good of each individual.

When men come so together they may unite under a king. I do not mean to say that no other form of government is possible for them ; nor do I even mean to insist, as might be done, that government by a king is the best form of government. It is sufficient for our purpose to admit that government by a king is one of the possible political forms. That is enough to enable us to inquire reasonably what it is in any particular man that enables him to fulfil worthily the offices of this more specific type of kingship.

If we abstract from the titles to power—that is to say, if we abstract from the question of whether or not a king may become such legitimately by the mere fact of being a child of the preceding monarch, or whether conquest will ever give a right to kingship, and other questions of the kind—if we abstract from these and similar considerations, we arrive at the striking conclusion that such kingship is based on nothing more than what serves as the foundation of the universal kingship of every man. Ultimately, and essentially, this kingship also is based on the possession of reason. For all that is required to govern a State well is to understand the end of the state and to direct its members in accordance with the dictates of justice. Whoever has a moderately well developed intellect can grasp the end of the state. He will be able to see also how this can be achieved by the co-operation of its members. He will see, therefore, how he should rule them. It may be necessary to ask the advice of experienced men when individual questions of exceptional difficulty arise. But this does not prove that reason is not a sufficient basis for kingship. It shows instead that, though reason may need to be fortified by reason, it has no need of anything foreign to itself. It is not for us to prove now that it is better to be ruled by one man—even if he does need to ask advice—than by many, who need advice just as much as the one ever will. Let us simply accept kingship as a possible form of government. Reason will be its basis.

When, therefore, God created man and endowed him with reason, He made him a king. He gave him a power of directing and apportioning based on reason's ability to grasp the idea of end and the subordination of everything that can be a means to what is an end. All men have this power ; there remains only in practice that the occasion be given them in which it will be physically possible for them to exercise it. Had man never fallen by the sin of our First Parents this kingship of his over the material world would have been one of his noblest titles. It is a splendid thing to be allowed to share with God the work of governing the universe ; to feel that the world is an instrument at the keyboard of which we stand, and that according as we touch key after key the divine melody of creation rings forth in obedience to our wills. It is a still more splendid thing to rule human souls, to share with God His moulding of eternal destinies. That is real power : to fashion an eternal work. Whoever is king over men is a fashioner of souls. His work will endure. His work will shine forth in the clear radiance of heaven for all eternity. All men will see what he has done and marvel that man could perform so stupendous a task. But man has debased his kingship. Whether in his rule of things or his rule of men, man, as sin has made him, tends to produce chaos. And so there arises what is known as the Kingdom of this world—the torment of the sinner and the child of his sin.

A point emerged when we spoke of the kingship of man over man which was still in the background when we spoke of his kingship over things : I refer to the need for justice in a king of men. To be a king of things seems at first sight to demand nothing more than intellect. But to be a king of men demands not only clarity of intellect but impartiality of will as well. The moment we even think of one man in control of others there flashes upon our minds the vision of power exercised tyrannically or favours conferred in disregard of merit, and we realize at once that great though be the king's need of prudence, no less is his need of justice. But what is so evidently true in the one case is no less true, though far less evident, in the other. There can be abuse of power over things no less than of power over men, and the reason of the former will be the same as that of the latter, injustice, namely, in the will. Where the will is allowed to follow the bent of a fallen nature, rule will always be bad, no matter what be the character of the subject. It is part of the dire consequences of sin, that man, who, if he had remained in God's friendship, would have ruled the universe under God and led it to its predestined end, has now an unhappy tendency to introduce into the world that lies beneath his hands as much as he can of the confusion that reigns in his own soul. Man who was made a king has become, and makes himself, a tyrant. Every man tends to be a fomenter of rebellion not only within himself, but within as much of this world as he can gather beneath his standard as well. Man is chaotic in himself and tends to produce chaos. And the root of this is once more his reason : but now a fallen reason ; a darkened understanding and a weakened will.

Having reason, man can set up ends. But his intellect being darkened he tends to err in deciding what is the true end, and his will being weak he tends to adhere to an end that offers an immediate and easy gratification rather than one that will afford true happiness at the price of sustained effort. The effect of sin was to turn the will of man back on man himself. Before his sin man sought God and himself in God : after his sin man seeks self and makes self his god. Whether man be fallen or unfallen he seeks happiness. But unfallen man seeks it in God and in all things in subordination to God, whereas fallen man seeks it in self and in all things in subordination to self. This is the truth so luminously set forth by St. Augustine in his memorable words : " Two loves have built two kingdoms : love of self, even to the point of contempt of God, the Kingdom of this world ; love of God, even to the point of contempt of self, the Kingdom of Heaven " (*De Civitate Dei*, Bk. XIV, Chap. 28). The law of man's being is to love ; and he cannot love without establishing a kingdom. If he loves God, and uses his reason, illuminated by faith, to see how to set all things under God, he establishes the Kingdom of God on earth : if he loves self and uses his reason, darkened by sin, to see how to establish all things under self he establishes the kingdom of this world. Left alone he can establish the one kingdom ; with the help of grace he can establish the other. But the underlying principle of both is the same : love of an end and the marshalling of all things else in its service.

The outstanding feature of the Kingdom of this world, in so far as the aspect of it which we intend to study at the present moment is concerned, is that the conscious aim of every man who lives for it is to be a king, but the inevitable effect is that he becomes a slave, and that of the very things which he imagines are the subjects of his will. There is in this a fitness so divine that we cannot conceive of any other logical issue to the machinations of human ambition. If man dethrones God from his soul, and peoples the court won by this sacrilege with what should be the servants of Him he has dethroned, it is not strange that the Almighty, Who allows foolish men to seem to have their day, should use the courtiers of the usurper, man, to detrone their master and make him taste the bitterness of quelled rebellion. And, in acting so, God acts as we feel He should. When we read in history that usurpers are undone by their own creatures we feel that that is the fate which justice demands for them. One rises to power by the brute violence of an inebriated mob, and dies after but a little while at their hands when their first fury is replaced by another no less base. Another rises by promises, and falls by greater ones. Again another rises, the choice of an army, and dies at the hands of another army's choice. It has always been so, and always will be so. Enslave what you may in the service of self, it will rise up against you and crush you. The lesson of rebellion which man teaches nature is one that nature learns easily.

Should we seek examples of this unvarying rhythm of rise and fall in the Kingdom of this world, we need but turn to the pages of the Gospel. St. Luke gives us one in the parable of the rich man narrated by him. " The land of a certain rich man brought forth plenty of fruits. And he thought within himself saying : What shall I do, because I have no room where to bestow my fruits ? And he said : this will I do : I will pull down my barns, and will build greater ; and into them I will gather all things that are grown to me, and my goods. And I will say to my soul : Soul, thou hast much goods laid up for many years, take thy rest ; eat, drink, make good cheer. But God said to him : thou fool, this night do they require thy soul of thee. And whose shall those things be that thou hast provided. So is he that layeth up treasure for himself, and is not rich towards God " (Lk. 12, 16–21).

The man in this parable is one who established the kingdom of self on the basis of riches. He began, perhaps, in a moderate way. He felt the need of happiness—or he may have termed it self-expression. However he formulated his ambition, it amounted to the kingship of his self. Looking around on the world he sought a means to establish his kingdom, and saw goods and riches. They could be made serve his purpose; his reason taught him that. With sufficient goods, with moderate riches—far be it from him at this early stage even to think of anything savouring of greed—self would be safe. Not only would it be safe, but acquisition, and still more possession, would be an exercise of dominion, and hence gratifying to self. If goods and riches be really things that count, and self has made them tributary, then self is a king in very truth. Goods and riches are not the end. No man is so great a fool as to make them an end in the absolute sense. They are but a means. Self is the end. They provide self with a kingdom in which to rule and with the weapons to overthrow whoever might dare interfere with that kingdom.

There is an amazing depth of human psychology in the way in which the parable develops. The land of the rich man brought forth plenty of fruits. His kingship is apparently secure beyond possibility of question. And yet it is at this precise moment that, unknown to the man himself, his enslavement is being brought about. For the very extent of his riches entitles them to dictate to their would-be master. He sees that he has no room for them; that he must make provision for them. He is no longer absolute lord. They, too, have demands to make. They are his riches; but he must busy himself about them and their administration. His life begins to slip from his grasp. Even the self for which he has laboured so long and so toilsomely recedes into the background. He may not live now as he wills, for there are barns to be built and crops to be gathered into them. And all that he can offer self is the measure of happiness that riches will dole out : times of rest, of eating, drinking, and good cheer. There is the royalty of the rich man : a dowager-like existence at a new and upstart court. Self sought expression through riches, by converting them into the docile tools of its higher nature. It lived to see them dictate first self's message, and then finally its very being.

This is the invariable sequence of events in the life of the man whose love of self leads him to establish a kingdom built on riches. Money seems at first sight to promise all that he desires. With a little money he will be independent of other men ; he will be able to provide for all reasonable needs ; he will secure his future ; he will, in other words, be raised above the servitude of the circumstances of life—he will be a king, in however small a way. And were God his aim in all this, it is true that he would arrive at the desired kingship. But with self as end it is impossible. For if the happiness of self be made to depend on the possession of riches—in no matter what amount (and that is what is meant in practice by building one's kingdom upon them) riches are invested necessarily with an absolute importance. If they, and they alone, will make self king, then self cannot be king without them. They are, therefore, from the very outset, of as much importance to our conscious life as self is. It is but a single step from this stage to that in which they pass from being the condition of happiness to being its measure. They are sought to cause happiness, but being sought exclusively they inevitably determine the nature and extent of the happiness that is sought. He who sets his heart on riches deprives himself of the possibility of finding genuine happiness outside them. He can be as happy as riches can make him, and no happier : and the day will come in his life when he will know that the happiness they give is sharpest pain.

In the person of Pilate we meet another type of the kingship of this world. History inclines us to believe that Pilate was a place-hunter. He was a man who sought to satisfy self by giving it the gratification of office. He was hardly by nature first and foremost an unjust man ; though being a weak one he could be guilty of injustice on occasion. But above all things else he desired to hold office. That was the one thing that really did count in his eyes. And he was capable of any act if only its performance was necessitated by some danger to his position. That is Pilate as we know him. Let us conjecture how he started on his path.

The glitter of Roman officialdom it must have been that first ensnared him. The story of a triumph awarded by the senate, the sight of a magistrate in all the glory of state ceremonial, a tale of the power of officials in the colonies—something of this kind must have gripped him when his mind was young and impressionable, and he felt with that rare certainty bred of desire as much as knowledge, that the life of a victorious general, or magistrate, or high official was the one that would yield him lasting satisfaction, and raise self to the pinnacle of glory. We can imagine the caution of his early years, the application to duty, the scrupulous fidelity to orders. These were the means to take possession of office and to hold it. He would spare no pains to make preferment his docile slave. Position after position would fall to him, until he would finally stand forth in his own eyes, and perhaps even in the eyes of the world, as a master and a king.

It is hard to say how much importance he would have paid to the Person dragged before him by the Jews that day of their Pasch, were it not that his wife upset him a little. It is true that he could hardly have failed to notice that the Jews, at least, seemed to think this occasion was one of more than usual importance. But he must have felt, around that time, that he was at the turning point of his career, and that should normally have made him either supremely contemptuous, or irritatingly inquisitive—we cannot say which, exactly. Procurator of a difficult province, he had everything to hope from his successful term of office there. His ambition was near its realization. He would be the king he wished to be. Now there comes before him this strange Criminal. And Pilate, inspired by the cries he heard on every side, troubled by his wife's message, asks the strange question which betrays an interest in the Jew before him he would normally have never felt: "Art Thou a King then?" What a depth of unplumbed irony in that question! One, whose unformulated will was to be a king, faces the true King and asks Him how could He by any chance lay claim to the coveted title. For not the first time in the life of Our Lord the two kingdoms were brought face to face. In Pilate was the kingdom of this world, built on love of self; in Jesus was the Kingdom of Heaven, built on love of God even to the emptying of self. Pilate did not recognize before him the true royalty which he so intensely ambitioned. And a cry went up from the mob, a sharp snarling threat from the priests, and Pilate, feeling that his kingdom reeled, condemned the King of Glory to death.

Poor Pilate ! To save office and self he condemned the Son of God. A few years later, office compelled him to exasperate the feelings of his subjects. They complained at Rome and he was deposed. His uneasy thirst for power led him of necessity to compromise his power. His very desire to make his position secure, issued in a brutality that made further tenure impossible.

The figure of Pilate at the trial of Our Saviour recalls inevitably him who betrayed the Lord, Judas. For in him, too, we see the battle of the Kingdoms, and the apparent triumph of the kingdom of this world producing the most complete and catastrophic overthrow of self its king.

Judas, like the rich man in St. Luke's Gospel, lived under the spell of money. He must, too, like Pilate, have felt the attraction of power, and probably looked forward, as did the more open sons of Zebedee as well, to the day when he would be somebody in the Kingdom of the Messiah. But the gospel account of his fall is most explicit in its references to his love of money, and it is on that therefore that we shall concentrate in this present study.

The chief suggestiveness of the story of Judas lies in the detail that he fell through a desire for money which, in point of fact, never succeeded in bringing anything even approaching affluence. The rich young man of Luke's narrative fell through the empire of possessed riches quite as much as through the desire of riches yet to be acquired. But Judas never succeeded in acquiring anything at all proportioned to the patient waiting and the real inconveniences of his three years of service among the disciples of the Lord. His betrayal, even, earned him no more than about five pounds, even at the most liberal estimate. We read that during the three years of the Public Life of his Master he had acted unjustly and appropriated part of the common funds which had been confided to his care and administration (Jo. 12, 6). But he cannot have become much the richer by what he could pilfer secretly from the already slender resources of Jesus and His disciples. It is probable, therefore, that he never experienced the thrill of power consequent on the actual possession of great wealth. There was never a moment when he could say that he had at length acquired sufficient money to raise him above the buffeting and uncertainty of life. He never was king in fact over any kingdom worthy of the name. And yet he had established a kingdom of this world ; for to do that demands nothing more than that one be a king in desire. He wanted riches, he trusted in them ; therefore he reigned by them, within his heart if not in the eyes of men. He had determined to rear a throne for self and had decided upon the materials out of which he would construct it. It would be a throne of jewels, a throne of gold (were he alive to-day it would have been that most abominable of abominations, a throne of banknotes). In his eyes self was already raised up. He reigned in his own esteem. And is not that the deepest and most lasting of all the ambitions of man : to be a king to oneself, and to warm with the fever-heat of power, felt within even though it burn without a visible glow.

St. Matthew tells us the sad end of Judas' Kingdom. Seeing the dread reality of his betrayal he returned to the Temple with the blood-money. The priests refused to take it back, "And casting down the pieces of silver in the temple he departed ; and went and hanged himself with an halter" (Mt. 27, 5). Reflection had shown him that if there really was a kingdom within him he was not its king. Money had enslaved him and forced him, as it were in spite of himself, into a course of action which now stood out in its true colours. What was still more—he had not even the satisfaction of the feeling that he had served a king worthy of so exalted a name. The money for which he betrayed his God lay where he had cast it, on the floor of the Temple. It was now in his eyes not money but the price of blood. He saw what he had served, and cast it from him. Nothing remained. Self had been raised on the shoulders of money and now it was being trampled under the feet of the price of blood. He went, as we are told, and hanged himself.

These Gospel incidents are either real life or based on real life : two are history and one is a parable. They are stories not without a lesson for all men. The motives that shaped the life of the rich man, of Pilate, and of Judas, are those that determine the lives of a multitude this very day. Two loves are still at work on the face of the earth, and they are the same which served as theme to St. Augustine : love of God and love of self. Love of self is the architect of the Kingdom of this world now as ever. Granted a will that is turned in on self and an intelligence capable of seeing how things may be subordinated to it, nothing more is needed to give a king, a kingdom, and a tragedy.

It is certainly well worth while to insist a little on the point peculiar to the case of Judas : that the kingdom of this world is possible even in the absence of great material achievement. The human soul, even without the gift of grace, is something immeasurably higher than all the lower creation taken together. It is spirit. Spirit is more than matter. Spirit is more than matter even if no matter be actually under its effective control. The poorest man has the power of rising in mind above this earth to despise it, to assert his superiority over it, and to arrest his act there without turning his face a little higher still and bowing down before the majesty of God. To despise this world is to be its king just as much as it is to control it. In fact, there is included in every act of control itself an element of contempt, and this is what makes it appear so royal to us ; for to use the world in the exclusive service of self is to put it far below self. Whether then a man have effective power over much, or over little, or over nothing at all, matters not in the slightest : His kingship is a matter of the spirit. What counts for him is the consciousness of the superiority of his self. Self is stayed up by the world, possessed in fact or hope, or simply used as a term of comparison. That is enough to constitute a kingdom, and it is called the Kingdom of this world.

One may be convinced experimentally of the existence of this kingdom (should it happen that one's conscience does not afford evident proof that there is such a thing) by simply opening one's eyes upon the world of to-day. It is unfortunately possible for each of us to learn that men exist who act as if nothing mattered but their own gratification, and this in matters of even immense moment which happen to be under their control. We need not refer further to such cases. What is of interest to the majority of men is to see how people, only moderately circumstanced whether in the matter of wealth or attainments, can establish a kingdom on their slender resources. For it is a fact that the type of person who can do so is not unknown. It is possible to meet poor men who despise the rich, not through any sense of religious values, but in sheer pride. It is possible, too, to meet stupid people who look down on those who are well-educated : feeling, and rightly, that they cannot compete with them in intelligence, they escape the unpleasant experience of learning anything by stiffening themselves into the attitude that there is nothing which it is worth their while to learn. Ordinary stupidity is but a natural defect and is in itself and necessarily neither a hindrance nor a help to spiritual perfection. But thought out and embraced stupidity stifles the action of the Spirit, because it is pride. Such people have their own private kingdom in which they rule. They have, therefore, no desire to enter God's Kingdom as simple subjects.

A man in a position of only moderate importance can fall into the same fault. It is not rare to meet inferior officials who deck out their persons with airs of business and trappings of circumstance which would be normal only in the head of gigantic concern. There is no question in their case of the air of dignity which is becoming in any Christian. One can sense something more in them. One notices that their peculiar dignity serves only one purpose : to keep all it can overawe at arm's length. It is a moat of defence, like Christian dignity ; but it differs from it in that the treasure it surrounds is not the image of God wrapped up in a human soul, but a self whose greatest joy is to feel that men wonder what exactly it is that the moat hides from them. An air of mystery, of inscrutability, and the shadow of a real power—this is enough to dress self as a king, and the dress is self's greatest concern.

Let the whole question then be summed up in a simple way by stating that wherever self is loved there is a kingdom of this world. This is equivalent to the affirmation that each and every man, as long as he remains on this earth a sinner and tending to sin, is the centre of either an established kingdom or of one in the course of growth or decay. For all sin is ultimately a form of pride. The sin of our First Parents was ultimately that they refused to be subject to God and sought their perfection by the free and unhindered use of some creature independently of God. Their sin, being a personal one which in some mysterious way became also a sin of human nature itself, is the model and cause of all subsequent sin. The man who sins to-day can find no way of doing so other than the old and tried one of turning away from God and drawing some creature to himself. Say if you will that sin is a turning to the creature : it is no less true that it is a laying hold on the creature, the invasion of the creature, a rape of the creature. The sinner turns to the creature that he may make it the instrument of his illicit pleasure. He seeks the creature because the creature can be made to serve. He turns to it in that petty, human, anæmic attempt at pride, which, even as sin, stands so far below the spiritual intensity of Satan's revolt, and glories in having found something weak enough to support his rule for a time—though strong enough, he will one day learn, to drag him from his burlesque throne.

It is part of the punishment of those who would reign in this way on earth that they become, by a natural necessity, the slaves of some creature. But there is a still greater punishment, of the character of which they often fail to be aware, even when it is the cause of their greatest torments. They little know that, even as kings of this world go, there is a greater than they can ever hope to be, one who is a spirit. To rule this world is, for a man, to be at most a tributary princelet. There is a King of this world, in the strictest sense of the term, to whom all other kings are subject. His name is Satan, and he rules to enslave.

CHAPTER II

THE PRINCE OF THIS WORLD

" To thee will I give all this power, and the glory of them ; for to me they are delivered " (Lk. 4, 6).

THE Psalmist, speaking of the dignity of man, indicates as one of his chief excellences that he is a " little less than the angels " (Ps. 8, 6). Man is not the greatest of the works of God, the Author of Nature. Higher than man is, is the angel —so much higher indeed that he need feel it no shame to glory in the mere fact of his resemblance to the angel. Compared with the fact that there is something he holds in common with the angel, all the other prerogatives of man may well seem to him to pale into insignificance. For the angels are so sublime that there is nothing in them except what is the best that is in man, and even this itself is in them in a way which the mind of man cannot fathom. The angels are pure spirits. They have no bodies. Their life is one of intellect and will : of intellect unobscured by sense, and of will unshackled by passion. God made them that, among the works of His hands, there might be some who would show forth in a faintly adequate way the transcendent perfection of His own life of knowing and loving. God's life is to know and to love. He willed to create beings who would share in this life, unhampered by the needs of a lower self ; for the might of the Maker is revealed in His works, and below the angels He had made no creature to show forth as they do, the inner mystery of His life. That there might, therefore, be as full as possible a manifestation of the mystery of the One God, He planned a universe in which He would be revealed not only in the being of stocks and stones, but in the life of men and angels, and more perfectly in the life of these latter than in the life of all men and beasts and plants taken in their rich totality.

It is an opinion favoured by weighty theologians that Lucifer was the highest of these spirits. He was an angel of awe-inspiring beauty and power. His intellect was inferior in range and depth to the Divine Intellect alone. He saw and probed realms of actual and possible being which till that moment had been hidden in the bosom of the Almighty, and which awaited the scrutiny of his piercing eye as the condition of their ever being known by a mind other than that of God. His will had in it something of the inflexibility of the will of God. By his intellect he had a wonderful power of perceiving what was worthy of love, and his will could fix itself with unbending finality on what the intellect approved of. He could have offered a wonderful tribute of praise and love to God. There was no other angel, not even Michael the Archangel, who could have known God as familiarly as he. There was no other will so attuned to the harmony of the Divine attractiveness as his was. He was, if we may so speak, simply made for God ; he had been given a will and an intellect that tended more to God than they did to Lucifer himself, for with their breadth and scope they could rest finally in nothing less than the Infinite. He would have led the other angels in their life of love and adoration. He who knew so much of God, and who would have been so responsive to the claims of the Divine Worth on his praise, would have communicated of his knowledge and his enthusiasm to the world of spirits into which he was born leader. He would have been their model, their inspiration, their teacher. He would have been next after God Himself, link between God and the little ones of the world of angels.

We know that Lucifer sinned and fell. His sin was the most terrible of all sins, angelic pride. The pride of an angel is something to which the most heinous of human crimes can only approximate. For since there is no darkness in the angelic understanding, the angel can never sin in ignorance, nor through ignorance. Neither is there passion in the angel, as there is in man. Man can be whirled, as it were, into sin. Even when he sins freely there can be the extenuating circumstances of the blind, headlong rush of unreflecting sense, that launched him on the way of sin before he was aware of the direction his soul had taken. But the sin of an angel is deadly calm and calculated. There is no headlong rush in the angel's sin. It is a measured step—and one step only—to a clearly conceived goal. All the angel's desire is concentrated in the object of his sin. There can be in man a kind of conflict between sense and will, even in the very sin itself—for sense can tend to what is evil with a violence behind which will can lag—but the angel's desire is fully unified. Its sin is its single choice, made without reserve and irrevocably.

The sin of Lucifer was pride. There was no other sin of which he was capable—no other sin so utterly perverse as to be connatural to a being such as he was. He had no body, and could not fall through a sin of the flesh. Having no body, nor bodily needs, it followed, too, that the goods of our material world could never have led him to sin either. There was but one object sufficiently sublime to ensnare him. That object was his own perfection. He was wonderfully perfect. There was no angel comparable with him. God could have made a greater angel than he, but God had not done so ; and Lucifer represented the summit of creation. God alone was above him ; and Lucifer, ensnared by his own exceeding beauty, willed to make himself like unto God.

The inner character of this angelic sin must ever remain a mystery to men who can sin only in the measure of their inferior capacity. It may be that Lucifer aspired by the exercise of his own powers to that resemblance with God which is obtainable only as a free and merciful donation by the infusion of sanctifying grace. If this be his sin, what makes it essentially diabolical is that he most assuredly knew when sinning that he could not raise himself by nature to what was of grace. His mind was too great to be deceived in this human way. His sin, on this hypothesis, could have been nothing other than the mad self-exaltation of willing to be God-like by a means known clearly as inadequate, and persisting in that will rather than accept a gift from the hands of Divine Mercy. " . . . thou saidst in thy heart : I will ascend into heaven, I will exalt my throne above the stars of God. . . . I will ascend above the height of the clouds, I will be like the Most High " (Is. 14, 13–14). He may alternatively have sinned by making his supernatural perfection consist in the normal exercise of his natural powers. That is to say, he may have turned his eyes away from the possibility that there could be for him a greater perfection than that which he already possessed. Though this sin, expressed thus, is radically the same as the other, there is still a shade of difference between them. The first consists in the desire to achieve grace by the power of nature ; the second is the denial of grace and the assertion of the all-sufficiency of nature. But even in this second form his sin loses nothing of what we have termed its essentially diabolical nature. He cannot have failed to see that God was throned above him on an unscalable height, and that, therefore, there were necessarily modes of participation in the Divine Nature higher than that, even, which he possessed by his magnificent being. His sin cannot have been occasioned by ignorance. It was quite clear to his intellect that a created perfection higher than his was possible ; but his will rejected it. His will would bow before no higher being than himself. God had made him : that he was forced to see. But that God would improve on him : that he would never admit. He could even see that God *could* improve on him : but this thought, too, was intolerable, and he willed the impossible in sheer pride. He willed himself as upper limit in the firmament of creation rather than admit in his own case, what he saw to be inescapably true, that there is no limit to God's creative power, and still less a limit to the power of His mercy.

The revolt of Lucifer spread wide in the world of angels : " . . . and behold a great red dragon, having seven heads, and ten horns : and on his heads seven diadems : And his tail drew the third part of the stars of heaven, and cast them to the earth " (Apoc. 12, 3–4). Here once more the human mind falls back baffled. How can the sin of one angel be the cause of another angel's sin ? And yet we know that it was so : that he who should have led the spirits of the heavens in a hymn of eager and triumphant praise, led many instead into the most barren of all revolts. To what blind futility did the angels' pride not lead them ! It led Lucifer himself to wish absolutely the impossible ; it led his adherents to follow him as leader rather than to submit to God—to submit to a fellow angel giving them the example of stubborn revolt rather than be subject to One on Whom, in any case, they could not but be totally dependent. But though many fell many remained faithful. "And there was a great battle in heaven, Michael and his angels fought with the dragon, and the dragon fought and his angels : and they prevailed not, neither was their place found any more in heaven. And that great dragon was cast out . . . and he was cast unto the earth, and his angels were thrown down with him " (Apoc. 12, 7–9). Michael led the faithful angels, to whom God allowed some share in the overthrow of their rebel brothers. His name is the key to the revolt, for his name means " Who is like to God ? " That name was the principle for which he stood and which Lucifer had assailed. The one accepted the inimitability of God ; the other aspired to share in some way in God's utter independence of being, in God's unique Royalty. The first of all struggles in creation was, in other words, a struggle about a kingdom.

The sin of the angels was ultimately the sin of the kingdom that is not of God : it was the love of self rising up in pride to the kingdom of self. Man will strive to build a kingdom on brittle fame or riches or some bauble of the kind ; for the angels there are but two elements in the drama of the kingdom : self and the powers of self. The Kingdom of the angel will be a kingdom built up by, and reposing upon the angel's mighty powers. Self will be enthroned on what self can be—not, as is the case with man, more on what self can do or self can acquire. For an angel, to be is to achieve its natural perfection. There is no slow process of growth in the angelic nature. In one act the angel is fully, essentially, achieved, and that act is the uninterrupted possession of its natural perfection. It was by that act that Lucifer, and his hosts, willed to reign. They willed that that act should be for them the limit of what was desirable. They willed that that act should raise them for ever above the possibilities of elevation inherent in what is weak and made and dependent. They wished to reign in and through that act of theirs. They would be kings, each angel in his own being ; king over the resources of their nature both in regard to perfectibility and utilization. The Kingdom they ambitioned was, however, insufferable because so utterly intolerant of the unsharable uniqueness of God. It represents the limit to which a created nature has been found capable of rejecting the dominion of the Almighty, and demanded a punishment proportioned to its stark deformity. "God spared not the angels that sinned, but delivered them, drawn down by infernal ropes to the lower hell, unto torments, to be reserved unto judgment" (II Peter 2, 4). God cast Satan and his followers down to hell. Hell was made for them first of all, for hell is that "everlasting fire which was prepared for the devil and his angels" (Mt. 25, 41). There was for them no question of another time of trial. The will of the angel is so strong, so impetuous, that it never renounces its choice. Having selected evil they became, by their own act, confirmed in evil. Evil would be their lot for all eternity. They would taste unendingly the bitterness of their kingdom. They had selected to reign without God, and they would be deprived of God. They would live with self—but now that self would be something very different from what it was before. They had willed badly ; they had willed in defiance of their nature ; and the result of their act will be that their natures, while retaining all their powers, will be strained with a warp of self-inflicted mutilation. Their intellect is as keen as ever : their will has lost nothing of its vigour. But that is no consolation ; rather is it the condition of their pain reaching its maximum intensity. For their keen intellect sees the agonizing vision of what they have lost and what they have become ; their strong will writhes in the grip of what they are and would fain not be. Their torments are the greater the keener their power of realizing what they are and how low they have been dragged by them. To blunt their faculties would be to deaden their suffering. But this condition of relief may never be realized. For it is necessary that a kingdom based on the powers of the spirit be cast down by the tyranny of those same powers over the spirit that tried to enslave them.

The will of the fallen angels is therefore obstinate in evil. They have selected pride, and pride will be their portion for ever. They willed the impossible and were thereby deprived of the possible ; while the impossible of its very nature can never be realized and hence can never yield them happiness. Men are inclined often to chafe at the limitations of their nature. They feel that they are weak, that their wills have but little of unshakableness—and in this they do not deceive themselves. But they forget that there is wisdom in all that God has done. If He made wills, which, viewed in relation to wills He could have made, were weak and unsteady, He gave these wills, in consideration of their weakness, the blessed power of retracting choice. Man is so weak that he may select evil : but God has made him so fortunately unstable that he may renounce this choice. He can select evil and then, under the impulse of salutary regret, turn from evil to good. There is no weakness in the angelic will other than that it may err in its first choice by adhering to evil rather than good. It is entirely free from that weakness of man's, which is an indecision at the core of all decision. The angel's choice is irrevocable. An angel never changes his mind in the matter of moral choice. The angelic nature is created in a state of relative perfection. The attainment of its full perfection is but the matter of a single act. Man is created in a state of humiliating imperfection. He is far from his real end. It will take him many acts to arrive at it. Human perfection, if achieved in the normal way, is not the work of a day but of a lifetime of days. The nature of man therefore allows for progress by slow and tedious stages, whereas the nature of the angel demands that progress be by one single step or not at all. Angels resemble those finely tuned machines which on their first trial will necessarily prove a breath-taking success, or shudder into scrap. Man is a simple and rusty piece of work. He can stop or go ahead ; little has been lost—nothing in fact that is irretrievable—if at his first trial he proves a failure, for his elementary type of motor will bear patching and can come out the better for it. By the very fact therefore that certain angels adhered to evil they lost for ever the power of turning to good. They were too wise to make a choice in ignorance ; too pure to make one in the heat of passion. They chose calmly, though madly. That moment of choice was the last they had of calm, and the first of sharp-toothed madness.

The state of mind of the fallen angel is, first of all, one of hatred of God. Their sin was an aversion from God. They thought to withdraw themselves in some way from their

being so weak, is a patent reproach to an angel if he proves faithful where the latter proved false.

The devils' envy leads them, then, to strive to effect the destruction of man. But it can be noted that in doing this they approach as near as they may to realizing as well what their impotent hatred wills. They cannot harm God in Himself : but they can reach unto Him in His creatures, and this they do by causing that He be banished from souls. The normal result of hatred is the destruction of the thing hated. The devils cannot destroy God ; they can only avert their gaze steadfastly from Him. But they can destroy that presence of God in souls which is rather a presence of souls in God. They can destroy the life of God in souls by grace. But even in doing this they do not touch God as He is in Himself, for grace draws the soul to God without God being changed in any way. And this is what we mean by saying that the presence of God to the soul in the state of grace is rather a presence of the soul to God. Grace sets up a relationship between the soul and God in which only the soul is changed and only the soul reaps an essential gain. God is, as it were, an ocean of life. To be in the state of grace is to be plunged into That Ocean ; but the Ocean remains the same whether the soul be plunged into it or not. The soul alone suffers if it be far from those life-giving Waters. All that the hatred of the devil for God can accomplish is, consequently, to keep souls from God. God does not suffer thereby in Himself. But it is enough for them if His influence in the world be a little less. They can endeavour to destroy what is of God in creation. If they succeed, their hatred will not have been utterly in vain. They will have achieved something, however far removed from their real aim, however petty and pointless considered as an attack on the Transcendent.

Both hatred of God and envy impel the fallen angels to seek the destruction of man. On the one hand they will banish God from the human soul, and on the other, they will wipe out the reproach of a nature weaker than their own rising with the help of God to a fuller understanding and acceptance of reality than was theirs. Their pride, too, enters in here directly ; and just as it sinned at first against the light of evidence, so now also it seeks a glory which is known to be empty. The devils sinned by establishing a kingdom of self in pride : they unfold and develop their sin in this world by attempting to establish, once more in pride, a kingdom over the souls and bodies of men. They know that such a kingdom, if they were to extend it even to the whole human race, could yield them no happiness, no consciousness of true achievement. They know that their fall has been complete. They know that a kingship which leads to the destruction of subjects is no title to self-esteem. But they are so utterly perverse that they persist indefatigably in the establishment of their reign of horror. The reward they seek is truly diabolical : success divorced from achievement ; glory without praise ; laughter without joy ; triumph without victory. Only the devil can seek what is evil just because it is evil—and evil is all he ever seeks.

If we wish to understand how it is that the devil can establish a kingdom over men, the end of which will be their eternal separation from God, it is necessary to recall that his sin, terrible though it was, left him still in the full possession of his natural powers, and that God allows him to exercise those powers in the measure in which His Divine Wisdom sees that to do so is compatible with the reign of His Glory on earth.

The devil retained after his sin his wonderful power of understanding the nature of man and the things of earth. He knows more about the secret resources of this world than do all scientists and all philosophers together. He has an amazing grasp of human psychology. When he came to deal with the very first man, Adam, he saw at once the flaw in his human armour and manœuvred into position most adroitly so as to launch an almost unerring blow. If his understanding of what was in man was such in the case of the first man that ever was—a man, be it noted, far wiser and far more prudent than we are—what is not his grasp of human frailty now after sixty centuries of probing and testing, of scrutiny and invention ? He has found out the weakness of the wise and the foolish. He knows from the way in which we reject one temptation that we are likely to fall in another. He has found out the foolishness of the strong and the weak. He knows from the way we view one attack that a different one will appear quite overpowering. It is true that he does not know all things. But it is quite as true that we, human beings, are the least qualified to determine the limits of his knowledge. It can even happen that Almighty God, or the good angels, will reveal to him things hidden from his view. This never happens except in accordance with the Divine Goodness and Mercy. But when it does happen it arms a foe who rages for our ruin and against whom we can fight only with the arms of God.

To form some idea of the knowledge the devils possess of human nature we need only call to mind the amazing knowledge which even a man can have of what pass as the secret motives underlying the actions of his fellows. There are men who can sum another up with great accuracy after a conversation of a few moments. The nature of man is limited : the number of ruling passions and ruling virtues is far from great. Once one has come to know the broad categories of character one can place men with little difficulty, and foresee their probable reactions to future events. If a man can do this, much more can Satan do it. Human psychology is not really a subject worthy of Satan at all. It is far too elementary for him. He has learned to his cost what angelic psychology is, and he needs but to apply this knowledge, making it more gross, and less uncertain than it is when applied to the angel, in order to have the soul of man as it were an open book before him. It should not be forgotten, of course, that he cannot read the intellect of man ; only God can do that. Neither can he read the workings of grace in our souls. But all that is of sense ; all the images that float through our minds and give body to the thought of what we intend to do and of what we fear, all the words we utter when we think we are alone, all the secrets we have confided to paper, all the words we have whispered in trusty ears—all these are things which he may come to know and understand : and if he can know all this how little of our lives will remain entirely closed to him ?

The devil's knowledge is accompanied by the power to interfere in the course of events here on earth. Spirit can affect matter. The soul of man—and it is the weakest of all the spiritual substances—can set the human body in motion ; can influence it for health or sickness ; can make it serve as the instrument of knowing or as the instrument of passion. The devil can do all this, and do it more completely than the soul can. Knowing as he does the inner natures of bodily things, he can utilize their powers to produce any effect of which they are naturally capable. We are even now only scratching on the surface of things in science and invention. He has long since seen down to the core of cosmic reality and has tamed forces which man will never learn of. He knows how images are formed, how they are recalled, how they are distorted by bodily conditions ; and his will can extend itself to effecting all that his mind can plot and plan. He can call up those nameless fears that owe their origin to a condition of the bodily organism. He can excite movements of passion by interfering with the hidden powers of the flesh. These are ways by which he can act inside man ; and he can act outside him as well. He can perform apparent miracles, can call up pretended visitors from beyond the grave, can overwhelm us with material calamities as he did Job with the permission of God. In short we may say that there appears to be no limit to what he may perform if it be not that he is unable to create or annihilate, and that he has no direct power over the soul and its faculties, nor over grace and its workings. But all that is material whether in man or outside man is his to change and modify in so far as this is possible by the utilization of the hidden powers and laws of nature.

Granted then, as we have shown, that the desire of Satan is the spiritual destruction of the human race, he is wonderfully equipped to take supreme command in the kingdom of this world. Man, even abstracting from the action of the evil one, tends to turn away from God. He does this, as we have seen, by establishing a chimerical kingdom in which self will appear to be king and God will be a foreigner, or rather an outcast. In other words, man tends of himself to do what Satan desires to lead him to do. Man has already a certain inclination towards the end that Satan wills. Nothing more is required then to make Satan supreme prince of this world and of all its petty princelets, than that he allow man to have his way when he follows the yearnings of self, that he spur man on his way when he seems to cool off in his quest of self, and that he oppose obstacles to the way of man when he makes a sincere effort to dethrone self from the heart that was made for God. He does all this by tempting him.

We have seen how he can tempt man. He can tempt him through his sense cognition by calling up, or recalling, images which provoke to sin. He can tempt him through his sense desires by inflaming him with passion, or by filling him with fear. He can tempt him too by surrounding him with calamities, by creating world problems that perplex his mind. Surround a man with strife and pain and you tempt him, as Job was tempted, to curse God and die. Show him a world where evil seems to come on top, where the good suffer, and that most cruelly, and you can lead him to doubt of the very existence of God. Satan can have a hand in all these sad events which make the path of the just man thorny, and widen the narrow way of the fool into the broad and straight road of perdition. Temptation is the devil's weapon for achieving world domination. By it he can direct—or at any rate attempt to direct—men in whatever direction he may will ; and the direction is always the same, away from God. Poor fools that men are ! When they will to be kings of their little lives they are but the pawns in the dire game of the spirit of evil. They think they have selected their path alone : he stood by, looking on at least, probably making it easier for them to see their way to ruin. If there be any kingship of this world it is his and not theirs. They are but his puppets. His hatred of God so far surpasses theirs that their petty bout of spite cannot but be engulfed in his gigantic plan of uncompromising godlessness. He is the ultimate ruler of the lives of sinners. His rule is an easy one while he is as yet kept at a distance by the barrier of dissoluble flesh. He means it to be easy, and knows that it will in fact be easy, for his greatest prudence is to allow men to have their way. He is hardly ever importunate in normal cases. He need but sit in state—with nothing but his fevered eye to betray the nature of that state—and men will throng his throne-room, wearing the while their own fantastic crowns with which he humours them for a brief hour or two. His glee must be intense—even if bitter—as his kingdom spreads. He sinned to acquire a kingship which he knew was chimerical, and now there unfolds before his eyes the wonder of a kingdom into which fools crush their way. As he gazes down into the crowded room he sees one or two grow anxious, he sees them finger their crowns and make as though to lay them aside and flee his presence : a word from him, the prince, and an image floats before their minds : they see the unpleasantness of a life of poverty, the difficulty of self-control, the cowardice of forgiveness : they cease to fret and question, for there is no course open to them but to see their venture to its issue. And Satan lets them be, and turns with interest to the latest pretender to royalty who struts across the floor.

It would be great folly indeed to imagine even for a moment that the case of man must be well-nigh hopeless if there be so powerful a spirit fully intent on destroying him. Satan can do nothing without the permission of God, and we know that God wills all men to be saved, and that He will not allow us to be tempted above that which we are able to support and overcome. Satan is quite powerless against souls who trust in the grace of God. The vision which the Little Flower had of the devil, when she was still a child, convinced her of this. What she learned in this experimental way to be true of herself, is true for all who are in the state of grace, or who are willing to co-operate with grace. The devil is not prince over souls of this kind. He attacks and molests them from outside perhaps, but he does not rule them from within. They are not his subjects ; they are his adversaries. To them he is Satan simply—the adversary. It is necessary to recall in this connection that he has no immediate power over the will of man. He can move sense desires by acting upon the body, but the will is independent of the bodily organs in its essential nature and hence escapes the possibility of falling under his power. God alone can move the will, and He moves the will positively to good only.

St. Thomas explains in his commentary on the words of St. John : " Now shall the prince of this world be cast out "

(Jo. 12, 31), who are the true subjects of the prince of darkness They are, he tells us, those of this world, who despising their true Lord submit themselves to the usurper. They alone are tempted by him in the very interior of their being. It is necessary to pause a moment here in order to understand what St. Thomas means by these last words. He does not mean to say that the devil has immediate power over the wills of sinners. Whether a man be a sinner or a saint the devil can approach no nearer than his sense faculties. But there is this great difference between his way of tempting the one and the other category : he tempts the saint from outside his rational and grace-endowed soul and meets from the soul with nothing but opposition, whereas, though he tempts the sinner from outside his rational soul also, he finds a friend within the camp of the soul itself and a door is opened at once to his emissaries, even if there be no possible entry for himself. The sinner compensates for the fact that Satan cannot rule his soul from within, by ruling it himself in obedience to every dictate issued by Satan from without. Satan is, in a sense, prince by proxy. He rules through his hirelings. But he manages to do so in a way that makes his triumph all the more impressive ; for his hireling is none other than the rightful king of each usurped territory. He rules each self through the possessor of the self, and deludes the possessor into the belief that he alone is ruler. There is a lesson to be learned from puppet shows ; it is that the devil holds the ends of many strings.

One of the many disquieting features of modern times is that the people have no longer a healthy respect for the devil. St. Jude warned us against this mistake in his little-read epistle : " When Michael, the archangel, disputing with the devil, contended about the body of Moses, he durst not bring against him the judgment of railing speech, but said : The Lord command thee. But these men blaspheme whatever things they know not " (Jude 1, 9–10). It is customary nowadays to treat the devil as a joke. If there is one thing which he certainly is not, that thing is a joke. The devil is a very serious person indeed : there is nothing at all in things, as he sees them, to invite him to merriment in his own mind or to pleasantness with others. It is a fact, we must confess, that one cannot come into contact with the popular mind of the Middle Ages without feeling that the devil was held in slight esteem there also. He appears in paintings in a most ludicrous form—at any rate the form appears ludicrous to us, though others might have been impressed—and even in the drama of the time he was used to raise a laugh. Whatever may be said in explanation of this, there is one very significant point of difference between the medieval and the modern laugh at the devil. The man of the middle ages laughed at the devil because the devil was made to look funny : the modern man laughs at him because he thinks he really is funny. And lest the medieval man should have ever been tempted to make the mistake of his modern brother there was always a reminder at the side of even the most ludicrous of devils to hint that he had claws : I refer to the gaping mouth of hell with its miserable victims urged on with forks, or dragged with chains, down into the very depths of a bottomless fire. If one will laugh at the devil, let the laugh be respectful. If one refuses to be respectful, one may guffaw, on condition of quaking a little interiorly. But there is no room for mere hilarity and less still for the knowing grin. Men have forgotten how to love God. They are unlearning that there is a devil. What chance remains of their saving their souls ?

Our Lord pointed out on one occasion, which has been described for us by St. John, what are the characteristic attributes of the devil in his dealings with men. It was the inveterate opposition of the Jews to His doctrine which called forth these words, which, though addressed to a limited audience, are true even if applied to all men : " You are of your father the devil, and the desires of your father you will do. He was a murderer from the beginning, and he stood not in the truth ; because truth is not in him. When he speaketh a lie, he speaketh of his own : for he is a liar, and the father thereof " (Jo. 8, 44). The devil appeared in his genuine colours on the very first pages of inspired history. He was a liar in the garden of Eden, and a murderer on the day that Cain slew Abel. These are his favourite weapons : not indeed that he has no other weapons, for he can use the world and the flesh to serve his designs, but because these two, we may say, are his very own. When he fights alone and in person he fights with lies and with murder : the man who can be overcome by the flesh or by the world hardly needs to be overthrown by the devil in person as well. That he should fight with lies is no strange thing, seeing that he stood not in the truth. He turned his back on truth ; he sinned against the light. He could not delude himself, but he can delude others. He can make them believe what he would like to be able to believe himself, and thus prepare the way for their downfall. He is the Prince of Darkness and of addled minds, and knows that souls captured by false ideas are an easy prey. He became the author of the first false philosophy of human life when he promised Adam and Eve all knowledge, and through knowledge, power, on terms that were simply deceptive. " Be disobedient," he said, " and you will know all things." Those accents are familiar in a thousand more elaborated systems : happiness consists in material progress ; happiness consists in the levelling of distinctions ; happiness consists in the triumph of what is racial ; happiness consists in amoral competition. He has never ceased to make promises. And he always promises the same thing, happiness, on the same condition, revolt. He is the great liberator ; mankind is fettered ; he will set it free. His years of dealing with men have shown him that it is unnecessary to adopt a new line of attack on the masses. A course of action and a promise linked together by a lie—there is his simple formula, and it almost always works. And when it seems to fail he has another weapon. For he is a murderer as well as a liar.

There is hardly any time in the history of the world when there is not slaughter and bloodshed in some country, near or distant, and the good as well as the bad fall victims. In this there is little or no reason to see a special intervention of Satan. But mixed up with such squandering of life there is always a certain amount of wanton extermination of the good which can never be traced back to anything other than an orgy of hatred, seizing individuals for a time and then passing when it has found its victim. And it is not even necessary to turn to times of war to find examples of this. It has been known in times of peace—if those times may be called times of peace when in the absence of a foreign enemy, the faithful were persecuted, hounded down, and put to death by their own fellow countrymen. Such wanton and blind hatred is not human. A man will kill for gain, for revenge, but a man will not normally kill just because he hates without knowing why he hates. When men do kill for this reason, one cannot but feel that the killers, for all their freedom and assent to their action, are urged on by a being who is by nature a hater and a murderer, and that the reason why they cannot understand their frenzy when once it has passed is that in its inner nature it was not their frenzy, but the frenzy of another, who can destroy for the sake of destruction and hate for the sake of hating. Such moments of unbridled hate have marred the course of history from the days of the first martyrs to the days of martyrs we ourselves have known and loved as friends. There is one example however which is unique and unassailable : the death of Our Saviour determined by a mob before Pilate's house. Our Saviour was a Man Whom Satan failed to rule. He had attempted to do so three times of which we have precise knowledge, and each time was repulsed. His rejection on these occasions did not make him lose interest in the Man Jesus. He noted His activities. He saw that were He to have His way, there would be an end to the kingdom of this world and to that of the prince of darkness. When deceit failed to conquer Him—for, after all, deceit was at the root of the three temptations—there remained the great, even if despairing, weapon, death. He must kill this Man, else he would be undone.

Before Pilate's house there stand the two kingdoms of evil, the Kingdom of this world, and the Kingdom of Satan, both identified in the persons of the Jews. The Priests and leaders saw that Jesus threatened their privileges and power, and they wished His death but feared the people. Satan wished His death absolutely. He could bring His death about only through the instrumentality of men, but those who would gladly obey him were held back by fear of the mob. The mob, consequently, must be swung round. Fill the mob with hate and the great ones of the Jews would do the rest. And

then, suddenly, as it were, the mob began to hate. Ask the
mob why they hate? They can only answer with a renewed
" Crucify Him! Away with Him!" Their hate exceeded
the measure of their reasons for hating. It was diabolical.
It was the hatred of Satan that spoke that day by the lips of men.

In spite of his making so many victims to his hatred and
envy, the devil never experiences the slightest feeling of satisfaction. His life is one of unmitigated pain. Pain, in so far as
it is an act of the will, is the will's revulsion from present evil.
The absence of what one desires vehemently, or the presence
of what is opposed to desire, causes pain to the will. The
devils suffer from the loss of God. Their being calls out for
Him. They have turned their wills away from Him, and
in doing so they have put their wills in presence of the evil
of a bad and irrevocable choice, they have given their wills a
warp which tears them asunder while still leaving them sufficient
cohesion to enable them to experience the deadly strain. They
suffer too from the presence of the object they have chosen :
self. Made for God, they are faced with a vision of failure,
and of a failure that is their own. They who had minds to
grasp and wills to adhere to What was noblest, are locked
in the embrace of what is most repulsive. That is a terrible
pain to their sensitive natures—for their natures are sensitive.
It is easy when thinking of the power and majesty of Satan
to forget that he, by the very fact of his sublimity, was made
more keenly susceptible than lesser minds to awareness of the
unutterable horror of evil. He lives now with evil. His
will, made to reject it, is chained to it. Every instant of his
contact with evil is agony—and there is no chance that he
may thrust it aside. Highest, with an almost infinite capacity
for happiness, he has become the lowest, with an almost
infinite capacity for pain.

To these two pains, which, with the pain of hell-fire, are the
essential pains the devils endure, must be added the pain of
seeing man passing unscathed through the trial of life. They
experience no joy when a man falls a victim to their plans :
but they are capable of experiencing pain, when, by the grace
of God, a man succeeds in putting them to flight. The will
of a proud angel revolts violently at the sight of a mere man

who can outwit him. It matters little that man's way of outwitting Satan is to fly to God. That by the grace of God man should fly to God is more than he can bear. He too was given grace and he rejected it. The sight of men who accept grace is a perpetual and humiliating reminder of his moment of folly. A proud man who is a failure cannot tolerate the success, however moderate, of another. If this be so for man, it is doubly so for the angel whose pride is stark and simple. Hence, the throne of Satan in this world cannot but be an uneasy one. The number of his subjects is no satisfaction while as much as a single man escapes. One human soul saved is enough to humiliate proud Satan. What satisfaction will be his if he proves by experience what he knows so well already, that man can fall? But what agony it is to learn by experience, what he wills should not be, that even a single man has been saved! His kingdom, like the kingdoms of this world, becomes his rack. It seemed to be an instrument of glorification : its insatiableness makes it an instrument of torture. Satan cannot escape any more than man the inexorable laws of creature-made kingdoms : he too must suffer at the hands of what he made his slave.

Such is the prince of this world and such is his kingdom. Considered from the side of God, his kingdom over men is a futile attempt to give vent to hatred of God : considered from the side of men, his kingdom is an attempt to work their destruction. As an attack on mankind the kingdom of Satan is something which makes our minds stagger. It is simply an attempt to gather all men into one organization that all may perish. We have had experience of human attempts to destroy the bodily life of limited sections of the human race. We have even experienced attacks on the minds of men, and local or widespread attacks on religion. Satan envisages something bigger than any man has ever attempted. He aims at the ruin of the souls of all men, past, present, and yet to be born. He makes no exceptions—men always do, for reasons of sentiment or through mere whim ; but he has no room for sentiment and he despises whim. His aim is too simple, his formula too elementary, to except any child of woman. All must be sucked into the one current, and dragged and battered by it up to and through the iron gates of Hell. As king, Satan rules with the most easily-stated of aims : destroy all ; let none escape. His kingdom is a web where he sits throned, spider-like, in a corner, never to appear till the victim is so immeshed as to have lost the power to flee. The corner of his web is just beyond the frontier of death. It is there he waits.

CHAPTER III

THE KINGSHIP OF GOD

" For the Lord is high, terrible : a great king over all the earth " (Ps. 46, 3).

IT is a fact of created psychology that there is no way of doing wrong except by copying and warping a way of doing right. There must, therefore, be a deep lesson concealed in the sin of angels and men. For both sinned in the same way, by making self king. And this lesson can only be that there is some self that is truly king, and that their sin consisted precisely in attempting to become by guile what some being was by nature. Their very attempt to become kings shows that not they but someone else is King in the way they ambition. This Person is God. All things are His. All things really do belong to His Self. He is King of Kings. The universe is His to rule and guide.

The kings of this world, who rule over peoples, are in a very true sense as much the servants as the masters of their subjects. The subject must obey the king in all his legitimate commands and ordinances, but the king has no right to command or ordain except in view of the common good. The king is the servant of the common good. His life should be devoted to procuring it. He is what he is for the sake of his people. We need not go far to seek an explanation of why he who is so high must bend so low, and how the king can be both master and servant. The explanation lies in the fact that though the king is in one sense the end of the people, another and higher end has been given to each citizen as well as the person of his king ; that the king himself is less than this end ; and that his function is to procure it for his people. In civil matters the king is the end of his subjects. They are bound under this respect to submit entirely to him. But outside and beyond civil matters are the matters of the soul. Every man, no matter how slight be his importance in the government of the state, has a soul which is greater than the state, for the sake of which the state exists ; and in what concerns the good of the soul—even its natural good—the individual, considered as individual, is greater than the king considered as king. The individual has his own perfection to achieve, and that he achieve it is of infinitely more importance than that he submit to a king, if such there were, who would seek nothing further than the exercise of kingly power.

If from kings of earth we turn our gaze to God we see that He is King in an utterly unique way, because He is a King Who is the total end of the subjects He rules. All things come from the hand of God, and all things ultimately must return to Him. They have ends of their own it is true. They have their own perfection to achieve, their own activities to pursue. But over and above the purpose they achieve when they realize to the full their individual capacities, there is a higher purpose to which all other purposes are subordinated. This higher purpose is the glory of God for which all that has been made came into being. God is King therefore in the unique sense that He is the Principle of all things and rules all things in a way that submits them in their every aspect to Himself. Nothing escapes His over-lordship. He is a Ruler Whose rights are so all-embracing that no action of His can be understood as interference, no demand as excessive.

Man's kingship, as we have seen, is based on the possession of reason. But God does not reason. For to reason, meaning to proceed from one thought to another necessarily connected with it, is an imperfect form of cognition, found only in a being incapable of grasping things otherwise than point by point. Nevertheless God is King ; and the basis of His King-ship is to be sought in the same direction as that in which we found the explanation of the kingship of man. For man is king, not because he knows in an imperfect way, but because he knows sufficiently well to have the ideas of end and means. Any being who can distinguish an end from a means can be a king, because he has, radically at least, all that is required to enable him to establish a hierarchy of values and to put some one value in the place of honour. God became King of a created universe, therefore, when, willing His own Glory as end, He willed the production of things as means to it. He brought a universe into being for a purpose. He subjected it fully to that purpose—so fully that the free beings Whom He created could not escape from contributing to that purpose even were they to abuse their freedom—making thereby His purpose reign over the works of His hand. He reigned Himself in the reign of His purpose, both because it was His, and because it was nothing other than His Glory.

Let us try to glimpse the Mind of God at the dawn of creation. Fulness of life and wealth of being had been His unshared possession since the unnumbered days of eternity. No one had partaken of His life ; no one had known of the treasures of wisdom and knowledge stored up in the Godhead. And God decided, in sheer generosity, to call forth created life and being, that there might be creatures who would share in the marvel of existence, and minds and hearts that would taste of the sweetness of knowledge and love. He willed that all that would come into being should show forth in some faint way His own Divine Nature. He could not but will this, since He was all Being, and to be could only mean to be like Him Who is. All things were destined therefore to show forth His infinite Perfection. Everything that would be would point beyond itself to the Fount of its being. God would be wonderful not only in Himself, but in His works as well. His unspeakable majesty would shine forth in a thousand made reflections as well as in the one great uncreated Ray.

God, Who is the greatest of all artificers, set about making the universe in the most perfect of all ways. He first gave the universe as a whole its end. Then He fitted the various parts into its gigantic framework. As the end of the whole He willed a certain manifestation of Himself. We cannot determine further than this what the end He proposed to Himself was. When we have said that He made all things for His Glory, we cannot go on to explain how much glory He expected from things otherwise than by stating that He willed as much glory as the things He made were capable of giving. Having therefore freely willed a certain degree of eternal glory, He next willed an organization of parts and a distinction of individuals by which this glory would be assured. He willed that there should be angels and men—and that these should be free ; that there should as well be animals and plants and non-living things, all determined in their activity. To all that He made He gave a law, because all that He made had its place to fill and keep in the realization of the purpose of creation. He made things as He did make them because He had decided on the place they were to hold in His scheme of things. The end comes first with God, and the means are selected in view of it. He made angels because He had willed for Himself an external glory which could not be obtained without them : He made them free, and hence capable of sin, because He had willed a glory that could come only from a universe that counted among its parts the miracle of a creature so like to God as to be free, even though so unlike Him as to be subject to abuse of freedom. It was the same with everything else that He made. He made all things as He did make them because if they were other than they were made they would not fit into His plan. He made then angel and man, plant and mineral, because His plan demanded angels and men, plants and minerals. And had He drawn up another plan and willed another glory He would have fashioned a different universe to meet its requirements.

The nature that God gave His creatures was therefore a law. He made them as they were because He wished them to have the manner of being and activity which their nature gave them. Judge the nature of a thing from the side of the thing itself, and the nature is not a law to its possessor. The nature of a thing is not greater than the thing : rather is it but an incomplete expression of its full reality. Consider it, however, as the expression of the Divine purpose, and it is a law. For the Divine purpose is itself a law ; it is what we call the *Lex Aeterna*, the Eternal Law—the order and harmony of things as existing in the Divine Mind, awaiting the moment chosen by the Divine Wisdom to express itself in forms, spiritual and material. We may say then that each thing is to itself the promulgation of the Eternal Law. It comes into being as that law will have it be. It does not first exist and then submit to a code that arises long after the thing itself has been produced. God does not force His Law on an unwilling world. To exist is to exist as the expression of God's idea of how the end of creation is to be brought about.

It is wonderful to think of the Wisdom of God grasping thus, in a single glance, the scheme of all things, past, present, and to come, grasping the conspiration of parts to end, the inner harmony of part with part. Than that Kingship there can be no greater. And what is most wonderful to human minds is not perhaps the way in which all— even evil—fits in with the end, but rather the way in which part fits in with part. For it is easy for man to submit things to an end ; but it is not easy for him to do so without violence to the nature of the parts which he uses to fill places of lesser dignity. In every great business concern there will be men of real talent wasted in positions of comparative insignificance, simply because it is not possible in a man-made scheme of things to place everybody without exception in the place for which his talents equip him. In God's scheme of things nothing is forced into a position for which it was not made. Plants will be sacrificed to the support of animal life. But their nature demands nothing more for them. Being lower they demand but to serve what is higher than themselves. Similarly, animals are subject to man in fact because they were made subject to him in nature. Certain men and certain angels fell from beatitude and would seem to have upset the Divine Plan. But in this too there is no insuperable difficulty—though there be inscrutable mystery—for, as God made them, they were capable of falling, and if they fell they did so through their own fault when they could, with the help of God, have been saved. God's Kingship is therefore just, as well as supremely wise. He gives to every nature the law that its being demands. He expects from every nature what it is capable of giving— that and nothing more. He allows no nature to fail in the achievement of its own peculiar end unless He has endowed it with that freedom by which, if it turns itself away from its end, it does so knowingly and loses thereby the right to accuse Him of injustice Who made it free. And thus He reigns over all things in wisdom and justice, leading them unerringly to the end of Glory which He planned from all eternity, and which neither the frailty of the things of sense nor the perversity of things spiritual can hinder Him from achieving as His Kingly right.

We are not concerned here however with God's Kingship of irrational things, sublime though that be and worthy of so many songs of the inspired psalmist. Our concern is His Kingship over those beings which He endowed with intellect and will. Even from among them we must omit the angels and speak most particularly of man. To understand man's place however it is necessary to retrace our steps somewhat.

The Vatican Council teaches us that God did not create the world to add to His own happiness but rather to manifest His perfection by the benefits which He would confer on creatures. His glory would follow on the manifestation of His perfection, as we have already indicated. But what the Council teaches us, though on the surface so simple, is really difficult to grasp intelligently. For if the end of creation be the manifestation of God's perfections, then to whom does He intend to manifest them? And if we say that He means to manifest them to angels and men, would a universe in which there were no rational creatures at all be possible?

To answer the second question first, we must admit in all simplicity that we do not know whether or not the Divine Wisdom could see a motive for creating a universe in which there would be no intellectual being. Though we can see little or no point in such a universe, we cannot claim to know enough about the things of God to be entitled to decide such a question without the aid of revelation. But there is something that we can say about the universe as God has made it —and this includes the answer to the first of our two questions as well as to the second—and that is, that in the universe which God did create, intellectual beings were not only necessary but were even the proximate end of all things else, and that whereas we can readily enough conceive of a state of things in which there would be angels and nothing lower, we cannot easily conceive of one in which there would be material objects and nothing higher. What we mean to say is that the glory which God sought in the creation of the universe He did make is something which is realized essentially through His intellectual creatures, and that others realize it fully only in so far as they are in some way drawn into the sphere of influence of the world of spirits.

That this is so follows upon the very notion of glory. Glory, as we understand it in the strict sense, is knowledge and praise. The glory which God sought from creation was that creatures might know and praise Him. Now angels can do that even if there be nothing lower than themselves in the universe. Knowing their own natures they have an altogether sublime understanding of the Divine perfections and are capable, as we have seen, of rising to ecstatic heights of praise if only their will submits to the burden of a necessary creaturehood. Hence it is understandable that we should consider a universe of angels as quite intelligible even if there were nothing else in it. Let that suffice by way of comment upon the angels' place in the Kingdom of God, and let us consider now the place of man which is our chief concern.

God could have been satisfied with the voice of praise of angelic hosts. Such a voice is sufficient to give Him glory. But He selected something different. He willed that material things should glorify Him in some way as well. Now, material things have no articulate voice of their own. We can speak, it is true, of God's being praised by birds and seasons and plants. But if we abstract from every implication of an intelligent being somewhere or other who grasps their message, we are indulging in mere metaphor. When we say that they give glory we must imply at least that God Himself understands their mute message. Seeing then that they had no voice of their own, He willed to give them a voice in a being who would be so far a spirit as to have a voice and so far material as to speak in their name. That being was man ; God willed therefore that the glory due to Him from the material universe should come essentially from man. That He should be King of material things meant ultimately to be King of man.

Material things were destined in the first place to support the life of the human body. In this way they contributed to man's praise of God, for without them he would not even have that existence which is the first condition of praise. But such a contribution, necessary though it be, is still far removed from the praise itself. So God in His wisdom made them such that they could excite man to praise God. This second purpose which they have within the framework of the world itself, is the real reason of their being. God made them that they might prompt man to lift his heart up in praise to their Maker. Of themselves they have no access to the inner sanctuary where those live who can give God the glory of a praise that springs from knowledge. But man, who has access to God, lives on the frontier of their world. They can press around the door of man, lie in wait for him with upturned faces, that he may say on their behalf what they cannot say, and that he may say on his own behalf what he has learned from them is his duty and his privilege. It is consequently exact to say that God made material things that they might excite man to give God the glory which was the end of their coming into being. All creation, and each part of creation, finds its meaning in what is highest in the whole or in the part to which it belongs. Man is the highest in the material part. He gives meaning to all that is below him. Through him what is below him arrives at its end. When God rules man, God has that kingship of matter which He desires.

When the universe gives God glory, God reigns in it, because in giving Him glory it subjects itself to Him. But we have seen that that part of it which is material gives Him glory principally through man. We are therefore entitled to conclude that the reign of God in the material universe is principally a question of His reign in man. This is a conclusion at which we might have arrived by more immediate processes of inference. But the way we have selected has its own outstanding merit ; not only does it show in what God's Kingship of the material universe consists most particularly—in the voice of praise of all creation becoming articulate in man—but it indicates too, in what God's Kingship of man consisted. It tells us that His Kingship of man is His right to man's knowledge and love, to the service of man's praise offered by man in his own name and in that of creation. And this is equivalent to saying that the Eternal Law was given to man by his Divine King in a way which differed essentially from that in which it was given to other creatures. The Eternal Law was given to material things as a necessity of nature ; they could not but obey it. It was given to man as something to be accepted consciously. God is King. He is Lawgiver. To accept His Law is to accept His Kingship. God's demand on man was that he accept God's Law for man, and this law was that man serve by praising, that he know and love. God's glory coincided therefore with His Kingship. If man accepts the Kingship of God, the world gives Him glory through man : if man rejects His Kingship, the world, as God made it to be, ceases to fulfil the purpose of its creation.

It is striking to note how the Law of God as participated in material things and as participated in man, though differing, as we have just now indicated, is fundamentally one. I refer to the fact that the law of God for man is no less the law of man's being than is the law of God for any other creature the law of that creature's being. God willed that man should be the voice of material things as well as of an intellectual nature. Hence He made man both spirit and matter. When therefore man becomes the voice of what is material he does what his nature demands of him. Being what he is, he cannot refuse to fulfil his rôle otherwise than at the price of frustrating the urge of his being. When he praises and serves God in the name of creation he is simply doing what his nature demands of him ; he is obeying the law of his being. But the full perfection of his service is that he should not rest in the idea of achieving himself, but should rise to the concept of the law of his being as the expression of the law of His Creator, and obey God as King, not just as the term implicit in his natural tendency. It is however none the less true that there is a remarkable parallelism between the two concepts of law, and that even though man be obliged to obey it as the voice of a Divine Lawgiver, he can profit—and that immensely—by the consideration of it as the law of him also to whom the law was given.

Adam was the first man to whom God gave His law. He was also the first to refuse to accept it. It is well to note that the precise prescription which Adam disobeyed was one bearing upon the purpose of material things. It could not have been otherwise when a wise God commanded a man whose very nature linked with the material. God forbade Adam to eat of the fruit of a certain tree. In God's idea that tree was intended to serve as a special reminder of His absolute rights. Paradise itself was a reminder of so many other of the Divine Attributes : of the beauty of God, of His wisdom, of His power ; and in being such a reminder it played its predestined part as fuel to our first parents' knowledge and love of their Creator. The tree, however, was intended most particularly to recall to them the attribute of His Kingship. It summed up in itself what all the rest of creation was intended to do cumulatively. In it was expressed in crudest terms the place material things should hold in man's esteem. Hence Adam's sin, being a denial of the meaning of that tree, was a refusal to admit God's Kingship over creation and over himself.

Adam should not have sinned against the law of God. He had too many motives for obeying it. There was in the first place the motive of reverence. Who was God, and who was Adam ? If God wills, should not Adam obey ? Is it not utterly unbecoming that nothingness should raise itself up against Being, even if there were no reason for subjection other than æsthetic fitness ? There was as well the reason of justice. Adam had received everything from God. God had therefore a right to dictate terms to him. The tree, too, belonged to God. He had the right to determine its use. Justice demanded that His will in the matter be respected. Were Adam to use his own powers, or the tree, in opposition to God's will, he would misappropriate God's property. There was finally the motive of love. For, after all, Adam, creature and subject though he was, was the King's friend. As friend he was bound by his friendship to lead the way in acceptance of the law of his King. Friendship does not exempt one from obedience to one's sovereign. Rather it makes one punctilious in regard to his wishes. Under all these heads therefore—and they are but a few of many possible ones—Adam was obliged to acceptance of the Divine Law. Adam should have allowed God to rule him.

Adam's sin was, therefore, a refusal to admit God's Kingship ; and he sinned, quite characteristically, by refusing to make himself the voice of a creature's praise, for he converted into an occasion of revolt the tree given him by God as symbol of his obligation to serve. His sin involved essentially a misuse of creation. Things had been brought into being that they might excite him to service of God : he, by his perversity, used the tree of knowledge of good and evil as an excitant to revolt. He thereby failed in the duty peculiar to his position in creation. It was his privilege to be the voice of creation's homage, and this by being responsive to creation's godward beckoning. By making creation the instrument of sin he perverted it to the utmost limit possible. Creation remained good in itself, of course ; but it had ceased to be what it was most of all intended to be, the occasion namely of God's being glorified by man. And to that extent the law of God and the Kingship of God had been rejected on the whole earth. God had endeavoured to enforce His Law by reverence, justice and love. His law had been rejected. It remained to find and impose a new motive for keeping it.

God found the new motive. It was fear. He cast Adam and Eve out of Paradise in anger—though even then there was mercy, too, in God—and bade them till the earth and bring forth children in pain. The old order had passed. A new order was come. But it was not till the law was given to Moses that man was allowed to see the full implications of the act whereby our first parents were banished from Eden.

When God gave Moses what we now term the Old Law, He inaugurated a new reign on earth. He acted then once more as King and Lawgiver. It was His will on that occasion to submit mankind to His rule. But the rule to which He submitted them through Moses was far different from that to which He submitted Adam. Now He ordered as an angry God, as an outraged God. He would have full mercy later and send a Redeemer ; though even now mercy was not entirely banished by wrath. But for the moment His reign would be rather the reign of a Master than that of a Father.

The characteristics of the Old Law are given us by St. Thomas.[1] He tells us that its motive was fear. We have seen that this characteristic of the Old Law was foreshadowed in the punishment of our first parents. It comes into full evidence when we consider the circumstances in which it was given on Sinai : how the people were threatened with death if they were to approach the Mount : how, when on the third day the Lord did speak " thunders began to be heard, and lightning to flash, and a very thick cloud to cover the mount, and the noise of the trumpet sounded exceeding loud : and the people that was in the camp, feared. And when Moses had brought them forth to meet God from the place of the camp, they stood at the bottom of the mount. And all Sinai was on a smoke : because the Lord was come down upon it in fire, and the smoke arose from it as out of a furnace : and all the mount was terrible " (Exodus 19, 16–18). That fear was the motive to obedience to the Old Law is no less evident when we consider the punishments meted out to them that transgressed it. When Ochozias the King was sick he sent a captain of his army with fifty men to take Elias in defiance of the respect due to God's servants, and at the word of the prophet fire came down from heaven and consumed them all. When David in pride ordered a census of the people to be taken that he might know the full extent of his dominion, God sent in punishment a pestilence which carried off seventy thousand of his subjects. One cannot read the Old Testament without being impressed by the fact that whenever the chosen people sinned God did not delay to recall them to obedience by defeat in battle, or by pestilence, or captivity. Fear of punishment was the motive He willed to employ. He would

---

[1] It is to be noted that, for St. Thomas, those of the Jews who were in the state of grace belonged to the New Law. The Old Law of itself was not the Law of grace, but was preparatory to grace. Hence what we say of it here and in the following paragraphs must be understood as referring to those only who lived by the letter of the Law and never rose to an understanding of its spirit.

submit them to Himself; and since they had refused to submit in the freedom of love they would be forced to submit in the bondage of fear. The God of the Old Testament is indeed a terrible God. His wrath, as depicted in its pages, defeats out understanding. We are so accustomed to the God of Mercy and Compassion that we almost dare to question the justice of God the Avenger of His kingly rights. But what we cannot understand is not, by that simple fact, unintelligible. If we fail to grasp the inner coherence of God's dealings with men, our reaction should be, not questioning, but reverence. God is in Himself a Mystery. It is not strange then if His Wrath appear shrouded in darkness when no soft ray of mercy or of love lights it for our frightened eyes.

In the second place the Old Law demanded, of itself and immediately, an external rather than an internal service of God. To see this it is sufficient to cast even a cursory glance at the pages of the Old Testament. But what entitles us most of all to make this point is that it was singled out time after time by Our Blessed Lord Himself as being the characteristic of the service rendered the Father by the interpreters of the Law. He spoke of their ceremonial ablutions, of their insistence on legal purity, of their zeal for the temple taxes, of their fanatical regard for the Sabbath, and put all this into sad contrast with their interior rottenness, with that pride whereby their outer acts, in spite of the appearance of religion, were directed all to the glory of self. As we shall have occasion to say later, the Scribes and Pharisees could not appeal to the Law in support of their interior attitude. But what did make them typical of the law under which they lived was that its directions were immediately concerned with what was exterior and that their lives were but a series of external rites and practices. They erred in confining the Law to the exterior, not in understanding it of the exterior. The reign of God, then, inaugurated on Sinai, was to be a reign in external activity. God demanded certain practices of His people. He willed to reign in them to the extent of forcing them to submission to ritual in fear. A dreadful sovereignty—but a just punishment for an ungrateful people.

In the last place St. Thomas points out that the reward of

the faithful observance of the Old Law was not immediately eternal life but rather temporal happiness. He refers us, in support of his thesis, to the account given in the Book of Exodus of the release of the chosen people from the captivity of Egypt. We read in the third chapter how God, seeing the suffering of His people, determined to deliver them. And He made at the same time the promise of the reward that would be theirs if they were faithful : " I have seen all that hath befallen you in Egypt. And I have said the word to bring you forth out of the affliction of Egypt, into the land of the Chanaanite, the Hethite, and the Amorrhite, and Pherezite, and Hevite, and Jebusite, to a land that floweth with milk and honey " (Exodus 3, 16–17). The years that followed the fulfilment of this promise are evidence of the fact that its immediate reward was temporal prosperity. Whenever the Jews were faithful to the Law God blessed them, and gave them victory over their enemies and tranquil possession of the rich territory of the Promised Land. Whenever they proved faithless they fell into the hands of their enemies, and, despoiled of their possessions, were carried into captivity. And when at length, in the times of Esdras, their crimes had reduced them to a state of indescribable misery, they themselves were con- scious that observance of the Law and temporal prosperity were connected, and that their misfortunes could be attributed directly to their disregard for the command of their Heavenly King : " Behold we ourselves this day are bondmen : and the land which thou gavest our fathers, to eat the bread thereof, and the good things thereof, and we ourselves are servants in it. And the fruits thereof grow up for the kings, which thou hast set over us for our sins . . . " (2 Esdras 9, 36–37).

There was nothing unbecoming in God's establishing a Kingdom of this kind. Man had fallen, and it was but in keep- ing with his weak nature that God should raise him only by degrees, were He to decide in His mercy to raise him at all. Man would profit by a period of prayer and patient waiting. In the meantime he would be given a law which would be simply imperfect, not evil. It would impose salutary obliga- tions on him, urge him to observe them by the promise of an immediate reward ; and, if he were to raise his heart as well

as his works to God, it would be possible for him, even in Old
Testament times, to receive the gift of grace and so enter under
the benign rule of the Law of the children of God, the Law
of liberty and love. The Law was imperfect, preparatory
to a higher Law yet to be given. But it was never the Divine
intention that man should rest in its imperfection and turn his
heart from the more perfect Law it prefigured. And yet
this was what men did ; and that in spite of the fact that the
motive of the Old Law was not only fear but hope as well.
For God had not imposed in it fear alone. From the very
beginning there had been a promise of a new law, of a new
reign of God on earth. And man had been given to understand that the purpose of the Old Law was to prepare the way
for the new, and yield it place when the fulness of time should
come.

Even our first parents had been told by God that He willed
to reign in them as much by the hope they would have in
His mercy as by the fear they would have of His wrath. He
revealed this to them when He spoke to the serpent : " I
will put enmities between thee and the woman, and thy seed
and her seed ; she shall crush thy head, and thou shalt lie in
wait for her heel." (Gen. 3, 15). Our first parents knew by
this promise that One was to come Who would establish a
new reign of God over their children, and crushing the serpent's
head destroy the reign of Satan. This hope, taking its origin
in the very establishment of the Kingdom of fear, grew as
successive ages saw an ever fuller revelation of the character
of Him Who was to come. David sang of Him, his Lord,
sitting at the right hand of the Almighty. Isaias spoke of
Him, Wonderful, Counsellor, God the Mighty, the Father
of the world to come, the Prince of Peace. Daniel saw
Him coming with the clouds of heaven, even to the Ancient of
days, receiving power and glory and a kingdom. In the hope
of such a Redeemer could the chosen people support the law.
They knew that their bondage would be but for a time. And
though they cried out in the agony of waiting, their hope was
unshaken. God had promised, and God was faithful and
true.

But the perversity of man corrupted even this Kingdom of

fear and hope. The Jews, taken as a whole, refused to admit that the Law was imperfect, and looked upon its temporal rewards as their greatest hope, its external observances as its highest demand, the misfortune it threatened here on earth as God's greatest sanction. Shutting their ears to the true accents of the prophets and their eyes to the evident meaning of the inspired word they understood the temporal rewards promised them by God as being all He had to offer, and the Messiah as a great King under Whom they would rise to world-domination rather than as an Incarnate God under Whom they would rise to world-contempt. Ideas of a golden age so crude as to be almost incredible were the equipment of the popular Jewish mind. Jerusalem would become as big as all Palestine ; the walls would be of gold and silver ; the Messiah would be conqueror of all pagan powers, particularly of the Roman Empire. It is not just to say that there was no excuse whatever for the prevalence of such ideas. A people, ground to the dust for centuries, contrasting at all times their present misery with their former greatness, could hardly have escaped entirely the snare that the glory of earthly magnificence constituted for them. It is true too that the terms in which the reign of the Messias Who was to come were described in the inspired writings abounded in images taken from worldly pomp—though what other images could God use if He wished to speak to men of kingly glory in terms that men could understand ? But even when we do make allowance for these, the extenuating circumstances of the Jewish national crime, it still remains a fact that their sin was enormous ; for it consisted in perverting the notion of the Kingdom of God into a Kingdom of men.

When the Jews spoke of the Kingdom of the Messiah, whatever the words they used may have signified, their mind contemplated a Kingdom of the Jew. And what was utterly fantastic in their position was that it was a Kingdom of the Jew established by God Himself. This is the peculiar enormity of their national sin. God can and will establish only the Kingdom of God. To conceive that God could have an essential interest in the earthly glorification of any people, however favoured they might be in His eyes, is to attribute to

God the desire to establish the Kingdom of this world. The Kingdom of the Jews was nothing else than the Kingdom of this world in one of its not uncommon forms, the enthronement of the race. The Kingdom of this world we have seen to be ultimately the Kingdom of self. But it may be realized through the glorification of the race no less than by the glorification of the individual as such. The individual is a member of the race. If the race rises, he feels that he rises with it. He will even be prepared to sacrifice a purely personal gain if only he is made to feel that he will triumph in some mysterious way after death in the ultimate triumph of his race. There is then no real distinction between the decadent Jewish idea and the idea which we have seen to be at the root of every kingdom that is not of God. It is always self that strives to mount the throne. It matters little whether self mounts openly, or whether it sneaks up under the self-effacing mantle of racial-altruism. The reality is always the same. And if it be possible to mark degrees of iniquity in the forms it may adopt, the worst will possibly be that in which the Kingdom of self is brazenly established upon a claim to divine rights There have been men who have built their kingdom upon the pretext that they were divine. This sin can be the sin of an individual. It can be the sin of a people as well. It matters little whether a nation does as the Jews did, or whether it does as race-philosophy would have its adepts do—claim a kingdom as God-given, or claim a kingdom as the right of a nation that is itself God—in either case the claim is blasphemy, and the result is inevitable humiliation.

The story of the Kingdom of God on earth is, then, a sad one. It was rejected by Adam and misunderstood and abused by his children. And yet, in itself the Kingdom of God is something easy to understand and something that should appeal to man. It is easy to understand : it means the submission of man to the law of God and the reward of man's submission by entry into the peace of God's realm. It should attract man : for man desires to be like God, and he will be like God when, submitting to rule of God, he is allowed to share in the treasures that lie hid in the Godhead. But man has always sinned by seeking obstinately something less than

God wished to give him, thinking that its price would be less than the one God asked him to pay. If Adam had been submissive to God he would have been rewarded by grace on earth and by eternal life after the life of time. That was the reward promised to service in God's Kingdom on earth. Every Kingdom offers something to its subjects : God's Kingdom offered grace and glory. Adam preferred some kind of independence of God, some knowledge of good and evil that would make him independent of God, to that real share in God's own independence of all that is not Himself which was offered him by grace. What God offered was divine. What Adam aimed at was human—it was nothing more than human independence. God offered more ; Adam selected less. Selecting less he sinned ; and learned that the less was impossible and that the more had been lost. With the Jews it was the same. They were called to live in a Kingdom which could offer them the hope of a Redeemer. They willed to live in one that offered nothing more than the hope of rich harvests, and fruitful cattle, and subjected peoples. Why should they reject the Divine offer ? Why should Adam reject it ? Why—except that the Divine offer was made on condition of the submission of self to God, and that man, loving self so dearly, has thereby the awful power of preferring self to God and to self's true perfection ? The price of entry to the Kingdom of God is one which man is so unwilling to pay that sooner than pay it he will forgo the alluring advantages it holds out to him. He will persist in seeing nothing in the Kingdom of God but the harsh invitation to submission. He will ignore the promise of the peace of God in the Kingdom of God, and make his unhappy choice—the torture of self in the kingdom of this world.

We have said enough to indicate the general structure of the Kingdom of heaven : the reign of God and the peace of God in souls. When Adam rejected the first offer of the Kingdom, God determined to reign in men through fear and hope. But it was never His intention that this Kingdom should be final ; for it was perfect neither in regard to the reign of God nor the peace of God. God reigns very little in those who serve in fear, even when their fear is to some extent quickened by hope. One who serves in fear is a bond-man. He gives as little as he must, and that little only in order to escape punishment. He will never dream of going beyond the letter of his terms of engagement. To do that is the property of love. Love is generous : fear is grudging. Fear expects but little from mercy and tries to keep back as much as possible in view of an emergency. It prompts us to do just the same thing in our dealings with God, even though there is no possibility that what we have kept back from Him will be of any avail against Him. The result is, that those who serve God in fear really submit to Him, and allow Him to reign in them, only as little as possible. He is their King, for He has made them and they belong to Him ; but they refuse to bend to the guidance of His Royal Law.

The Kingdom of God in the Old Testament was imperfect also in the matter of the peace of God which should reign in the Kingdom of God. We have seen that the Old Law promised immediately nothing more than temporal prosperity. Now temporal prosperity is a divine blessing. But we say that it is the last and lowest of all God's blessings, and is never given by Him to a soul He loves except as preparation for the blessing of grace. God was not satisfied therefore with what the Kingdom of the Old Law offered to man. It offered external peace, freedom from want and persecution, but not that peace of soul which surpasseth all understanding. Whether then we consider the Kingdom of God as the rule of God or the peace of God, it was God's intention to go beyond the Old Law and establish a new one which would be perfect both in the submission it would demand and the peace with which it would reward. And He would do this by gathering all men under a King Who would be both God and man : man that He might rule over men, and God that He might rule them for God. This King was Our Saviour, Whose yoke is sweet and Whose reward exceeding great.

CHAPTER IV

CHRIST THE KING

" The Kingdom of this world is become Our Lord's " (Apoc. 11, 15).

WHEN God invited Adam to enter His Kingdom He placed no prince of the race of men or angels over him. Adam was invited to serve and be subject to God Himself, and to have dealings with Him directly and without intermediary. God followed this same plan in the Kingdom of the Old Law. Though He demanded and promised less in it than in the Kingdom which He had offered to Adam, He abated nothing of His will to immediate control and immediate service. If anything, we may say that, taking the circumstances into consideration, God was more jealous of His position as sole King under the Law than He had been before. The familiar story of the Jews' petition to Samuel to give them a King of their own race to rule them is evidence of His mind : " Then all the ancients of Israel being assembled came to Samuel to Ramatha. And they said to him : Behold thou art old, and thy sons walk not in thy ways : make us a king to judge us as all nations have. And the word was displeasing in the eyes of Samuel, that they should say : Give us a king, to judge us. And Samuel prayed to the Lord. And the Lord said to Samuel : Hearken to the voice of the people in all that they say to thee. For they have not rejected thee, but me, that I should not reign over them " (I Kings 8, 4-7). The request of the people displeased the Prophet Samuel. Perhaps the crude reference to his sons' scandalous lives and his own declining years contributed not a little to his displeasure. Even if left to himself he might therefore have refused the people's request. But God, Who saw the mind of the people behind their words, was still more angry with them and ordered Samuel to give them a king in punishment for their sin, knowing that such a king would become a burden to them and lead them to regret the day they wished to serve any master save only God.

But though God wished to reign immediately over both Adam and the chosen people, the reason why He so willed

differed essentially in the one case from the other. He willed
to place Adam under Himself directly through love. He wished
to honour Adam, whom He had made. Adam was so far a
masterpiece of His that He would make him subject to nobody
less than Himself. The angels, of course, were higher in nature
than Adam, and God would not disturb that order of perfection in which their place was at the very summit of creation.
But though they were at the summit, Adam represented a kind
of sovereign petty state—less than the angels but directly
dependent on God alone, God's peculiar possession in the world
of space and time. It was not, however, because He respected
fallen man, that God willed to have no king reign over the
fallen people but Himself only. Rather was it because He knew
so well the frailty of Israel and of the man that would become
its king. He knew that His people would use their king to
achieve earthly greatness and to forget their utter dependence
on Himself. He knew that their king would be only a man, and
a fallen one at that, and that he would tend to make of Israel
a kingdom in which he, rather than God, would reign : that
he would, in other words, use his power over the chosen people
to establish for himself a kingdom of self. He would see that
he and not God would be glorified ; that his ends and not the
ends of God would be pursued ; that his will and not the will
of God would prevail. It was to avoid this evil—and to spare
His people the punishment that would follow it—that God
willed to be sole King of Israel. Hence, Israel's desire of a
king was rightly understood by Samuel as an attempt to shake
off the yoke of God, and his refusal to accede to it aimed at
preserving their true allegiance. God, however, was displeased with His people, and for their punishment He commanded Samuel to accede to their desire. They would have a
king, and they would suffer under him and his successors.

There was therefore something in the very nature of a fallen
man which made it difficult for such a one to be a king after
God's heart. Fallen man tended to establish a kingdom of self.
His heart was closed up within him ; his will was bent back
serpent-wise upon himself. He would almost infallibly submit
his subjects to the indignity of serving his own glory. He
would use them as steps to self-realization, rejoice in the sub-

mission offered him by men his equals, feel Godlike through
the vision of God's image prostrate at his feet. And, yet, in
spite of every difficulty in its accomplishment, there was a deep
fitness in man's being led to God by man. What could be
more consonant with human nature than that men should be
gathered into a kingdom by a man like themselves, knowing
their aspirations and feeling their impulses, and that gathered
under him they should offer themselves, a united people, to
their God ? There was deep-rooted in the nature of man the
desire of such a kingdom of God on earth. Not only should
each man be subject to God in the inner throne-room of his
own God-inhabited soul, but all men should be united in a
visible and social group ; in that group there should be one
who would be the voice of all the rest ; and he, leading the
rest in mind and heart, should reign over them that he might
offer them to God. He would not reign over them for self,
but rather for God. He would be a king ; but not so much for
himself as that he might make what was chaotic and formless
in the submission of man into order and beauty, and that man's
voice might escape from his lips as one voice of praise to the
glory of the Almighty. Man had need of such a king even
though he was not sufficiently conscious of his need to formulate it as I have just done. It was a need of his nature, not
a need arising from enquiry. It was deep ; and God respected it.

If we now consider the Incarnation as God's answer to man's
need of a king Who would be also man, we find ourselves
breathless at the beauty of its inner harmony. A human king
of the race of Adam tended, as we have said, to establish a
kingdom of self. By the Incarnation we are given a King
Whose Self is God. The Incarnate is a King Who in drawing all
things to Himself, draws all things to God. O felix culpa, we may
cry with the Church, O happy fault, which has mapped out the
plan which God would adopt to wipe out all faults. Sin is
an attempt to establish a kingdom of self ; it will be destroyed
by One in Whom, though He is truly Man, the Kingdom of
self and the Kingdom of God are identical. For the Incarnate
Word is a Divine Person : the Self of the Incarnate Word is
God. And yet the Incarnate Word is God made man, and
therefore can be a King of men such as we have seen to be the

desired of men. Sin is undone by the Incarnation. The Incarnation gives men a Brother Who can never sin, for He has no human self to which to draw things away from their Master. If we but submit to Him He will take possession of us for God, and the Kingdom of God will be restored, and from His heart and lips there will ascend to the throne of the Almighty in our name a hymn of love and praise such as man had never offered, and earth had never known.

. . . . .

The plan of the re-establishment of the Kingdom of God was therefore very simple. The Incarnate Word would be King of men, and subjecting all men to Himself would offer them to the Father. On the side of men this plan had the advantage— proof if ever proof were needed of God's tender consideration for human frailty—that it would be One of their own to Whom they would be subject in the first place. It would be easier for them to understand and love a human king than it had been for them to subject themselves to the King of Ages. And there would be the feeling of pride, too, that man could be elevated to such a dignity—an extraordinarily delicate appeal to the feelings of a fallen and humiliated race. The Incarnate Word being a King was given all the requirements of kingly rank. These requirements amount in last analysis to two : dignity and power. We shall consider them in this present chapter.

. . . . .

Let us consider now the royal dignity of Christ Our King. The Incarnate Word is Man. But Man in such a way that the dignity of royalty pervades His Humanity. There is in the first place the personal dignity given to Christ by the fact that He is a Divine Person. Now we speak here of the dignity and royalty that are His as man. His dignity and royalty as God are those of which we spoke in the preceding chapter. What we mean now is that Christ the Man is a Divine Person, and that this fact gives to Him, again as Man, a royal dignity. He Who is Man is God. Hence, He Who is Man is raised as far above men as God is above them. Christ the Man is not mere man, though He is true man ; because the Person Who is Christ the Man is God the Son, the Second Person of the ever Blessed Trinity. Were it then possible that Christ have nothing of the Divine Nature at all, nothing of the Divine Power—and this is impossible since a Divine Person cannot be conceived of without all the attributes of Divinity—He would still be of transcendent dignity. Even could He think but the thoughts of a man, and will but as a man wills, He would be more than man, more than all men, because of His value as a Person. As a Person He would be God, even though as a source of activity He could do nothing more than the merest man ; for personal worth is a real worth in its own right, giving its bearer a value in the universe which is independent of every other consideration, entitling him to respect and service in proportion to its elevation.

The dignity which is the Man Christ's in virtue of His Divine Personality is not easily grasped by our minds because we are not accustomed to the idea of personal dignity as opposed to that which is consequent on nature or essence. When we speak of the personal dignity of man, for example, we have usually in mind nothing more than the extraordinary perfection of the powers of man, intellect and will, as opposed to the more limited powers of the animal, and our contention that human personality is something that should be respected amounts usually, in last analysis, to nothing more than the belief that man's great powers are too great to be wasted without our feeling a sense of irreparable loss. But the personality of man is not the nature of man. The nature of man is what we define when we say that he is rational animal. The person, on the other hand, is the possessor of the nature. The person is, we may say, greater than the nature, since the nature belongs to the person as that in which it is and expresses itself. Being and reality belong to the person first of all : the nature follows as sharing in the being that is the person's, and determining what will be its outer expression and its manner of action upon other beings. What makes it so easy for us to confuse nature with personality is the fact that human nature, as we meet it, is always in a human person. It really matters little then, in ordinary cases, whether, when speaking of the dignity of man, we have his nature or his personality in mind, since in either case the dignity will be human ; for the dignity of human personality expresses itself connaturally in a human nature and imposes upon the world in the force of human powers. But such confusion is altogether out of place when we speak of the Incarnate Word. In Christ human nature subsists in a Divine Person : that is to say, He is a man in nature, but God in Person. Hence, considered even as man, considered even as acting in virtue of His human powers and expressing Himself in human terms, He retains His Divine dignity and worth. His personality therefore considered as personality, and abstracting from every Divine Attribute, raises Him above mankind, entitles Him to their submission, makes Him their King.

Though it is impossible to find in human experience an exact analogy to this mystery of the Incarnation, one can still find something which is sufficiently similar to it, to illustrate it in a certain degree : I refer to the dignity which we feel to belong even still to one who has misused and warped his nature beyond hope of human rehabilitation. The mind can—whatever we may think to the contrary—recognize in such a man a dignity which is not just that of his nature. It happens from time to time that certain men, either through vice, or sickness, or some other cause, lose the use of their rational powers and seem to have no prospect of ever regaining the capacity to exercise them. This can happen as a result of intemperance, or through some kind of stroke. Considered from the side of their nature such men have lost their worth. It is true, of course, that their soul remains substantially unaffected by the illness of the body and that their nature is thus pure in its roots. But the value of that nature here and now, its chance of expressing itself in appropriate activity—all this is nil. And yet we realize that there is something inviolable about such men, even as they are here and now. We do not lose from view that, being immortal, their fall may be only temporal, that they may have an eternity of complete activity before them, and that this gives them worth. But it is not to that that I refer. Even independently of such worth we feel that there is something in them as they are here and now which entitles them to our respect. We feel that they have a value which is but inadequately expressed in what remains to them of their humanity, and that this value is real and awe-inspiring. No matter what they may appear to be we know that they are persons ; persons wrapped up and smothered, it is true, in opaque folds of uncongenial flesh, but still persons, with all the dignity of human personality, with all the right to respect that personality commands, with all that sublime fulness of being which is man's in what is highest in man.

If this analogy be applied—with all the respect which the occasion demands—to the question of the Personal Dignity of the Incarnate Word, we shall be able to see something of what is meant by saying that Christ the Man has the worth and dignity of a Divine Person. Each Divine Person possesses all the Divine Worth and Reality. But it is possible for Their outer expression to fall short of Their inner fulness. A Divine Person, while remaining Such in Himself, may manifest Himself inadequately. To do this it is only necessary that He should assume to Himself a nature lower than the Divine (Which is the only Nature That is the adequate expression of Divine Personal Reality). If the nature assumed be human—and this is the nature which in point of fact was assumed—the Divine Person assuming will thereby be made man with human powers of activity and achievement. As subsisting in that nature the Divine Person will be efficient cause of nothing more than what lies within the ambit of the powers of a mere man ;[1] but as final cause He will be God. He will act on others as a man can act ; but others will be obliged to act for Him as for God. He will divest Himself, as it were, of His might, but preserve His dignity and worth. Of more than His might and His external trappings of Godhead He cannot be divested, for while He acts at all He acts as Divine Person and must retain His worth as a Person. But that much He can renounce : and then we have the mystery of which St. Paul speaks—that emptying of Himself which the Incarnate Word embraced, when He Who wa in the form, and enjoyed the perfection of the powers of God expressed Himself to men in the form of a servant, veiling His Personality behind the coarseness of flesh, moving among mens in the weakness of human nature, acting as a man, appearing

---

[1] We are, of course, still abstracting from the Divine Nature, which, accompanies Divine Personality necessarily.

in all things a man—and still being King, since God, still being royal by His Person though a servant in nature.

Though we have spoken so far as if the Personality of the Word subsisted in no nature other than the human, in fact the Divine Nature was not and could not have been laid aside, but rather was a human nature assumed to union with the Divine in the unity of one Person. Hence, His Divine Personality is not, therefore, the only title which the Man Christ has to royal dignity. He is King too, because One and the Same Person subsists in the two natures, the human and the Divine. Hence He Who is man, with the limited powers of man, is also God with the infinite powers of the Godhead. The Word did not become Man precisely to perform activities in which His humanity only, to the exclusion of His Divinity, would take a part. In all that would be essential to the achievement of the purpose of the Incarnation the Humanity of Christ would be the instrument of His Divinity and act in the power of the Divinity. Hence, when Christ as man presents Himself to the human race for their acceptance, He comes to them as a man Whose Humanity is reinforced by Divinity. By this we do not mean to say that in such matters as the processes of the vegetative life the humanity of Christ was the instrument of His Divinity. What is under discussion here is His intercourse with men : and we say that He never approaches them in His Humanity except in so far as that Humanity is the instrument of His Divine Power. Hence, even when He comes to them in the power of a man, His power is perfected by that of Omnipotence. He comes therefore as Lord and Master even when He comes as Brother. His created love for them is the instrument of an uncreated love. His human words are the bearers of a Divine message. His finite acts have linked to them all the significance of the acts of Omnipotence Itself.

It is easier to find an analogy to explain this aspect of Christ's Kingship than was the case when we spoke of His Personal dignity. The human Nature of Christ is elevated and made royal by the Divine Nature in much the same way as any instrument is elevated by the principal cause that uses it. A violin considered in itself is a thing of little intrinsic worth. A certain amount of wood, some glue, some gut—that is a violin. A violin in the hands of a master is something different ; it is the bearer of beauty ; it can throb with passion, melt with tenderness, fret with waywardness. United to one who knows the secret of wooing melody in wood, the violin has a worth commensurate with that of the Lady Music it holds willing captive ; it is no longer just wood and glue and catgut. Smash a violin in the very instant that the artist holds it, and you destroy beauty. Use it as firewood when he has laid it aside, and your act would have little of the barbarian in it were it not for what the violin could be made to do by the artist : considered in itself its value at that moment is slight. An instrument then, of whatever kind, receives dignity from the fact of its union with a higher cause. The total effect belongs to the instrument as well as to him who moves it ; and by the fact of participating in the production of a noble effect and receiving into itself, even though in a passing way, the power to produce it, the instrument becomes the bearer of an added worth which belongs to it as long as it remains in use. It is entitled to a share in the respect due to the being who moves it. It participates in his power to act ; it has a right consequently to share in the dignity that power carries with itself.

Now the human nature of Our Blessed Lord is the instrument of His Divinity. On that account, when He, acting as man, is moved to His act by the Divine Nature, He is entitled, even as man, to participate in the reverence due to the Divine Nature Itself. His human nature becomes, as it were, the instrument of the Divine Harmony—and to say " as it were " is almost superfluous in this case, as He is in all reality the channel of the harmony of divine life to discordant souls. His Human Nature is ennobled therefore by the harmony it bears. That harmony really resides in it, even though it be not fully of it. His Humanity is touched, quickened, enkindled by His Divinity. It is all lit up with the Divine. We cannot divorce Christ the instrument of the Divinity from the Divinity. We cannot will to honour Him just for what His Humanity is in itself, for from the moment that it is elevated by the Godhead it ceases to have a merely human value. The violin is more to us than wood and glue and catgut when music pours into our ears : Christ the Man is more to us than mere man when His Humanity gives us life in the power of His Divinity. He is not just man, and therefore not to be equated to man. He is Man, but greater than man ; One among men, therefore, but One Who is their King.

This peculiar elevation of the human nature of Christ due to its being the instrument of His Divinity, is not something which comes and goes according as it is or is not actually being used as the instrument of salvation. The peculiar dignity of the violin is something that lasts while the violin is in use and then is lost. The instrumental dignity of the humanity of Christ never passes. The reason for this is clear : the Sacred Humanity is not an instrument that can be laid aside ; it is an instrument joined on permanently to the Divinity—what theologians term an instrumentum conjunctum. The two natures in Christ—the human and the Divine—are permanently and intimately united in the One Person. They are not confounded or merged the one in the other. But neither are they side by side without essential subordination. The Human Nature of Christ was so assumed by the Person of the Word that it was placed under the Divine Nature as Its instrument. Thus, it is always Its instrument, just as the hand is always the instrument of the arm, even when the arm is not actually moving it. And being thus united to It, it shares always in Its dignity, just as the hand is always to be respected for what the arm can communicate to it. We may say that the Humanity of Christ, while remaining really human, has no function of its own in regard to men, in which it ceases completely to be the instrument of this Divinity. It is not like the violin which can be used—and that because its nature so permits—for uses other than that of providing music. The Humanity of Christ has but one use for men : to save them. It cannot be made to serve a merely profane use. Thus it can never enter into human experience otherwise than as divinized by the Godhead. It is always the nature of a King, even when the King acts as man.

Christ is King of men, too, in virtue of His created grace of Headship. His human soul was adorned with created grace to fit it for the task of co-operating with the Divinity in the work of redemption. It is inconceivable that a human nature should be raised to such familiar contact with the Divine—whether Person or Nature—without being prepared by the greatest created divinization possible for man in the present order. The Man Christ was also God. How Holy must He not have been as man to bear the sense of such an awful nearness? The angels standing away from God veil their faces for reverence and cry: "Holy, Holy, Holy." The Man Christ could not veil His face from the Divine Presence, because He Himself was God and was, as Man, endowed with the Beatific Vision. Had there been in His manhood the slightest fibre of ungodliness, He would have been consumed entirely by the white fire of the Godhead, so intolerant is It of all that is not God. Our God is a burning fire where nothing can survive but what is burning as He is, and with a flame as bright as His. We say on this account that it was necessary that the Sacred Humanity should have all the fulness of created grace, because grace is created likeness of God in the image of His inner being.

We arrive at the same conclusion if we consider that Christ, even as man, needed to be full of grace, seeing that it was the divine intention that we should receive of His fulness. He was predestined to be the source of grace and supernatural life to the whole human race. He could not therefore have been given grace in stinted measure. It was necessary that He should be a true Sun of Justice—One, this is to say, possessing not merely more grace than any other man, but possessing grace in such wise as to be the source which lights up the soul of every other man. If all were to receive of His fulness without diminution of that fulness, He needed to be an inexhaustible fount of grace. Our grace is therefore related to the grace of Christ as effect to cause, not precisely as what is quantitatively less to what is quantitatively greater, even though this latter relationship does exist in some form. Just as all being depends on God as fount of being, so, in somewhat the same way, does all human sanctity depend on the sanctity of Christ as fount of sanctity. In neither case are the two terms of the relations strictly commensurable. The Being of God does not bear a mathematical proportion to the being of any creature, but exceeds it essentially and necessarily inasmuch as It is its source. Neither is the grace of Christ strictly commensurable with the grace of any man, however holy. Christ is the Fount of his grace ; and it is easier to weigh the drop of water against the well from which it sprang than to weigh the holiness of man against that of Our Saviour. As measured against Christ every man is essentially dependent in the Supernatural order. Christ, by His created grace is the source of all the supernatural life of man : that is to say, He is a King.

It is worth our while to consider this last point still further : we say that Christ is King because His created grace is the source of all human grace. And we are entitled to do so because all rights whatever to royalty are based ultimately upon the power to provide what is essential to life. God is the Source of all that we have. We depend on Him for every moment of our existence. Because of this total dependence on Him for all that we are and have, we are bound in justice to submit to Him in all that we can do, whether with the powers of soul or of body. That is the meaning of what is known as the virtue of religion. By it, God, the Master and supreme King, is honoured. In the next place we depend on our parents. Under God they have given us life. They have been responsible for our education. We are placed thereby in their debt. The debt must be paid in service. This is a matter for the virtue known as piety (pietas). We depend too on our native land. Our life has been, and is still, supported by it. We were made beneficiaries of the experience, and learning, and virtue, of its people. We owe it some return in strict justice. This duty is regulated by the virtue of patriotism. Now there comes in the last place our duty to the head of the state ; and what we should notice most particularly here and now is that, like every other duty of the kind, it is based upon our dependence in the matter of certain benefits. The head of the state directs the state. We profit by his guidance. Therefore we are placed in his debt, and are bound in justice to repay him by service and recognize his relative superiority to us by paying him honour. Kingship is then something simple to understand. It is nothing more than a certain share in the right to that service and respect which is due from man to God, a particular application of the general principle that wherever there is subordination and dependence there must be honour and service.

We are now better able to understand why it is that Christ is King because of His being endowed with the fulness of created grace. The reason is that we are indebted to Him for all that we have in the spiritual order. All that we have comes from His fulness. We owe Him in the spiritual order all that we do to father, fatherland, and king in the natural order. To speak of Him then as our King is not to exaggerate. It is rather to understate the reality. He is more than a human king. We depend on Him for more than any people depends on its king. However, it is still permissible to designate Him King rather than Father or Fatherland—though neither term would be inexact—and that for the reason that dignity is more palpable in the idea of King, even though dependence is less so. It is the name to which we have attached the greatest honour. It is therefore most fitting for Him Who is so far elevated above man, as expressing, better than any other name would, His transcendent dignity. He is King by reason of His majesty, though Father, and more than Father, by reason of the life He gives.

There remains still another title which Jesus has to kingly rank, and that is His merit (we omit for the moment, as being irrelevant to our present purpose, the question of His title by right of conquest). What this title means is that Christ by His Passion and Death acquired merits so altogether eminent as to rank Him at the very head of mankind and make Him King of men. But this is not a title which we understand easily. We are inclined to consider merit as being rather in the person of whom one deserves well than in the person who merits. Thus, when we say that Christ merited by His Passion and Death we understand this as meaning that God will reward Him for what He did ; so that if the reward takes the form of His being placed at the head of the human race, He would be at the head, it is true, but the real power would be in God, even though exercised in favour of the One Who seems to be King. What we are neglecting when we express in this form the mystery of Christ's Kingship by merit is that He really did suffer and die, and that what He endured makes Him different from other men, even if He rules them only through the Divinity. A man who has gone through a severe trial and borne himself with manly fortitude receives a psychological stamp which lifts him out of the rut of humanity. He has done something difficult. He has come out of his experience a different and a fuller man. He has evolved in the process. Now we may say that something like this is true for the Man Christ. He endured what no man was ever called to endure. He Who was conscious of His Godhead was treated as a criminal because of His justice. Alone He faced the world and Satan. Two Kingdoms were ranged against one Man. Even though that Man was God, He waged war in His Humanity. As Man He faced the greatest forces that could be arrayed against Him, and triumphed over them. Is it untrue then to say that this Man has shown Himself to be, or made Himself to be, a King among men ? Even though He rule but through His merits, is He not a King in worth ? If men have been called the Fathers of their people, and given honour that fell short in little of what is doled out to God, is not Christ, judged by the same standards as they were, fully and really King ? What He did was no less heroic than what they did. Were He nothing but a mere man, what He did would have marked Him out as the greatest of all men, a King among men. If He be God as well, does that lessen the rights of His Humanity to our honour ? Christ the Man is King then, no matter what be the criterion of Kingship we adopt : King as Hypostatically united to the Person of the Word : King as instrument of the Divinity ; King by the fulness of His grace ; King by way of merit. He is One of Whom we may feel proud, One Whose Kingdom we may feel privileged to enter. He is God's claimant to the throne of men on earth. And if we only know Him, can we offer the throne to another ?

We have spoken so far of nothing more than the dignity of Christ the King. But Kingship includes more than dignity or excellence. It includes also, as titles to honour, the power to govern others and the actual exercise of government. We shall speak in a later chapter of Christ's government of souls from His throne at the right hand of the Father. But to complete what we have begun in this present one, it will be necessary to speak here of the more proximate principles of His power over souls.

Christ's power to govern and guide comes ultimately from the Divinity to which His human nature is united, and the created grace with which His soul is filled. We have indicated these principles of His power sufficiently to make it unnecessary to refer to them once more. The exercise, however, of Kingly power demands something more than the remote principles of power. A certain psychological equipment is required as well. We can conceive readily of human kings, having at their disposal all the power their state demands, but lacking that clarity of mental vision which opens up the way to its beneficent exercise through the tangled undergrowth of national and international life. There are other kings, too, lacking neither power nor vision, but failing in that spirit of generous self-sacrifice which is a necessary condition for the fair distribution of charges and emoluments. Over and above mere power there are therefore two great kingly requirements : prudence and justice. If Our Saviour has these He is a King indeed.

Prudence is the virtue which orders moral activity well in view of the final end. Its act is to command : its object is those moral actions which lead to the attainment of the end of human life. In its narrowest sense it is a virtue peculiar to the individual in the direction of his own life. But it is transferred, by a very legitimate process of extension, to include all the cases in which there is question of directing human lives to the attainment of the end of human life. There is therefore a prudence proper to the father of a family, who needs to be able to direct those under him in such wise as to obtain for them all the benefits of family life. And there is in the same way a prudence proper to kings. For the concern of kings is ultimately that their subjects may attain their end as men, and the kings' commands are so many indications of what should be done in view of the attainment of the end of human life in the various circumstances of social intercourse and effort. Hence prudence as a kingly virtue presupposes knowledge of the end of the kingdom and signifies understanding of the bearing of means upon that end. To be a prudent king one needs to realize these two require-ments.

It is almost superfluous to ask if Our Divine Saviour and King understands the end and purpose of the Kingdom of

Heaven. For if we consider Him as God we find that the peculiar appropriateness of the Incarnation of the Second Person of the Blessed Trinity rather than any other Person lies in the fact that, being the Divine Wisdom, He is the Personal expression of the end of all that God has made and of all that God wills. The Word is the Personification of all that the Father sees to be good. Hence the Word is the Personal archetype of the end of creation. When the Father uttered His eternal Word He uttered in Him every word expressive of a Divine intention. It was fitting therefore that when the first plan drawn up by the Father for man on earth, and expressed in the Word, should have been frustrated by sin, the Word Himself should come on earth to restore to man what continued to exist all-glorious and undiminished in Himself. God's plan would be restored by the Plan of God.

But it is of Christ as man that we are now speaking. The understanding of the purpose of human life embodied in the Person of the Word concerns us only in so far as it overflows somehow into the created intellect of Jesus. And this takes place in two ways.

The first way is that implied when we stated already that the Sacred Humanity was the instrument of the Divinity. The Humanity of Jesus is used by His Divinity—Which is the Divinity of the Word—to perform a work planned out by the Word Himself. Christ as man will have His own thoughts, and these thoughts will direct Him in all that He will do. But what He does is not a merely human work. It is a work of God, a kingly work to which God is moving Him. Hence His thoughts, even though they be the thoughts of a Man, are the thoughts of a Man Who is being actually directed by the Divinity of the Word. His thoughts are in that sense instrumental : not that He does not grasp them, not that His mind is filled with nothing more than a great unknowing, but that even the midday light of His mind is itself lit up with a more glorious splendour, and that in what He sees and judges He has been moved, not against his convictions, but beyond them and with a force and sureness to which they could never give birth. No human mind can bear the burden of the thoughts of God. Even the human mind of Christ is too weak for this.

What alone is possible is that a human mind be carried to its judgments with all the sureness of God, but without full understanding of the grounds of God's certainty. This is what happened to the prophets. They could give their own reasons for what they said, could offer their own guarantees of its truth. But ultimately, its truth was greater than their guarantees. Its truth was Divine; their guarantees were human. They had not been forced to a blind assent. But they assented to something for a reason which while utterly convincing did not lay bare all the implications of their assent. Now it is in much the same way that we may speak of the created intellect of Christ as being instrumental to His Divine Intellect. We shall see shortly that His created intellect was extraordinarily perfect. In this He surpassed all the prophets, even the most penetrating. But in so far as His created thoughts were the expression of the uncreated Mind they were instrumental and prophetic. They carried with them a guarantee that was not that of a merely human mind : they had the guarantee of Eternal Truth—of Eternal Truth in its most perfect human expression.

Christ as Man had, therefore, in virtue of the Hypostatic Union that knowledge of the purpose of man necessary in a King of men. He had it no less by the fact that as man He enjoyed the Beatific Vision. The Man Christ always saw the face of God, always looked into the mind of God. His human mind being finite, He did not comprehend or exhaust Its message. But it is axiomatic that every created mind sees in the Beatific Vision, when it attains to It, as much of the things of God and men, as is becoming to one of its rank and position. It follows that since Christ came as He Who would restore the Kingdom of God on earth, He would see its full meaning in the Beatific Vision, in so far as any created mind could be said to grasp it fully. We are not speaking now of what we termed in the last paragraph the instrumental or prophetic knowledge He had of the end of man. We are speaking now of a knowledge which was fully explicit, fully conscious. And we say He had this fully conscious knowledge of the end of man as seen in the Divine Essence by the Beatific Vision. He grasped in the Divine Essence Itself the purpose of the Kingdom of which He was

King. There was nothing conjectural about this knowledge. It was dazzlingly clear. There was hardly anything created about it even, for the act of the Beatific Vision is one which while being the act of the creature is still more the act of God Himself. It gave Christ a wonderful fitness for His position of ruler. No earthly king sees the scope and purpose of his kingship as clearly as Christ did. The Jews were accounted happy to live under the rule of a king as wise as Solomon. But what was his wisdom when compared with the beatific wisdom of Christ? Solomon could err. Solomon did err. Christ the King cannot err. He sees His aim in God; and in God things are clearer than they are in themselves. He will rule then not as a steersman who steers by a clouded sky, but as one whose gaze is fixed on the Eternal Sun.

In the last place Christ knew the purpose of His Kingship by infused and acquired knowledge. We group these two forms of knowledge together because they are both created, even though one comes immediately from God and the other is acquired by experience. To treat of but one point, we may say Christ had the fullest experimental knowledge that man can have in human concepts of the Kingdom of God and of the duties of its King. His keen mind read into the scriptures as no mind had ever done before. He saw in them what God had spoken of the Messiah, what God expected of Him. He saw, too, why men needed the Messiah, and the end to which He should lead them. It is beautiful to think of the human mind of Christ brooding on the words of the Father. What reverence, what divine curiosity! His reading of the scriptures alone would have fitted Him to be King even had He had no other understanding of His duties than what He obtained thereby. He must have learned from His holy Mother; from men of the type of Zachary, and Simeon, too, for there must have been others like them in Israel at the time. Their words were but sparks to enkindle His mind, it is true. He thought beyond their thoughts before ever they had finished their words. But a spark does contribute something. He really did learn by occasion of the words of men, though they could never be termed His teachers. For how could men who lisped of kingship be said to teach the King of kings?

It is unnecessary to repeat the principles we have just laid down concerning Christ's knowledge of the end of His Kingdom by applying them in detail to the question of His knowledge of the means to be adopted in order to attain it. He knew these means by His[1] instrumental, His beatific, and His created knowledge, and that for the reasons we have given in the respective sections. There is one point, however, which it is well worth while to stress, and that is that He knew the means in their most concrete details, and that in this He is distinguished from even the greatest and wisest of human kings. It is the duty of the king of a people to make laws and give commands which will ensure the well-being of the people as a whole. He must be sufficiently prudent to foresee whether or not a certain law will result in advantage or disadvantage for the greater number of his subjects. He must be able to estimate whether or not such a course of action as a declaration of war will be justified by the losses inevitable and the gains possible. But it is not his duty to know whether or not any particular law or practical decision will entail loss or gain to any one individual. If he declares war a certain individual will be killed. But that is not his immediate concern. He fails in kingly prudence only if the gross result to the whole people be a loss he could and should have foreseen. The individual as such is no concern of his. Now Christ is a King of such a kind that the individual is a concern of His. He guides individuals to their individual ends in addition to guiding the whole Kingdom of God to its end. He does not draw up laws that will ensure merely a gross profit. His laws are of profit to each unit as well as to the whole. He does not make decisions which will result in the sacrifice of some for the good of most. His view embraces individuals as well as groups, and His plans are laid in such wise that if followed out each and every soul will grow to its full stature of grace. When saints have had the conviction that Christ died for them personally they were not deluded by their piety. For while it is true to say that He died for all men, it is even better to say that He died for each man, so far was He from

---

[1] It will be recalled that this knowledge is not different in its substance from the other forms of knowledge with which the Man Jesus was endowed.

regarding men as merged in the human mass when He entered
upon the great battle for His Kingdom. As it was in winning
the Kingdom so it is in administering it—at all times Christ
has the individual in view. He is the only King so prudent
as to find this possible. He is therefore a King to Whom
His subjects owe allegiance as much for what they are as
individuals as for what they are as members of a group. No
king is as near as He to His subjects.

Our Saviour has the second of the two great kingly virtues
as well as the first. He is just. We may say of Him : " Thou
art just, O Lord : and thy judgment is right " (Ps. 118, 137).
Our Saviour's judgments are not only prudent, they are just.
It is a fact, of course, that a judgment cannot be truly prudent
if it be unjust. But there is a semblance of prudence, which
is really short-sighted capitulation, and which men flatter
with the name of prudence, or realism. And there is another
which is brutal fear, and which in its turn is misnamed prudence
or caution. And it is because these two masquerade as
prudence, whereas they are really folly, that it is necessary to
make explicit mention of justice as well as of prudence as
being a kingly virtue. When therefore we say that Christ
the King is just we mean that in His rule He never allows
Himself to be turned from the end of His Father's glory either
by yielding to the strong or by oppressing the weak, but that
He gives to all His subjects their due and leads them, blessed in
the peace of His reign, to pay their just tribute of service to
His Father and theirs.

The principles of His justice are parallel to those of His
prudence. Considered as man He is just because of the subordination of His human will to the Divine Will, because
His human will is fixed beatifically on the Divine Goodness,
and because His human will has all the fulness of created charity.
It will be sufficient to touch very briefly on these different
points. The details may be filled in by referring back to what
has been said of His prudence.

Christ as man is just because His created will is the instrument
of the Divine Will. God is just. What He wills is always
just. But there is this difference between God's justice to
man and man's to man, that man's justice can be based upon

a real debt to man, whereas God can never be in man's debt. If two men enter into a contract in which the one is bound to certain services on the condition of similar services being rendered him by the other, we have a case of justice based upon a real debt. But man, having nothing which is not God's, cannot render God any service such that God will be bound to repay him in virtue of a strict obligation in justice contracted in regard to His creature. Whenever then we say that God is bound to act in a certain way in justice, what we mean is that He is so bound, not in justice to man, but in justice to Himself. It would be unbecoming in God to fail to give virtue its supernatural reward. Granted that He has given man the power of acting virtuously it would be ungodlike in Him to neglect to approve of its exercise. Hence when we say, as we have just said, that God is not bound in strict justice to man, we do not at all imply that man has any reason to be insecure in his hope of justice from God. God will always be just to man not because of His debt of justice to man, but because of His debt of becomingness to Himself. Considered therefore from the side of God, justice in the divine dealings with man is as necessary as is the Divine Essence Itself. God would cease to be God were He to act with man in the way we term unjust. From this it follows that the justice with which Christ as man is just is an instrumental participation in the necessary justice of God Himself. Christ must be fair in His dealings with men since He acts as the instrument of the Divine Justice. It is metaphysically impossible that He should favour the great or slight the lowly. Such action simply cannot proceed from Him, seeing that He is a Man in Whom is incarnate the Justice of God.

As His human will is fixed immovably on the Divine Goodness in the Beatific Vision we have a second reason also for asserting that He is supremely just. The Divine harmony of things is revealed in its entirety to His intellect by its vision of the Essence of God. His will embraces This Essence, and the harmony It expresses, in an act incapable of change. Hence it embraces this harmony, which is the Justice of God on earth, in the self-same act in which it adheres to God Himself. He cannot therefore be unjust without averting His face from God.

And that can never be. That He be just is a necessary consequence of His being in the possession of God.

There is finally the justice which follows upon the possession of the fulness of created charity. When one gives to each what is his due one is said to be just. When one loves one gives what is due and gives it freely and with desire. Christ being full of love of men is necessarily just in their regard. To be just is less than to love. He who loves is just and more than just. We may, in fact, even dare to say that Christ is not just in His dealings with men but loving. He is therefore more than a competent King. He is a King and Brother. This is a Kingship such as only God can devise for a man.

The foundations of the Kingdom of this world were laid when Adam abused a creature of God in the garden of paradise. And when the fulness of time came God sent His Incarnate Word into the world to destroy what Adam had built up, and to re-establish what Adam had destroyed. There is beauty as well as power in God's works. God is not limited as man is, who advances the claims of the ugly on the platform of the efficient. Hence He undid the Kingdom of Adam in a beautiful way, piece by piece, using the circumstances of his sin to provoke new circumstances of omnipotence and mercy.

Adam sinned by love of his human self. God willed to re-establish His Kingdom in the love of a man Whose Self was divine. Adam sinned by contempt of a word of God embodied in the tree of life. We shall enter the Kingdom of God by acceptance of the Word of God incarnate in living flesh. Adam sinned in the weakness of human indecision ; we shall be saved in the weakness of human endeavour. But above all else there is the fact that in Eden man was lost by the desire of a false Kingship ; in Bethlehem man was saved by the gift of a true King. And God made that King as attractive in our eyes as only He can ; a King of flesh and blood, splendid with the glory of the divinity ; a King of flesh and blood, splendid with the glory of every human grace ; a King Whom to know is to love, to love is to serve. He is the pride of our race, the Glory of mankind. And we revere Him not only for what He is to God, but for what He is to us as well. In Him God has restored the confidence and self-respect of man. Satan had defeated man : but God reserved for man the triumph of the final defeat of Satan. He has given man, too, what the fallen angels rejected when it was offered to them : One of his own number to be the leader of his hymn of praise. Lucifer could have led his fellow angels in their songs of glory, but he preferred to lead them in their senseless revolt. Man alone among the creatures of God has a Brother Whose praise is always acceptable, Whose voice is always sweet in the Divine ears. And God, Who gave him this Brother did so in His Mercy, that he who had sinned in the weakness of mortal pride in self, might return to his allegiance unashamed, in the joy of pride in Another.

CHAPTER V

THE TWO KINGDOMS

" *And He was in the desert forty days and forty nights, and was tempted by Satan . . .* " (Mk. 1, 13.)

IN the fulness of time God sent men their King, Who would rule them in His name and lead them to Himself. He was born in Bethlehem, the city of David. His life as a Child is hidden from us in its details, though its spirit is revealed in the passage which tells us that He lived at Nazareth with Mary and Joseph and was subject to them. After thirty years of obscurity the time at length came that He should be proposed to men for their acceptance. They had been prepared for His coming by the preaching of John the Baptist, who baptized them in the baptism of penance. And that He might receive at once the approval of His Father in heaven and of John, His precursor, Jesus went to the Jordan to John to be baptized, as the first step towards the establishing of the Kingdom. His Baptism was signalized by a voice from Heaven telling that He was the beloved Son of the Eternal Father and that men should hear Him ; and the Holy Ghost, the Love of God, descended upon Him.

The events which we have so briefly recalled were not hidden from Satan, the prince of this world. His own intelligence enabled him to know of some of them ; God allowed him to learn of others that would normally have escaped his notice. He was unable to see that the Child Who had been born was God, for he had lost for ever the power of perceiving the Divinity. All the created supernatural life of Jesus was hidden from him too, and for the same reason. But what he did see was sufficient to convince him that he was in the presence of a Man like unto none other. And piecing together the prophecies, he had good reason to believe that this Man could not be other than the Messiah promised to mankind after the fall of Adam, and destined to be his own great adversary and the challenger of his power. Whatever doubts remained in his mind were dispelled on the occasion of Jesus' Baptism by John. He seems to have heard the voice from Heaven saying " This is my beloved Son," for when the time came to tempt, he insists strangely on the idea of " Son of God". He realized that there was no time to be lost ; that if a trial of strength was inevitable it had better be now than later when the Newcomer would have had time to voice His ideas. So Satan, blinded by his pride to the point of not knowing that it was the Spirit of God Who prompted Jesus to do all that He did, seeing Jesus go into the desert and fast and pray, thought that events had played into his hands and that his victory was as good as assured.

There had never been such an encounter as this on the face of our earth since God met Satan in the form of the serpent in the garden of Eden and cursed him. It is bewildering even to think of the bare fact that there once was on this earth of ours, an encounter such as that between Jesus and the tempter. We are easily astounded at the strength of opposing armies, less easily at the strength of opposing ideas. But far exceeding such encounters was that of Jesus and Satan, of the King Who was God and the Prince who was the Devil. Events of untold importance hung upon its issue. Satan was no mean adversary. He came to the desert as a king, and one at that who was determined to fight for his kingdom. He had often fought before. He had often been victorious, had sometimes been worsted, but never as yet had serious inroads been made into his possessions. He had proved that he was more than a match for even the holiest of men if only he were given an open field. He could look back with pride on his victory over Adam. Adam was the greatest of mere men. There never had been another to compare with him. Yet he fell to Satan's strategy ; and if later he was partially extricated, that had not been his own unaided doing. David too had tasted the humiliation of defeat at his hands. And Solomon, the wisest of men, how complete had his overthrow not been ! Even at that very moment that he moved towards the desert he counted almost the entire world as his subjects. Here and there a few eluded him for reasons he could not grasp, except to believe that God had something to do with such rare cases. And now this Newcomer ! Poor, uneducated—though gifted —friendless, it was time to test Him, to explore His armour, to find His weakness and overthrow Him. Satan knew what it was to fight, and this was a call to battle. He could not have wished for a better place than the bleak, inhuman desert whither the Man he hated had so foolishly withdrawn.

The other Figure in that encounter was the King of Whom we spoke in the last chapter. His glory was hidden, perceptible only to the eye of the Beatific Vision and of faith. He had not as yet His Kingdom. For though born a King He had willed to win it at the price of His blood rather than by a display of power. But whatever may have been His appearance in the eyes of Satan, He was more than a worthy opponent of even so great a prince. He was the immortal God as well as mortal man. He could have annihilated Satan. He could have blinded his intellect by His power. He could have made him act foolishly—could have played with Satan, as Satan does with man. But He elected to fight him in a way worthy of Himself : He willed to overthrow him by the power of His humanity and nothing more. Satan would taste the humiliation of trying all the wiles of his persuasiveness against Jesus and being defeated each time by nothing more than what man could do with the help of God. And so the conflict would be, as it were, equal. On the one side the greatest of the rebel angels, on the other a Man, as full of loyalty to God as man could be. Created grace would be pitted against created iniquity, infused virtue against acquired vice, gifts of the Holy Ghost against the force of hate. The struggle would be, therefore, not God against Satan, but regenerated man against Satan. And the question to be decided would be : can man, with the help of God, enter the Kingdom of Heaven in face of the opposition of the Prince of Darkness ?

It is at first a little perplexing that the account of the conflict between Our Saviour and Satan should be presented to us in the Gospel narrative before we have been given a clear idea of the issue under dispute. We can gather from the circumstances of the conflict, from the bleak arena and the two lone combatants, that a Kingdom must be at stake. But Jesus has not as yet announced His Kingdom. Nothing more than penance has been preached so far. All we have been told is that we have need of a change of mentality, of revaluation of life, if we are to find a place in the scheme of things He came to inaugurate ; but it is not till afterwards, on the occasion of the sermon on the Mount, that the nature of His aims is clearly revealed. And yet, the very meagreness of the information about the details of the issue makes its essential nature all the more clear. What the three temptations in the desert are intended to reveal to us is the struggle involved in the mere fact of entering a kingdom of God at all, and the principles which determine success or failure in it. It is not so much question here of the difficulty of entry considered from the side of the nobility of the work as from that of the strength of the opposition it will meet. Our Lord's first purpose therefore is to warn us that if we wish to follow Him we shall meet opposition. But His warning is also an encouragement, for He reveals to us in His own Person how that opposition is to be met. At one and the same time He indicates the danger and the means of overcoming it. He fights first and alone that we may fight the better afterwards with Him. What He does, we can do with His help, because He acts now as man. He is answering now for us the question we must answer later for ourselves : to which Kingdom do I belong. And since it is for our sakes He willed to be tempted, He willed that the temptation should take the form in which it usually assaults our weakness. He Who was all Holy allowed Himself to be tempted at first as if He were a beginner in the ways of God, because He knew that there would be beginners who would be heartened by the example He gave them. He allowed Himself next to be tempted as one who had made a certain amount of progress, because even proficients—though human proficients are but beginners—would feel the weight of a diabolical attack. He allowed Himself finally to be tempted as one far on the way to perfection, for even such souls have the old and weak Adam within them. He was tempted three times that He might point out the dangers besetting three stages in man's incorporation into His Kingdom,[1] and He overcame each temptation that men might know that at no time has Satan power to wrest them from their allegiance to God.

The first temptation is introduced significantly by St. Matthew in the following words : " And when He had fasted forty days and forty nights, afterwards He was hungry " (Mt. 4, 2). Satan may have been in some doubt about the human nature of the Man He feared. He noticed in Him a certain dignity of bearing, a certain sureness in action, that no man had ever exhibited before. He might be more than man. Were there not prophecies that seemed to hint that One would come Who would be more than man ? Whatever doubts he had were dispelled when he saw that Jesus was hungry and weak after His fast of forty days. That was a sure sign of humanity. Man depended for life and vigour on food. Whoever was faint after fasting was a man. God had no need of food, and to be deprived of it would make no difference to Him. It would be safe therefore for Satan to tempt. He had nothing before him but a man. And he knew how to deal with men.

---

[1] The three temptations deal with the whole field of temptation, the world, the flesh, the devil, and the self. From this it follows that they contain, each and every one of them, a lesson for all men at all stages of their spiritual life, seeing that man may be tempted through any or all of the four channels of temptation no matter how little or how far he may have advanced in the things of God. Our purpose therefore in the present chapter is not to indicate the only lesson that can be drawn from Our Saviour's temptations, but to point out that one which bears most directly on the question of the Kingdom of Heaven.

The weak and famished condition of Our Saviour indicated at once what the matter of the first temptation should be. He would play upon man's need for food and man's objection to physical pain. But Satan does not tempt in one matter only at a time. He can weave the thread of this world and the thread of self, or of the flesh, into an alluring temptation-pattern. One colour will lend charm to the other. The man who might perceive but little that is attractive in the flesh if it were alone will become victim of its spell if it be backed up by the appeal of self. Hence he determined to play upon love of self as well as love of bodily satisfaction. He would make ability to satisfy the needs of the flesh the test of whether or not the name which Our Saviour claimed for Himself was really His. "Do what I ask you," says Satan, "if you really are what you pretend to be." "If thou be the Son of God, command that these stones be made bread" (Mt. 4, 3). The temptation is not to inordinate desire of food alone. Behind it there looms the shadow of the temptation to pride. A hungry man will feel the craving for food. If his ability to provide it be used to test his right to respect from others, the craving for food will become the instrument of the deeper craving for self-esteem and self-expression. That was Satan's idea in wording his temptation as he did. He wished to make it as strong as possible while still confining himself in some way to what was, after all, the least vital of man's needs, that of food for the body.

In this temptation Satan regards Our Saviour as one who has but set foot on the path of the service of God. The first difficulty which encounters the soul that has accepted the doctrine of penance as the condition and companion of entry into the Kingdom is that to do so involves a certain amount of physical pain. This difficulty does not make itself strongly felt from the very start. At the beginning God so arranges things that the new life of grace is sweetened by consolations. Did He not do this, there are but few of the race of man who would ever make the slightest progress in the spiritual life. But after a time He begins to withdraw the feelings of fervour and enthusiasm and perceptible joy which He had lavished so freely at first. He acts so because He wishes the soul to serve Himself more exclusively and to make less account of a possible reward in this world. But this wise intention of His is not at all clear to the soul. What the soul notices most of all is that certain sacrifices it had once made without feeling the pinch become unexpectedly painful. It forgets that they would have been just as painful before the time of conversion had it attempted to make them. It forgets that were it not for the pleasure felt in the strange experience of tasting for the first time that the Lord is sweet, they would never have been other than bitter to the taste even when they were swallowed down with seeming relish. The one thing that is evident to it is that to serve God involves suffering, and that suffering is not a thing which can be accepted lightly.

This first refusal to enter the Kingdom of God comes naturally from the body, for it is the weaker element in the combination of matter and spirit that goes to make up man. The body has its own tendencies, and being a body its tendencies are far from God. They are not necessarily opposed to Him : in fact they are never opposed to Him except in so far as they result from sin, original or actual. But they fall far short of Him. Their demand is in time. What He offers is for eternity. Their demand is for what can be seen and heard and felt. He offers what eye hath not seen nor ear heard, nor the mind of man hath ever conceived. The body can see no point in fasting, in enduring cold and heat, in patience under pain, in self-restraint. And as soon as ever it ceases to be lulled to sleep by the voice of God speaking to it in words of human sweetness, it will start up, querulous and snappy—indignant even—at the first waking experience of the strain of righteousness. And with the body will start up the whole man. For the body is the body of the man. One cannot remain unmoved when the cry of the body is heard. Its voice is not one that comes wafted from afar on an unkind breeze. It is a voice from within. No matter how much a man may feel that he is spirit he cannot grow insensible to the fact that he is matter too. The soul can dominate the body ; it can stifle its voice. But it dominates it only after it has rebelled, and it stifles its voice only after that voice has made itself heard. To turn to God does not mean to be relieved of the onus of having an ungodlike body. It means chastising it and bringing it into subjection.

So important a part does the body play in the commencement of the spiritual life that the great danger of the soul that has begun to enter the Kingdom of God is that it may be led insensibly by the body into entering the Kingdom of the world in one of its many forms as well. The body does this by persuading the soul to aspire to make self secure by turning the stones of life into bread. The first spiritual experiences are wonderfully exhilarating. The soul never felt so full of life before. There is therefore much in these experiences for self to feed on, and self will not be slow to appear on the scene. For a brief space God is in the limelight on the stage of the soul—not perhaps as much as the soul thinks, but still He is there. Gradually however self worms its way to His side. It finds that spirituality makes something of it. It can share the light thrown on God. When God raises the soul He raises what belongs to self. When He raises a soul, He raises *my* soul and I can feel as much pleasure in the fact that it is I who am raised as that it is He Who raises. In short, it is possible for the beginner to look on the spiritual life as having no greater value in practice than that it exalts self. This is simply the antithesis of the true idea of the Kingdom of God.

The next stage in this process is to notice that certain elements in the spiritual life are unpleasant. They may seem to cramp self or they may seem to cause it unnecessary pain—in any case they do not fit readily into a scheme of things in which everything is subjected to self. It is much more pleasant when the hard things of life—the stones—are subject to self, are made the bread which sustains it. Self really rules only when everything has its place beneath it. Hence one or other of two things may follow : the soul may give up the Kingdom of God and devote itself *ex professo* to the kingdom of self ; or, alternatively, the soul may establish a kingdom of self under the high patronage of the Kingdom of God, by carefully eliminating from the latter everything that is hard. It is this latter course of action which is meant by changing stones into bread—leaving out of life what is hard, though willed by God, and keeping only what agrees with one's personal taste.

Nothing is more sure than that the soul that loves self will object to the difficulties inevitable in serving God. It comes easily to regard moral goodness as something which will raise it above the storms and buffetings of life. It has always wanted to be a king, to meet with no opposition. Its first experience of loving God had seemed to indicate that to do so would lead infallibly to mastery of the trials of life. And yet, after a while the trials came back, as acute as ever, perhaps even more acute. There could be but one explanation of so paradoxical a situation : these trials did not really form part of the spiritual life. The soul begins to see that the doctrine of the necessity of mortification is altogether exaggerated ; that a great deal of human comfort is needed to facilitate virtue. It cannot rule all the rough out of life ; but it can ignore it as far as possible, avoid it as far as possible, avert it as far as possible. This is to make the stones of life into bread. Stones have their purpose in life : so has bread. But a life in which there are no stones is as purposeless as one in which there is no bread. It is pure delusion to claim to be in the Kingdom of God and still to avoid doing what is hard. To do this is to be in the kingdom of this world. It is worse— if there can be worse—it is to be a subject of self and to cherish the illusion that one is a subject of God. It is to be the enemy of God, and, refusing to admit the fact, to rule out the possibility of ever becoming His friend.

Our Saviour laid bare the inner meaning of this temptation when He replied : " . . . man liveth not by bread alone, but by every word of God " (Lk. 4, 4). His answer amounts to the affirmation that both the rough and the smooth have their place in God's Kingdom. Man does not live on the spiritual level by merely accepting what is pleasant and escaping what is hard. Everything that God sends him has a sanctifying power within it. Hence, if the spiritual man finds that there are hard things to be done, difficulties to be encountered, he knows that that is no indication that he is on the wrong road ; he knows, in fact, that it is in its own way a proof that he is on the right road. To live for God means the cross in some of its forms ; and the cross is always painful, even when it is made light to bear by the strength of love. A man who finds that his life contains all the human comfort he wants, has reason to ask himself does he really serve God at all. It may be that he had turned the stones of life into bread, not realizing that every stone is type of the Cornerstone, and that it is on and with the stones of life we must build. Satan did not strike blindly when he tempted Jesus as he did in this matter. He aimed a blow at one of the really vulnerable points in man's defences. Jesus parried the blow, but so as to leave Satan the strength to attack once more in force. And so he advances a second time, conscious that he cannot now treat his Adversary as a mere beginner, but must adopt a different tactic which in the past had often succeeded with those who accepted the stones of life but believed that in doing so they became something in the Kingdom of God.

"Then the devil took Him up into the Holy City, and set Him upon the pinnacle of the temple, and said to Him: If thou be the Son of God, cast thyself down, for it is written: That He hath given His angels charge over thee, and in their hands they shall bear thee up, lest perhaps thou dash thy foot against a stone" (Mt. 4, 5-6). This temptation, like the first, is not directed from one point only. It includes an attack by the door of pride: "If thou be the Son of God"; and another by way of that presumption so characteristic of people who think that they are now in a position to venture on the spectacular: "Cast thyself down, for it is written: That He hath given His angels charge over thee . . .". But what concerns us most of all here is that it is a temptation to vain-glory. For vain-glory is the second of the great obstacles in the way of entry into the Kingdom of God, and it is the one which awaits those who have been so far docile to grace as to have overcome their natural repugnance to doing things that cost.

When the soul is first tempted to give up the service of God because to serve Him is difficult, God's grace comes to help it to surmount the trial. It will reflect on the glory of the cross, on the cross as a sign of the divine friendship, on the cross as an instrument of character-formation, and heartened by these considerations and drawing new strength from the

Source of all strength it may embrace the cross to the extent to which it will have been revealed to its eyes. The soul enters now on a new phase of life. Not only must it love God, but it must suffer for Him as well. And this new phase, like the first of all phases, has its own peculiar sense of exhilaration, its own sense of finality, with the result that having done so much the soul imagines that nothing more remains to be accomplished. Unless the soul is very foolish it will, of course, admit as a speculative principle that it can advance still further in the way upon which it has now entered. In all probability it will admit this even as a practical rule of life. But what it will not so readily admit is that there is still a possibility of something, as it were new and yet untasted, of which it has to learn. It believes that it has found at length where God abides, and that there remains now but to move towards Him with sure and steady step.

It is, however, a fact of human experience that when once a person is convinced that he is perfect in his own line, he considers nothing more natural than that others should give him due honour. Spiritual men are not free from this danger. On the contrary, they are particularly open to it, precisely because it is so very easy for them to become prematurely convinced of their heroic virtue. Figure to yourself the enthusiastic beginner who has just renounced the world, the flesh, and the devil. How can he escape the gratifying feeling of a day's work well done ? He has lifted himself out of the rut. He has seen what the world is and has despised it. In the first temptation he has decided even to suffer for his convictions. The flesh and the devil will always be there : he is not afraid of them now. But the world simply is no longer, as far as he is concerned. And the world includes all the less enlightened men and women whom it is able to ensnare. He has meditated, too, on all the virtues, even the most rare. He forgets, of course, that it is not quite so easy to grow in them as to think about them, and that it is hardly likely that they mean quite so much for his will as they do for his mind. But nothing is easier than to confuse much thinking with much doing. A man who is a hero every morning during his half-hour's meditation will easily gloss over the prudential motives that activate his daily life. He will look on the half-hour as the reality : the rest will be oversight, never to be repeated. And so he lives in an imaginary world, glowing with an imaginary perfection, a worthy object of the respect and esteem of the good, a patient bearer of the unreasoning hatred of the very-obviously wicked.

In other words, he is tempted to set up a new kingdom of this world. Self will be glorified by the praise of the good and the opposition of the bad, both of which, praise and opposition, he regards as his due. The man who has triumphed over the first temptation will be willing to suffer a certain amount ; he will practise some mortification and will be patient in the trials sent by Providence. But he will expect some recognition of all this. He will seek a glory from men that will be vain and fictitious, and neglect the glory that comes from God—Who is quite as capable as man of recognizing merit and praising it, Whose judgment is more likely to be correct than man's will be, Whose praise is more sincere. But the man who has never really dethroned self—and no man ever does it fully in this world—will not be satisfied with faith's assurance that God appreciates him at his true worth. He wants something more palpable, something more vivid than faith. Self is impatient : self wishes to be quite sure. Hence, self will neither wait till after death for the full revelation of God's esteem, nor be content now with the knowledge that He is probably satisfied with His unworthy servant. The expressed approval and admiration of one's fellows is something self can understand, and that alone will satisfy it. That makes it a king. Its excellence wrings from others the tribute of their praise if they be candid and unbiassed, the tribute of their hatred if they be so dull and stockish as to relish nothing of the spiritual. But whether the result be praise or hatred, it is no less a tribute in the one case than the other. Provided only people take notice of us we are happy. By that fact alone they admit that we are to be reckoned with.

This pursuit of vain and empty glory leads necessarily to indiscretions, to spiritual displays calculated to make an impression. It is not easy to find words to describe the deformity of such manœuvres, whereby holiness, which means devotion to the glory of God, is made the tool of the glorification of self. It is the sin of the showily pious Pharisee, and Our Saviour spoke of it in terms so indignant as to close discussion on it for all time. In a mild form it is the sin of most other men as well. It is hard to be God-fearing and yet to be ranked as one of the herd. There is something about holiness, as about all true nobility, which entitles it to recognition : of that there is no doubt. It is hard to believe that God's recognition is sufficient even if not a single man appear aware of the existence of anything at all praiseworthy. We are tempted to make sure that our virtue will get its meed of praise from men by drawing their attention to it by quiet displays of righteousness. In this we exceed the Gospel command to let our light shine before men ; for we have never been commanded to flash it on their windows. And if we are unevangelical in our way of letting our light be seen, we are no less so in the end we have in view. For the Gospel tells us to let it be seen to such effect that men may praise Our Father Who is in heaven. Our light must appear as His rather than as ours, and that is precisely the reason why we have not the right to hide it at will. But the whole purpose of vainglorious display is to bring credit to self. It consists in displaying God's gifts as if they were our own. And that is to tempt God, to make trial of His patience, to use His gifts as if their whole purpose were to enable us to strut around with success. If a man who has been offended by a friend forgives him, only to find that advantage has been taken of the forgiveness to get into a position where it will be still easier to give offence, no one will think it extravagant that he should withdraw his friendship for ever from the ungrateful one. The latter has presumed too much on the patience of his friend. The case of the soul who angles for self with the line of God's gifts is of just the same kind. That soul is tempting God, testing the extent of God's patience. It will have no reason for surprise if it finds one day that grace has been withdrawn, for the moment at any rate, and that nothing stands between it and the gulf of sin. Our Saviour's words in this second temptation hold for all time : " It is written again : Thou shalt not tempt the Lord thy God " (Mt. 4, 7)

It is surely an act of brazen impertinence to build such a kingdom of self on the foundations of the Kingdom of God.

Even when the spiritual man has encountered and overcome this second temptation he has not as yet reached peaceful possession of the Kingdom of God. There is a further temptation, which assails, most naturally, souls of a certain intellectual and moral greatness, to which not all are submitted in its full fury, but which does manifest itself for every soul in at least a mitigated form. This temptation is the third of Our Saviour in the desert : " Again the devil took Him up into a very high mountain, and shewed Him all the kingdoms of the world, and the glory of them, And said to Him : all these will I give thee, if falling down thou wilt adore me " (Mt. 4, 8–9).

Students of the inspired word often find it hard to see the meaning of this temptation. It appears to them too utterly fantastic to have had even a chance of succeeding in the circumstances. It is hardly possible that any decent Christian whatever would fall down and adore Satan, much less One Who had overcome the preceding temptations so completely as Jesus had. Was this last temptation a final parting shot from a beaten spirit, who realized it had no chance of reaching its mark but was determined nevertheless to make it ? It is hardly in accordance with what we know of the intelligence of Satan to believe him capable of such folly. Neither is it appreciative of the Gospel to think that one of the three temptations could have so little to do with life as this one would have on such a supposition. One feels that the third temptation came third and last because it was the greatest of all, and that Satan retired after it and not before it because, not until it had failed was he really defeated. It is our duty now to explain its meaning for the doctrine of the Kingdom of God. This will not be its full meaning, nor will our present treatment give its only possible application. But having learned one of the lessons it is intended to drive home, we shall be all the better equipped to find out other ones for ourselves in private study and meditation.

The peculiar meaning of this temptation for us follows from the fact that it is the third, and hence presupposes that whoever undergoes it has overcome the other two to some degree at any rate. It is the temptation of a man who has realized that the spiritual life demands real sacrifices, and that virtue can easily be ignored this side of the grave. It might seem that a man who had come so far would have nothing further to fear from temptation. But to reason so is to neglect the pertinacity of self-love. One never cuts it off at the roots in this world. The most that we can do is to strip it of every leaf and shoot and endeavour thereby to condemn it to a slow death by starvation. While the root remains, however, it is capable of an intense effort to live. New leaves, new shoots, will continually appear upon what seems to be a withered trunk. The survival of any one of them will mean eventually the full growth of the root of self. Hence having, in the first two temptations, lost the shoots of softness and vanity, it makes one more supreme effort. The soul begins to feel that the spiritual life is a kind of moral annihilation ; that there is absolutely nothing at all to be got for self out of the Kingdom of Heaven. Two things rise before the mind's eye : the bleakness of what is spiritual, and the fulness of this world. And there arises within it a sickening revulsion for the spiritual and it feels the magic of the world as never before.

This temptation really resumes in itself all that is included in the first two. Man is led on to embrace suffering partly by the conviction that there is a certain glory attached to it. He is next led to renounce seeking that glory from men by display of goodness. But he has never renounced the desire of glory itself : all he has renounced is its fevered quest. Deep down in him, therefore, identified with his love of self and his love of the exaltation of self, is an intense desire of being valued as a somebody. And now that the position has been clarified by two temptations there remains but one alternative as issue to the third : either to give up all idea of glory in this world, or to commit the hypocrisy of affecting to despise it while being in reality its slave. And there is only one way of following this latter alternative successfully. It is to meet the world half-way.

What brings the second temptation to a head in the ordinary man is the conviction that it is quite possible to be spiritual and to remain unnoticed both by the virtuous and by the vicious. He sees that while remaining within the limits of what is allowed him he will probably fail to attract attention. His virtue will excite no comment. He will hardly be made a lord mayor or a managing director on the strength of his spirit of mortification. Even his natural talents, if kept well in control in their exercise by the supernatural, will tend to pale in the light of the world's day. He will not be pushful to excess. He will practise a certain modesty, will hold back when he can see no supernatural purpose to be achieved by coming to the fore. That again is not the recipe for quick success in life. If he does all this the result may well be oblivion. Whatever chance there is of attracting attention if one tempers one's spirituality with a little vain-glory, there is absolutely nothing to be got from pure and unadulterated spirituality except suffering and neglect. There appears to remain but one course open. Meet the world and Satan half-way. Do not give up the service of God. But make sure of success here and now by a sufficient dose of the service of Mammon. Serve the two masters. Have what you want both here and hereafter. Give way on some little point. Curtsey to the devil—he does not ask you to remain prostrate for ever before him—and the kingdoms of this world and their glory will be yours. And who knows but that you will have an eternal reward hereafter ? " Again the devil took Him up into a very high mountain, and shewed Him all the kingdoms of the world, and the glory of them, and said to Him : All these will I give thee, if falling down thou wilt adore me " (Mt. 4, 8–9).

I have said that this is most obviously the temptation of souls endowed with great gifts of nature or circumstance—not that anybody who merely thinks he has them may not fall into it as well—for its sting lies in the clear realization of what exactly men are called upon to renounce when they enter God's Kingdom : they see that they are asked to give up a lot ; that they could have made themselves a success here below and that they are asked to be indifferent as to whether they succeed or not. Satan knew, when he showed Our Saviour all the kingdoms of the world, that he was offering Him something big in the eyes of a man. We may say what we will of the hollowness of the world, of the vanity of riches, of the dead-sea character of earth's choicest plums, yet there is always something in this world that can quicken the heart-beat of even the holiest of men for some little instant. And while the world holds that thing—whatever it may be—the holiest of men can fall through too great a desire of it, because it will be always as plain to him as daylight that he can never be sure of getting it while he remains uncompromisingly holy. If there is anything in this world that does not offer the slightest guarantee to be a paying proposition in terms of the world's cash, it is holiness. And the one thing self will always demand is to be paid. This temptation will therefore be greatest when the soul sees clearly that it has certain definite worldly advantages within its grasp if it but bestir itself to get them. Needless to remark, this is not the problem of the beginner. It is the problem of someone who has tried himself and sees what he is capable of, and sees too that if he keeps on unswervingly in his course of unyielding fidelity to principle he will, at the very least, not be the success he might be. It is a hard temptation. And what makes it all the harder is that a very slight unbending in one's allegiance to God is all that appears to be required to set matters right. If a business-man takes part in just one slightly shady undertaking he will never need to do the like again. If a bishop lets one little matter pass without comment he will earn the undying gratitude of the government. If a priest say "yes" to a rich man when he would certainly say "no" to a poor one, he will be sure that his parish will not be forgotten. It is idle to say that these are slight temptations. Success in business, peace with civil powers, a parish free of debt—these are things that can shake the most firm. And then—it will be only this once! The rest of life is for God if only by this simple act you make sure of the world as well.

As is always the case, Our Saviour gives us the clue to the meaning of the temptation in His manner of meeting and rejecting it : "Then Jesus saith to him : Begone, Satan : For it is written : The Lord thy God shalt thou adore, and Him only shalt thou serve" (Mt. 4, 10). He insists in the text He quotes, that God alone has a right to adoration. And that is the kernel of the whole matter. To fall under this temptation is to assert that there is somebody or something other than God that deserves to be treated as a value. In saying this I do not refer so much to the self—even though whatever is done is done in view of self's gratification—as to the object which gives rise to the temptation. To pay the devil even the tribute of a passing nod of recognition is sufficient to constitute surrender to him. As weighed against God he simply is not. Neither are governments, nor success in life anything when weighed in the same balance. They have their own worth ; but to set them over against God is to filch it from them. It takes faith to see that nothing counts as against God. Very few men have faith so as to see that fully. We all hold back something, have some little bit of territory over which we still rule in our own name. We waver long before we enter upon the path traced out in the words : " Fear not, little flock, for it hath pleased your father to give you a kingdom " (Lk. 12, 32). We can see the reason now in the light of what this third temptation reveals to us. The reason is not so much that we do not want the kingdom that God has given us—though there are of course souls who sin by refusing it—but that we are not content with the part of the " little flock." We do not want to be a " little " flock. We want to be something big in men's eyes ; and still more do we want to be something big in our own eyes. Our sin is not that we do not want God's kingdom but that we want our own as well. There is one text of the gospel which appeals to us when we take it out of its context. It is that of St. Mark : " Amen I say to you, there is no man who hath left house, or brethren, or sisters, or father, or mother, or children, or lands, for my sake and for the gospel, who shall not receive an hundred times as much, now in this time . . . " (Mk. 10, 29-30). The reason of its appeal is that we do not believe that virtue is its own reward. We are convinced that it deserves a reward here below, and we will even deviate a little from the path of virtue to make sure of finding it. We do not see so clearly that the grace of God on earth is more than the hundred-fold promised. We pass over the final words or the text which promise us all these rewards " with persecutions." We are dazzled by what the world can offer and what appears to be our own worth, and falling down ever so little we adore Satan, and get from him all that he can give while still hoping from God all that He has promised.

If we abstract from what is its very essence, nothing is more characteristic of Christianity than the notion of the *pusillus grex*, the "little flock." In this world the Church and the individual will always be the "little flock." The moment any group of members of the Catholic Church attempts what one calls "cutting a figure" in the eyes of the world at large, the individuals concerned have succumbed to the third temptation. Our Lord's words to the contrary are altogether too explicit to admit of any doubt in the matter. He has promised that the world would hate His disciples. Never once did He promise that the world would give them its grudging but unqualified approval. In the eyes of the world the Church will always be a crank, because no matter how good the world will think itself, and no matter how fully the Church will approve of part of its schemes, there will always be some differences between the two which the Church will refuse to ignore. And there is nothing on earth more bitter for a Catholic than to see his Church put forward by well-meaning individuals as the ideal tool of schemes which, no matter how good, are still but worldly. The Church is its own recommendation. It has no need to be padded out with the majesty of states and kingdoms, with the dignity of philosophers and movements. We could, if we but willed, have what the world has. Who knows better than we do what the world is and how to woo it? But to have it we must first bow the knee. That we shall never do. As individuals too, the members of the Church could make for themselves a name that would ring wide across seas and continents. With our age-old knowledge of man and God, with our philosophy, to what might we not attain in fancy schools of thought and daring schools of art? Knowing what is right we could give what is wrong that peculiar tinge of reality which makes all the difference between a nightmare and what may be. The price however is still the same. Bow the knee and all these will be yours. Pass me by and your virtue will be your only reward—and you won't think so very highly of the reward, either !

These were the three temptations which Our Saviour endured for our instruction and encouragement. Let us consider in conclusion one point of instruction which they contain and one point of encouragement as well.

The manner in which Jesus met Satan teaches us that whoever enters the Kingdom of God will overthrow the kingdom of Satan within himself—and in the world too—rather by suffering at its hands than by any display of power. Why should this be so ? If we say that it is so because God has so determined, we have given the best reason that man can formulate. God has decided to allow Satan to attack us while we live, and has guaranteed us the power to resist and to repel for the moment, but He has never promised us, while we are still wayfarers on earth, the power to inflict such a defeat upon the powers of darkness as to render them powerless against us for the rest of time. Our Saviour could have disarmed Satan from the very start. He could have allowed him sufficient semblance of strength to induce him to tempt and could then have reduced him to impotence. Instead, He allowed Him to renew his attack time after time ; and even the third attack was not the last of all, for we read : "And all the temptations being ended, the devil departed from Him for a time" (Lk. 4, 13). If for a time only, then he returned later. It was for our instruction therefore that Our Saviour endured this repetition of Satan's assaults. He wished us to know that we should have to endure the same. It will never be permitted us to build up a kingdom of self—even one based on the power to overthrow the devil at will. We shall have just as much power over him as God will give us and no more. Whatever we can do will be not to our sole credit but rather to that of Him Who strengtheneth us. Our great contribution to the struggle will be our patience : "My brethren, count it all joy, when you shall fall into divers temptations ; knowing that the trying of your faith worketh patience. And patience hath a perfect work . . ." (James 1, 2-4).

Our Saviour's manner of meeting temptation encourages us, who must encounter Satan, by the fact that He did so as man, and used the weapons which God places at the disposal of every man. His method of defence was always to take refuge in His Father's will. Whatever could be shown to be the will of the Father must be right. That is the meaning of His appeal to Holy Scripture. In other words, the way to defeat the kingdom of Satan is to remain within the Kingdom of Heaven ; and this because, as we have seen in a general way already, to be in the Kingdom of Heaven means to obey the law of God. God's plan for us is therefore very simple. We are not obliged to wage a war at the same time on two fronts. We are not even obliged to divorce our warfare from our inner growth. We defeat Satan by growing in grace, and we grow in grace by defeating Satan, and we do both by being submissive to the will of Our Father Who is in Heaven. Satan refused to submit in his own person. It is part of his punishment that he can be infallibly defeated by whoever will submit. He can pinch out the strength of human wisdom and pride between his thumb and forefinger. Humility defeats him because there is nothing in it on which he may lay hold. Pit your wits against his and you are lost. Pit your steadfastness against his power to cajole, and again you are lost. Take refuge in the wisdom and steadfastness of God, and Satan is powerless against you. His kingdom is powerful only against another made with hands. He falls back before the city that hath foundations ; whose builder and maker is God (cf. Hebr. 11, 10).

After the temptations, Satan departed from Jesus. It is with reason that the Evangelist adds that he departed from him only for a time. Satan had tried his wiles in vain. But there still remained to him two weapons as yet unused. He, being a liar and a murderer, could fall back on lies and death to complete what wit had botched. He would use the weapon of death only at the very end. The weapon of lies would need a fair and lengthy trial. If Christ really intended to establish a kingdom of God then Satan might succeed in hindering His work by a systematic campaign of lying, undertaken to poison men's minds against Him. That is the meaning of the false accusations of the Pharisees and Scribes. When they said He had a devil, when they said He cast out devils by Beelzebub, the prince of devils, when they said that His disregard of the Sabbath proved Him no man of God, they were the tools of a new temptation of Satan's. The time would come, however, when he would see that even lies were of no avail, that in spite of all that he could do, the whole world seemed to be following after the Saviour. He would be a murderer then, and suffer thereby utter defeat. But that is as yet a distant event. For the moment it remains that Jesus has wrestled with Satan. He has shown us the conflict which entry into the Kingdom entails. And it is now time that He should speak to us of the Kingdom itself. Going up into a mount He will speak of it. But His greatest sermon of the Kingdom will be one yet to come, preached from the pulpit of a cross.

CHAPTER VI

THE LAW OF THE KINGDOM

" I am not come to destroy, but to fulfil " (Mt. 5, 17).

MARY at the feet of Jesus in the home of Bethany, and the disciples gathered about their Master on the Mount of the Beatitudes—here are two scenes widely separated in their placing in the Gospel narrative, but near in the spirit that animates them. Mary, the sign of Christian perfection, was not idle at the feet of Jesus. The silence of her soul was filled, though still unbroken, with the deep peace of Jesus' voice. Nor were the disciples in any state other than that of breathless contemplation. They were not an uneasy, jostling throng, hearing chance words and commenting upon them in light accents. They could sense the majesty of the Law of God, and under the shadow of its wings they too found rest. They, no less than Mary, symbolize perfection. For it is of His Father's Law that Jesus spoke to them, and they like Mary, accepted it in joyful docility.

True though it be, however, that Mary and the Apostles

heard the same message of Divine Law, and ready enough though we be to assent to its identity in the two cases, there are many among us who would find it hard to explain how Mary in a few, perhaps, and deeply personal words, could have heard the same message as the disciples did in the many and general principles exposed to them on the mountain-side. And this is so because we concentrate our attention too exclusively on the mere words uttered. We do not see that what identifies Mary with the disciples is, before everything else, her attitude to what was said to her rather than what was said, considered in itself and in its superficial meaning. What identifies her with the disciples is that she, as well as they, accepted God's will in loving submission. It did not really matter so very much to her whether she heard much or little of its behests : she would have accepted it in any case. The disciples on their side showed the same readiness on a later occasion when, the meaning of Jesus' words escaping them, they yet cried out by the voice of Peter : " Thou hast the words of eternal life " (Jo. 6, 69). They confessed by these words their conviction that Jesus set more store by their readiness to believe and accept His word than by the completeness or incompleteness of the word which He happened to communicate to them. How this can be—how the all-important seems to be the readiness to accept rather than what is offered for acceptance—though it be at the same time the explanation of something else, is in its turn too a mystery, until we go still further in our consideration and arrive at length at what is a very obvious principle : that God has had but one idea of what He expected from fallen man, that willingness to accept the slightest intimation of this idea implied willingness to accept its totality, and that no matter how diverse the intimations made to different people at different times might at first glance seem to be, they become one in their acceptance, since one is their totality. Mary accepted not so much what Jesus said as the idea of God's right to rule. This was what the disciples had accepted before her. She, no less than they, was sanctified by the acceptance of a King and Lawgiver. God always approaches souls by leading them into a Kingdom.

We must bear these general considerations in mind if we hope to obtain any clear view of the meaning of the Sermon on the Mount considered as an exposition of the New Law of God as distinguished from the Old. For though there have been two Laws since the fall of our first parents, there has been all along but one mind in God, but one end to all Law, namely His rule in men through the Redeemer. The Old Law does not differ from the New as do intimations of distinct purposes. It differs from it as the imperfect outline of the mind of God does from the complete masterpiece. At all times God wished to rule fully in men, and that through the Redeemer. In the old law He wished to rule through faith and hope in the Redeemer to come ; in the new Law He wishes to rule through faith in and love of the Redeemer Who has come. Corresponding to these accidental differences in the position of the Redeemer, there are differences too in ceremonial and in judicial procedure. But the core of the reality is one. As we have seen in the case of Mary and the disciples, what really does count in God's eyes is our attitude of acceptance of His Kingship. His Kingship in Christ is the reality proposed us by the Old Law just as much as by the New, though so much more perfectly in the New than in the Old. What the Old needed therefore was not destruction but completion.

This is the key to Our Saviour's striking words at the opening of His discourse : " Do not think that I am come to destroy the Law or the prophets. I am not come to destroy, but to fulfil " (Mt. 5, 17). The Law and the prophets had given imperfect utterance to the legislative word of God. They had spoken in terms sufficiently explicit to lead a fallen race by the path of patient waiting to the day of the coming of the Promised One. They had even been so clear as to lead men of good will to a certain degree of intimacy with this as yet unborn Redeemer, so great as to lift them by His grace bodily, as it were, out of the Old dispensation and transfer them into the Kingdom of the glorious Son of God. But clear though they had been, God could speak clearer still. He could speak in His incarnate Word. " God, Who at sundry times and in divers manners, spoke in times past to the fathers by the prophets, last of all, in these days hath spoken to us by

His Son. . . ." (Hebr. 1, 1-2). When this Son would speak He would do so, not as saying something altogether new, but as saying explicitly what had been said in figure, as saying completely what had been said in part. The core of His message would be what God's had always been : accept the Kingdom of God. What would make it new would be the perfection of its detail and the majesty of Him Who spoke. Can we find a clearer proof of this than that encounter of His with the lawyer, who replying in words taken from the Old Testament to his own question about the terms of eternal life, heard the disconcerting reply : "Thou hast answered right : this do and thou shalt live" (Lk. 10, 28). Does not Our Saviour state in equivalent terms that His mission is not so much to inaugurate as to restate, not so much to teach a new lesson as to explain a lesson already taught ?

It would however be a mistake to think that Jesus' fulfilling of the Law meant nothing more than perfecting the imperfect. That is what He did if we consider the Law as a written code. But when we turn to the law as understood and lived by the Jews, we find that He did more than to perfect : there was a great deal of positive error, of perversion of the mind of God, to be removed. His legislation considered from this standpoint was much more a return to the original divine intention than its fuller exposition. The mind of God had become obscured by the abuse of the letter of His law. This was the evil that wrung from the lips of St. Paul his "For the letter killeth, but the spirit quickeneth" (2 Cor. 3, 6). What Moses had allowed because of the hardness of men's hearts came to be understood as the expression of a maximum demand : "Moses by reason of the hardness of your heart permitted you to put away your wives : but from the beginning it was not so" (Mt. 19, 8). What had been prescribed in the Law as a rule of conduct for judges in the exercise of their official duties, came to be taken as the norm to be followed in the interior attitude of a man to one who would have offended him : "You have heard that it hath been said : an eye for an eye and a tooth for a tooth. But I say to you not to resist evil" (Mt. 5, 38-39). And then there were as well the confusing array of man-made prescriptions in the observances of which the Pharisees seemed to make all perfection consist, and whose observance seemed to justify interior rottenness. All this was the Law as it was lived in the souls of those whom Jesus addressed. To fulfil the Law in their regard was to save it from them. They had lost sight of what God intended when He gave them His Law. His mind must be revealed once more. That was the second purpose of the Sermon on the Mount.

Were we to ask now what the immediate message of the Sermon on the Mount may be to us who live almost two thousand years after its delivery, we shall find our answer rather in its second purpose than in its first. The message of God to man is too simple to allow us to demand a lengthy exposition of its content. It amounts to a mere " Submit to the rule of God." But each individual does for himself what the Jews did as a race : he perverts God's Law ; he understands submission to God as meaning just what it suits him to have it mean. And when we understand that simple fact, the two thousand years that separate us from the pronouncing of the great Sermon cease to be. The Sermon is directed against what every one of us is doing to-day rather than against what was done once upon a time by some now-dead party. The Law of God needs to be saved from our perversion of it as much as from its perversion by the Jews. The great St. Thomas Aquinas was keenly aware of this when he proposed to answer the question of the essential difference between the Old Law and the New. That point of difference which would be the first to come to the mind of many an intelligent man— that the Old Law preceded the New in time—receives but scant attention at his hands. The difference between the two is more than temporal ; so much more, in fact, that it was possible to be under the New Law while living in the time of the Old. It is one between a perfect and an imperfect acceptance of God's rule. For St. Thomas those Jews who accepted God's rule fully, and submitted to His grace, were under the New Law not the Old. For the New Law is nothing more than the Law of grace, the Law of the Spirit. And we may add, as an obvious corollary to what he has said, that those Christians who understand the Law of grace carnally—

that is to say as a Law of externalities and not a Law of the spirit—when they deign to consider it at all, are still under the Old Law. The Sermon on the Mount is intended for such ; and we are all to some extent such. While we are not yet ruled completely by love we are not yet fully of the New Law. While we are as yet ruled by fear and give grudgingly, we are as yet of the Old. Nothing will cast out fear but love. Nothing will cast out all fear but perfect love. And perfect love is not of earth. It is the prerogative of the blessed in heaven. All men without exception are therefore ruled to some extent by the Old Law. For nobody is the Sermon on the Mount a fully-learned lesson.

Let us come then in spirit with Our Saviour to the Mountain, and stand near Him, with His disciples in the plain place (Lk. 6, 17). If we have faith we shall see His right to command. He is a King. His face has a majesty not of this earth. He is meek, peaceful, gentle ; but there is about Him an atmosphere of intangible, unknowable infinity. His forbearing calm casts a mighty spell upon the good ; the wicked regard it as weakness. His possessed anger fills His own with peace ; it sends a deep thrill of terror through those wicked ones who a moment before thought Him negligible. He looks a peasant, but He speaks like a King ; and when He speaks, one is not so sure that He had ever looked the peasant. Many a man might dare to harangue a mob on a hill-side, but when this Man speaks what were else a chance-gathered mob becomes, in some mysterious way, all humanity, lettered and unlettered, cultured and uncouth ; and what might have been a harangue, sounds a continuation of the mighty and creative " Let there be " of the first pages of Genesis. It is more than man Who speaks ; for it is the Head and King of men. His words are not just the advice of a counsellor ; they are the will of a law-giver. The Son of God has come into the far country of this world to receive a Kingdom, and He waits to see if His subjects will receive their King.

The continuity of the Old Law with the New is evident from the fact that the whole of Our Lord's teaching is contained in germ in the words of Deuteronomy : " Thou shalt love the Lord thy God with thy whole heart, and with thy whole soul, and with all thy strength, and with all thy mind ; and thy neighbour as thyself" (cf. Lk. 10, 27). The Sermon on the Mount teaches us how to translate the terms "whole" and "all" into daily life. It is as it were a commentary on the two great commandments of the Law. It is easy to admit that one should love God with the whole heart. But very few people succeed in seeing what this will mean for them when they set about earning their living or doing whatever duties fall to their daily lot. And since to love God is to allow Him to reign in our hearts, that is equivalent to saying that, whereas the average Christian will admit God's right to complete control, he will have an altogether inadequate idea of how all-embracing complete control really is. It was to be expected then that Our Blessed Lord would insist on the necessity for God's subjects of clear vision of the things of God. They must be able to see just what He has a right to. He reserved therefore a special beatitude for the clean of heart, because it is they alone who have the power of seeing God.

The world in which we live is darkness. Each soul has been given a light to enable it to make its way safely through life's night to the eternal day of heaven. That light is the eye of the soul (cf. Mt. 6, 22-23). But the eye of the soul lights up the soul only to the degree to which the soul makes good use of it. It must be kept single, or simple ; that is to say, it is strong enough to light up one narrow way before us, and to make that way safe to walk ; but if we flash it here and there, if we use it to peer into corners, to search out the filth of life's night, to follow the alluring progress of some intoxicating presence that brushed us as we toiled along our way—if we try to do all this by the light of our soul's puny flicker, we shall miss our path and be involved in those regions of outer darkness where the soft brightness of God's dawning day never rests upon a widening view. Only the pure of heart can see this dawn as they trudge through life. There is only one path that is flooded from time to time with the light of God's presence. And there is only one way of keeping to that path; and that way is to keep our hearts off every other one. We must be pure of heart to see God whether here on earth or hereafter. For purity of heart means ultimately freedom of heart from all that is not God, and the only soul that will see God consistently in everything is the soul that does not want to see anything else. The soul that wants pleasure will see opportunities for pleasure in almost everything ; if it is put some place where opportunities for pleasure are non-existent it becomes simply miserable. The soul avid of praise will find a way to turn almost every conceivable event to its own glory ; and if it ever fails to do so, it too is miserable. The soul which has constituted God its only treasure will be ingenious in finding ways of serving God where others will see only an opportunity of serving self ; will be responsive to intimations of the Divine Will where others will see nothing more than an opportunity of doing what they like. "If thy eye be evil, thy whole body shall be darksome. If then the light that is in thee be darkness : the darkness itself how great shall it be : " (Mt. 6, 23). If the eye of the soul be wasted in searching out what is not God then the whole soul will be left in the pitiful condition of being unable to see God. There will be no question then of pretending that one obeys God's Law. How can one obey when one hears no voice ? Set your heart on anything that is not God and the belief that God reigns in you is sheer delusion. You are still in the kingdom of this world. You still have a king, it is true. That much has not been taken from you. But the king you have is Satan. God is a King you have lost.

Were it not that we are already convinced of the intrinsic likelihood of any human frailty we should possibly be surprised at Our Saviour's next remark on the subject of cleanness of heart. Those, He tells us, who have least of it in themselves are far from being the very last in the power to detect and criticize its absence in others : " Why seest thou the mote in thy brother's eye ; and seest not the beam that is in thy own eye?" (Mt. 7, 3). A recommendation to mildness in our judgments on others, you may say, and in saying so you will not be wrong. But it is easy to miss another deep lesson contained in the same question—one, namely, concerning cleanness of heart. We see the mote in our brother's eye. But do we fail to observe further that our brother is quite ignorant of its presence ? He gazes on the world, and sees

things as he believes them to be, and is quite convinced that
his view-point is the one which reveals the truth ; and yet
we who stand outside him are at no great pains to notice that
his vision labours under a serious defect. We who have
detected the mote in his eye understand why he sees things
as he does and why his sight is not reliable. It is not necessary
that we should feel forced to accuse our neighbour of bad
faith every time we notice him acting unbecomingly. There
are times when his good faith is evident and his action must
be attributed to ignorance, or moral blindness. We notice
that a certain person often says sharp and cutting things. If
we credit him with the explicit desire to hurt on each such
occasion we shall probably be mistaken. It is more than likely
that he is unaware of the latent cruelty in what masquerades
in his mind as pleasant jesting. And thus it happens that, often,
when we detect the presence of a mote we detect as well
ignorance of its presence in him whom it blinds. Could we
go one step further we should do our souls much good. It
is not far from this to the final admission that if a brother
can have a mote in his eye and be unaware of its presence,
it is more than likely that there are not a few motes in our
own eyes as well ; and that the fact that we are unaware of
them, so far from being a proof that they are not there, is
part of the burden of having ourselves introduced them by
turning the soul's eye incautiously upon the regions of dust-
laden darkness. " Who can understand sins ? From my
secret ones cleanse me, O Lord " (Ps. 18, 13). While it is
unquestionably true that God gives all men light enough to
see what stands between them and their eternal salvation with
sufficient clearness to enable them to surmount it, it is
nevertheless a fact that no soul can pride itself on accepting
His rule fully, because no soul can be sure that it sees His will
fully. The first condition of entry into the Kingdom of God
is submission to the absolute necessity of dependence upon His
light even for the power of seeing what He wants us to do.
Cleanness of heart is the condition for seeing the words of
His Law.

To the soul whom cleanness of heart has led to the threshold
of His Kingdom Our Blessed Lord addresses a second beatitude :

" Blessed are they that hunger and thirst after justice : for they shall have their fill " (Mt. 5, 6). Just as the beatitude of the clean of heart indicated the general condition of intellect required for membership of the Kingdom of God, this second beatitude lays down the general attitude of will demanded in the same circumstances. One should come to the Kingdom anxious to perform the duties of citizenship. The Kingdom of God is not meant for those who regard its claims as matter for one's spare time. Even were it possible to serve two masters to the entire satisfaction of both, it is impossible for the human servant to do so, because of the extreme limitedness of his power to serve. The only way a man can give *genuine* allegiance to God, is to throw up every other allegiance which is not included in the greater one, and then pour out every drop of his life-blood on the altar of his great choice. God deserves more than that we serve Him alone : He deserves that we serve Him well ; He deserves that we hunger and thirst to serve Him. Our hunger will not remain unappeased, nor will our thirst torture us unslaked. Nothing more is demanded on our side than that we do hunger and thirst, and then, by that simple fact, we are nourished by the Kingdom of Heaven. To hunger and thirst for God is to serve Him, and that alone is sufficient to make one a member of His Kingdom. To possess God therefore, in His Kingdom, nothing more is asked than that we want Him, just as to lose Him it suffices to want something else intensely enough.

Hungering and thirsting after justice we shall enter in by the narrow gate : " Enter ye in at the narrow gate " (Mt. 7, 13). There is another gate, too, open before us ; a wide one through which we can pass with all the trappings and retinue of earthly royalty. If we enter by the narrow gate we must leave all our finery behind, for it is just wide enough to permit of the passage of body and soul, and even then the body will suffer bruising as it enters. It needs vision to see that the narrow gate is the better of the two, and it needs deep desire of God to make one follow one's vision. It is not even sufficient to know that the wide gate leads to eternal pain : " Wide is the gate, and broad is the way that leadeth to destruction " (ib.). For in spite of the evil reputation that wide gate has, it is true that "many there are who go in thereat" (ib.). They all go in thereat who insist on keeping self's little show intact. We cannot say, to reassure ourselves, that from the very start they had made up their minds to reject God. What determined their path was probably their not having any thirst for Him, because they knew they could drink to their heart's content at a thousand other streams.

It is necessary for us therefore, that we hear Our Saviour's words and DO them with desire. "The charity of Christ presseth us" (2 Cor. 5, 14) should be as true of us as it was of St. Paul. Hunger and thirst of the Kingdom is, after all, a matter of love of the Kingdom. There are many who wish to pass as willing to enter the Kingdom of Heaven, but whose great subconscious desire is never to fall a victim to the folly of loving it. Love takes one outside oneself, and self is the last thing man will consent to give up. The love that is most congenial to fallen man is the love of self. It combines the mock heroism of a sham quest of the good with the reassuring consciousness that the goal is already possessed ; for the love of self is of that serpent form which reaches out only to coil up again all the more readily. It was a commonplace of medieval theologians that original sin had as effect on the will of man to turn it back upon itself. God had made Adam erect, facing upwards to God. Sin bowed man down. The will which turned outside itself to God by grace, turns inwards now to self in concupiscence. We all come into this world tainted and weakened by Original Sin. Nothing will draw our wills away from self but thirst. A deep and true thirst cannot be quenched at the broken cistern of the thirsting soul. Such a thirst forces the will, as it were, Godwards. And such a thirst, implying as it does some knowledge that the Lord is sweet, and even some anticipated experience of His sweetness, cannot come otherwise than as His gift. One cannot by taking thought add to one's stature. Neither is it possible by just willing, unaided by grace, to enter the Kingdom. It is God Who gives us both to will and to accomplish. Our thirst will come from Him, as will our hunger of His Justice. Our part is to experience both thirst and hunger with joy, and to refuse all meat other than the will of Him Who made us.

The result of our vision and ready acceptance of the will of God will be that our virtues will be interior : " My little children, let us not love in word, nor in tongue, but in deed, and in truth " (1 Jo. 3, 18). It is not sufficient to say to God that we love Him and serve Him ; we must really do so : " Not every one that saith to me Lord, Lord, shall enter into the kingdom of heaven : but he that doth the will of My Father Who is in heaven, he shall enter into the kingdom of heaven " (Mt. 7, 21). God has no need of words, nor of our material achievements, nor of our possessions. There is ultimately but one gift which we can make to Him, and that is the gift of our free wills. It is precisely because these are free that they can become the matter of a gift. Words, achievements, possession, and suchlike things, mean nothing to God if man does not present them with his will. It is only when the will offers them that they share in something of the will's inner freedom. Our goods, for example, belong already to God. Considered in terms of the value they have as things they cannot belong more completely to Him than they do by the facts of creation and conservation. It is only as considered in terms of the value they have for us that they can really be offered in a new way to Him, and we do that by withdrawing our wills from them except in so far as God allows and desires their use. That is the meaning of poverty of spirit. It, too, is said to be an element in the constitution of the Kingdom : " Blessed are the poor in spirit : for theirs is the kingdom of heaven " (Mt. 5, 3).

We have already given the key to the understanding of poverty of spirit when, in an earlier chapter, we pointed out that the kingdom of self may be built up on riches possessed in desire no less than on riches possessed in fact. It is even correct to say that of the two, the only riches which are really important are those possessed in desire. To be rich in fact is no obstacle to loyal service of the Heavenly King, if justice be all that one hungers for. The vitally important thing is not to be *of* the world ; whether one be *in* it or *out* of it makes little difference. We have every right to use this world and all that it contains on the condition that we do so as if we used them not (cf. 1 Cor. 7, 31). This beatitude is no glorification of human misery considered as such. It is praise of a heart in which there is no misery because there is no love of what can cause eternal pain. And the point of its message is that the kingdom of heaven cannot cohabit with the kingdom of self, and that it is vain to hope to have the former while one strives after the latter by love and desire of riches.

" Be not solicitous therefore, saying : what shall we eat, or what shall we drink, or wherewith shall we be clothed ? " (Mt. 6, 31). Our Lord wishes to put us on our guard against solicitousness in the matter of the goods of this world, even when they are such as are necessary for the sustenance of human life. We claim to have submitted ourselves to the law of God. Nevertheless we fear the possibility of some privation in the matter of food or clothing or drink—let us say, for brevity's sake, in the things necessary for life ; or it may even be that we fear no privation, but we see the possibility of obtaining some considerable advantage. Desiring as we do to submit in all things to the will of God we tell ourselves that it is certainly God's will that we should have what is necessary for life, or that He gave us what we have that we might put it to good account and better our position thereby. How are we to know if we deceive ourselves in all this ? Is it the kingdom of heaven we seek, or is it the kingdom of self ? Our Saviour's answer to the doubt is amazingly simple. " Be not solicitous." There is no reasonable use of riches incompatible with membership of the Kingdom, provided only that one is not deliberately worried about how the venture will turn out. 'Having a treasure in heaven we should be indifferent to the fate of that other treasure which the rust and the moth consume and which thieves break through and steal (cf. Mt. 6, 30). If we treasure God alone our hearts will be in heaven with Him, and the rise or fall of our earthly possessions will seem of little moment. Even if the worst— or what passes in the world as the worst—should happen, we have a Father in Heaven Who clothes the lilies of the fields and cares for the birds of the air. He knows what we need and knows how to provide it. Our welfare is no cause of worry to Him Who has no doubts about the extent of His infinite resources. The sincerity of our identity of will with

His will is tested by our sharing or not sharing in His confidence in His power to provide for us. That is poverty of spirit—attachment not to goods but to God. It is a virtue for the rich as well as for the poor, for all are called to the Kingdom.

In the course of the Sermon on the Mount Our Lord gives one example of the poverty of spirit He demands, which is more eloquent in its simplicity than any learned discussion of the notion of spiritual nakedness will ever be. It is as follows : " Give to him that asketh of thee, and from him that would borrow of thee turn not away " (Mt. 5, 42). There is this peculiarity about lending and borrowing, that borrowing is in itself legitimate and the man who refuses ever to lend is unreasonable, but that he who does lend because he knows it is a good thing to do so is never quite sure that what he gave on loan will ever be returned. Lending, we may say, is the one great duty in the fulfilment of which the man who has goods of this world runs a continual risk of being deprived of them. The ordinary layman is well acquainted with the harmless ne'er-do-well type (who, by the way, never gets all the credit due to him for being a ne'er-do-harm in addition to a ne'er-do-well) whose arrival on the scene is followed invariably by a request for a loan of a few shillings—more or less as circumstances vary. Our Lord recommends that if we have no reason for refusing the loan which would sound other than futile in the ears of a fair-minded man, it is not upright to slip across the road before the would-be borrower catches sight of us. Money lent to such a person—making all due allowance for exceptional circumstances which will justify refusing a loan—is committed to the care of Providence. There is no other power on earth to look after it. If therefore we refuse habitually and unreasonably to lend, we may be sure that our hearts are set on our money for its own sake rather than because God wills us to make good use of it. There is no reason for confining this matter of borrowing to money. One can betray oneself by unwillingness to lend books, tools—anything in fact, which it is inconvenient to be deprived of. Neither is there any reason for confining it to the category of laymen. It applies equally well—in fact, with still greater force—to religious who have taken a vow of poverty. For even such have the use of certain objects for their personal use or for their work. It is very disturbing to be troubled by importunate fellow-religious for a loan of such things. The very least evil that will result will be that the lender will have to do as best he can without them till they are returned ; it will often happen that through human thoughtlessness they will not return till he asks them back. But such inconveniences are no reason for searching out some excuse that will repel the borrower. It is in the nature of things that borrowing and lending should find their legitimate place in religious life, and whoever refuses to shoulder this little burden confesses that though the vow of poverty deprives him of the fact of possession, his heart has never really renounced the desire. He is poor, but not in spirit. He possesses nothing, but he claims the exclusive use of all that he can of the common stock. Poverty of spirit is something very radical. It is not possible to see at the outset of one's life just how far its demands will reach. But though it be a price that exhausts our powers of giving it falls far short of what it purchases. And it is no mere chance that its reward is spoken of as obtained here on earth : " Blessed are the poor in spirit : for theirs *is* the kingdom of heaven " (Mt. 5, 3). The spiritual life cannot create a void. If the soul be free from self and its train the King of Glory will not delay to enter in.

We have just seen how it is possible to deceive oneself in one's attitude to riches. It is still more easy to be guilty of self-deception in the matter of self-love. The reason is that renunciation of self is necessarily so much a matter of saying to God that one has ceased to love self. It is so easy to pray (forgetting in characteristic fashion to make of it a prayer of petition) : " My God, I renounce henceforth all love of self. I belong to Thee alone, and will seek Thee alone in all things." A beautiful prayer in itself, but how meaningless it can be on human lips : " Not every one that saith to me, Lord, Lord, shall enter into the kingdom of heaven " (Mt. 7, 21). When one has determined to renounce self in all things, the renouncing still remains something to be done. And since " all things " become a part of a human experience not all together but one after another, the practice of self-renunciation means a continued conquest of self in a ceaseless daily struggle. It is possible to link together two of the beatitudes which still remain to be considered under the aspect of their place in the daily conquest of self. (It is of course clear that all eight beatitudes are ultimately rewards of some form of self-renunciation.) These two are the beatitudes of the meek and the merciful. It is easy to see why they are so closely dependent on the idea of the struggle with self. The reason is that they deal with our relations with other men, and it is most of all when we come up against our fellows, and feel that they too have selves which they are pushing to the fore, or that they have slighted the self which we value so highly, that the struggle of the kingdom becomes so radically simple as to be a matter of God or self, with no world, flesh, or devil, to complicate the issue.

" Blessed are the meek : for they shall possess the land " (Mt. 5, 4). This is the first of the two beatitudes we are about to consider. It is hard to define meekness ; but it is sufficiently described by saying that it is the contrary of pushfulness. In saying this the opposition between the two kingdoms is once more brought out into clear relief. The quality which ensures possession of what this world can give is pushfulness. The quality which ensures the possession of what God can give is its contrary. Could opposition be more marked ? Not unless it be that of love of self and love of God ; and this is not a new opposition but the root of the first ! A man is pushful when he keeps self well to the fore, especially when plums are going. Meekness is, then, nothing other than a certain disregard of self manifested in what the world takes for lack of initiative. It does not exclude initiative in business. The initiative it excludes is that which is quick to seize on an opportunity for praise and recognition. A successful business-man can be meek if he does not use his success to help him make a stir where there is a chance of his being unnoticed.

It is meekness that Our Lord recommends when He tells us : " Let your speech be yea, yea : no, no . . . " (Mt. 5, 37). There is a time for chattiness. A good talker can do a lot to cheer up even the most confirmed pessimists. But there is also a time for silence, and—what is still more difficult to recognize—there is a time for speaking not more than a little.

A loud voice proclaims its possessor as effectively as any trumpet. Even though the loud-voiced will disgust many they will usually draw sufficient attention to themselves to make their little performance worth while. If a person be born with a loud voice meekness asks him to make some attempt to muffle it. The attempt is sufficient to make him meek, even if he never succeeds in becoming dulcet. It is not he who is the real sinner against meekness but the man who wills to use his voice to best advantage in the service of self. God does not mean very much to him for a great part of his day.

It is probably harder to limit oneself to saying at all times just as much as the occasion demands than to correct a loud and pushful tone. We have an innate dread of being passed over or of being thought ignorant or ill-informed which makes us longwinded and insistent even after we have expressed ourselves with sufficient clarity. The meek man is satisfied to give his opinion for what it is worth and to leave it to his hearers to accept it or reject it at will. He does not indulge in those uneasy repetitions, corollaries, illustrations, so beloved of the man who is afraid that his point may be missed or may not get all the attention which is its due. When he can state the truth by saying no more than "yea" or "no" he says no more than "yea" or "no." There will be one exception, and even in this he does not cease to be meek : if it be his duty to stand up for the truth he will have no fear of being considered importunate in his attempts to get a fair hearing. But then it is truth and not self that stands at the bar. Truth is worthy of attention ; he himself is worthy only of as much as he can by no reasonable means avoid. In pushing the claims of truth he gives evidence of the most genuine meekness, for he goes so far on the way of forgetfulness of self as to run the risk of even a certain loss to his reputation. The truly meek man is capable of initiative ; but he keeps it all in reserve for a more worthy object than himself.

The beatitude of the merciful, like that of the meek, is concerned with regulating love of self. There is however a perceptible shade of difference between them. The meek are they who do not make sure that their rights will never be ignored : the merciful are they who do not mind if their rights have already been ignored. The meek refuse to look to the future ; the merciful refuse to look back on the past. Self calls out for revenge if snubbed or injured. The merciful man triumphs over self by ignoring its voice. This matter provides us with a very clear example of how the Sermon on the Mount is directed towards revealing anew the mind of the Divine Legislator. " Eye for eye, tooth for tooth, hand for hand, foot for foot "—so do we read in the Old Testament (Exodus 21, 24). Good as a principle of legal procedure, this was never intended by God to be understood as regulative of the interior attitude of the offended party. Yet, it had come to be understood by many in this way. The idea grew—and is it uncommon to-day ?—that the individual has a right to exact retribution in kind from an enemy. Fallen man feels that the balance in favour of self will never be restored short of making the aggressor suffer a defeat at least equal to that he inflicted. It is simply a question of how to put the Humpty-Dumpty of self up on his throne again. The merciful man does not resist evil. He is ready even to turn the other cheek (cf. Mt. 5, 39). If somebody takes away one thing belonging to him, he will allow even something else to be taken as well (ib. 40). He loves his enemies—those who think least of his self are loved by him, because he too rates it at a low value (ib. 44). A man cannot do all this without being very dead to self-love. The beatitude of the merciful is that of the very perfect. So perfect are they, indeed, that Our Saviour does not hesitate to sum up His recommendations with the strong words : " Be you therefore perfect as also your heavenly Father is perfect. . . . Who maketh His sun to rise upon the good and the bad, and raineth upon the just and the unjust " (ib. 48 and 45). Such indifference to treatment at the hands of others can find no adequate parallel short of the infinite forbearance of the Father of all mercy.

This beatitude is given an unwonted accent by the strange form of the corresponding promise : " . . . . for they shall obtain mercy " (Mt. 5, 7). Mercy is recommended to all because all have need of a higher mercy. If we are called to be so far forgetful of self as to pardon those who despise our human majesty, it is because we ourselves have despised a greater Majesty than that of man : by our sins we have despised the majesty of the King of heaven and earth, and we stand in need of a more undeserved pardon than we shall ever be called upon to accord. We have injured the Divine Self, and still dare to hope for pardon ! Where, then, is the sense of proportion in acting as if an injury to our human self were irreparable ? We have dared the authority of the King of kings, and still trust one day to enter into the benefits of membership of His Kingdom. Are we then to hold that the man who helps to cast down our self from its usurped throne is for ever to be excluded from the paltry sunshine of our human love ? It is characteristic of the kingdom of God on earth that its best subjects are the most keenly aware of their unworthiness to be included in it. It is a kingdom of redeemed sinners. No one else is wanted in it. It was not established to group the already just together, but to be a haven for them who were lost. The mere fact of being in it is a sign that one was lost ; one could not be in it otherwise. It is an institution of God's mercy. It is a divine settlement, in the world, but not of the world, into which those who labour and are burdened may crowd. The only condition of being allowed to remain in it is to take up the light yoke of its laws. That is but another way of saying that the only condition for remaining in it is to have determination to profit by one's stay. It is under such a dispensation of mercy that we all live. If we are deficient in mercy towards others, that can only be because we are insensible to the atmosphere of mercy by which we ourselves are surrounded—that we are members of the kingdom in name only, but not in spirit. One who breathes in mercy must himself be merciful ; one who prays for forgiveness must know what it is to forgive.

And from this idea of our living in grace by the mercy of God and of our radiating mercy on our fellows we pass over insensibly into another beatitude : " Blessed are the peacemakers : for they shall be called the children of God " (Mt. 5, 9). The peacemakers are those who radiate the peace of Christ which they themselves enjoy in their own souls. We could not now, without anticipating what will be the matter of a later chapter, explain the relationship between the peace of Christ and the kingdom of Christ. For the moment we must rest content with noting that as, in any state, internal peace is the result of wise and just government, peace of soul is the result of Christ's government in the kingdom He won by His death. Every true member of the kingdom of God becomes a centre of peace to all other members, just as the good citizen of any state is a support to his fellows. God does not save us as isolated units, just as He did not make us isolated units. He wills that we, being saved by His mercy, should be founts of salvation to all men. He wills that we should share in His sanctifying as well as in His sanctity. The Kingdom of God is not one in which each individual works for self alone. If no earthly kingdom worthy of the name is such, how can we expect that the greatest of all kingdoms should tolerate so grave an abuse ? Sanctity is not a school of selfishness ; it is rather a school of selflessness. The holy man is not indifferent to the rest of mankind ; they become instead his special and all-important care.

He who has enthroned God in his soul becomes a centre of peace ; he who has enthroned self there becomes a centre of unrest and revolt. Satan, the first and greatest devotee of self, led the angels, and tries to lead men, in revolt against God to their own destruction. The man who has enthroned self in his soul tries to do no less than Satan did. He will chafe against the moral law and lead others into sin ; he will rise up against the bounds set him by charity and justice, and enlist an army of the discontented on his side in defiance of the will of God ; he will perhaps prosper in his iniquity and the example of his success will cause the foolish to follow in his footsteps ; he will certainly create a milieu in which it will be difficult to live otherwise than at enmity with God. The solidarity of the human race is something that works for evil no less than for good. We necessarily radiate what we are. Others are free, of course, to submit to our influence or to reject it at will. But our influence will have been included among the forces capable of moulding the world even if no one ever profited or suffered by it, and that alone is sufficient to establish our responsibility. We did what was in our power.

It was through nothing of our doing that our efforts remained unrewarded.

When Our Lord blessed the peacemakers He did not mean to draw attention to what was nothing more than a useful or profitable side in the character of the spiritual man. He indicated something He expected from all spiritual men without exception. The truth of this statement is evident from the considerations we have just adduced. But we have as well, in support of it, the explicit teaching of Our Lord Himself in the course of His great Sermon. The following words are nothing more than a vivid description of the rôle of the Christian as peacemaker : " You are the salt of the earth. But if the salt lose its savour, wherewith shall it be salted ? It is good for nothing anymore but to be cast out, and to be trodden on by men. You are the light of the world. A city seated on a mountain cannot be hid. Neither do men light a candle and put it under a bushel, but upon a candlestick, that it may shine to all that are in the house. So let your light shine before men, that they may see your good works, and glorify your Father Who is in heaven " (Mt. 5, 13-16). A strange recommendation, this last one, we might think, to men whose greatest characteristic should be their desire to draw nothing whatever to themselves, not even the attention of men which their good works could hardly fail to excite ! But the strangeness is only apparent. Man's light must shine, but in such a way that attention will be drawn, not to him in whom it is, but to God Whose it is. The light of grace and virtue burns in us, but comes from God. It is His more than ours : it is ours only as belonging to Him. He who so waves his light as to draw attention to himself is no peacemaker. He is a fomenter of revolt. He is attempting to gather God's subjects around himself. Is there any greater act of renunciation asked by God of His subjects than that their very spiritual life, that which is best in them, which they have purchased at the price of the cross, which of all they have is alone worthy of being gloried in—that it like everything else is subject to the universal law of God's proprietorship, and that to use it for the benefit of self is to have no further share with Him ? We must be peacemakers, and that we cannot be otherwise than by disowning all right to human praise for what God has worked in our souls. This is an immense sacrifice. It means utter spiritual nakedness. Do we feel too weak to make it, there is a course still open to us ; we must pray that He Who gave us grace may give us, too, to see that it was given, not discovered within us. God did not give us His grace that we might attract souls to ourselves but to Himself. His grace is our final consecration to contempt of self, for it turns the best efforts of man from the exclusive desire of his own profit to that of the glory of another—God. A candle is not lit to be placed under a bushel. God has lit up our souls with His grace and He does not intend their splendour to pass entirely unnoticed. But the function of the candle is to give light to the Master and to show forth the beauty of His house. The flame of the love of God should burn us out in the service of God. But God Who clothes the lilies of the fields will know how to clothe our dead bones with a glorious immortality.

There remained still two beatitudes of which Our Saviour wished to speak : the beatitude of those who mourn and that of those who suffer persecution. Though these two beatitudes are clearly distinguishable in their purport it will not be amiss to consider them here only in so far as they combine to drive home the one lesson, that namely of the hatred of the kingdom of the world for the kingdom of heaven and of the continued assaults in which this hatred manifests itself.

The cross, under its aspect of suffering, is not the essence of Christianity, but it is so closely connected with it as to be its invariable companion. Our Blessed Lord came on earth that we might have the right of entry to His Kingdom. But being what we are we cannot submit to its law without the use of violence to our fallen and sin-infected nature. We do not wish to submit to His gentle rule, and the soul which, strengthened by grace, wills to submit itself, must suffer a veritable persecution from the body which perforce it must submit to the yoke it takes upon itself. The body does not want to follow the life which the soul maps out for it. It will endeavour to have its own way ; it will rise up threatening in the might of passion, and, seeming to invade the very inner strongholds of the soul, will fill this latter with fear and pain ; it will try the persecution of the crying nagger—how can it stand the strain ? it is worn out already, it is only fair that it should get a little of its own way some time. There is a persecution, too, from the outside world as well—less spectacular than many think, and most valuable when least clearly heroic. There is, first of all, a persecution to be borne at the hands of nature. We must put up with the attacks of cold, and heat, of fair weather and foul. And as these are attacks which can be averted by such simple precautions as always having warm clothing in winter, or cool clothing in summer, it is possible for most Christians to reduce their value as proof of their Christianity to the most schematic of syllogisms. For the man who has a warm pair of gloves, for instance, it would be well to rejoice when he forgets them on a really cold day. But the usual thing is to regard such forgetfulness as a dreadful nuisance. There is persecution also from the men who fill our world. It may be safely said that the average man is not persecuted by the evil members of his milieu half as much as he should think he deserves. The most testing persecution may well come from the best among our acquaintances. What makes it so testing is that, being good people, they have the best intentions in the world in what they do. They are frequently apologetic, but quite sure that they are right and that you are wrong, and they make no bones at all about your seeing that they oppose you in this particular instance not because your justice will interfere with their nefarious designs, but because they are convinced that you yourself could be better than you are. There is nothing very spectacular about this kind of persecution, no sense of the heroic, no strutting in triumphant righteousness across life's stage. It is exhilarating to bare one's sinless bosom to the storm, to oppose one's simple virtue to the oppressor. Offer the owner of the bared bosom a mackintosh, or him of the simple virtue a pat on the head, and you create an impression akin to that made by the patronizing persecution of the good. St. Paul and Barnabas fell out. St. Paul saw that Barnabas was going the wrong way about his work and Barnabas saw the same about St. Paul. Both became saints, and one at least of the two did his work superlatively well; but that did not prevent either from making the other feel something of the sting of being well-meaningly misunderstood. We all feel the same sting, and it will do us no end of good. Our patience will be termed lack of interest in our work, our meekness a real damper, our cheerfulness nerve-wracking, our helpfulness annoying. To be so misunderstood can be a great consolation. It may be a sign that we are on the right path. It certainly is such a sign if what consoles us is that we do not even get credit for what we do well, and that God is glorified in our pious persecutors whom we succeed in exasperating into His more active service.

"Blessed are they that suffer persecution for justice' sake : for theirs is the kingdom of heaven" (Mt. 5, 10). If you are just you will be persecuted—that we have seen. We may go still further and say that if you endure persecution for the sake of justice you have every reason to believe that you are in the kingdom of heaven, for in no other way could you obtain the strength to act with such supernatural courage. "Every one therefore that heareth these my words, and doth them, shall be likened to a wise man that built his house upon a rock. And the rain fell, and the floods came, and the winds blew, and they beat upon that house, and it fell not for it was founded on a rock" (Mt. 7, 24-25). The reason why the house withstood the storms of life was that it was built upon a rock. To withstand the storm of persecution we must be grounded on the rock, Christ. It is in Him that we overcome the world. In no name other than That of Jesus can we trust for victory. To be persecuted, then, should be a source of tranquil confidence and of joy. If we resist as we ought, it is Christ Who resists in us. Without Him we can do nothing. Our victory over self is therefore our greatest guarantee of the reign of God within us. If self has never suffered it may well be that our holiness is imaginary. If self has been crucified, if with Christ we have been nailed to the cross, we may believe in all humility that God does mean something in our lives. Suffering has its own beatitude, its own happiness. And in some divinely-understood way its happiness is the deepest and most true of all. It is a guarantee of the truth of every other happiness ; the companion of every joy of earth, which can change them to bitterness in our mouths or give them the sweetness of the triumphant Crucified.

These are the eight Beatitudes—Jesus' restatement and explanation of His Father's Law. Though but a few were gathered on the Mount to hear Him speak, His words were addressed to all men without exception. Those words were a law ; and to believe them was to enter a Kingdom and to accept a King.

THE PRAYER OF THE KINGDOM

" Thy Kingdom come . . . ." (Mt. 6, 10).

IT is not a little disconcerting to souls whose ideas on prayer are unbalanced, to hear those words of Our Saviour in the Sermon on the Mount : " Not every one that saith to me, Lord, Lord, shall enter into the kingdom of heaven " (Mt. 7, 21). And if we add to this the fact that His first reference to prayer was introduced in so casual a way, rather as a warning against ostentation than as a recommendation to pray (" And when ye pray, ye shall not be as the hypocrites " —Mt. 6, 5) and that His second and last one is to the form of prayer known as the prayer of petition (" Ask and it shall be given to you. . . ."—Mt. 7, 7) rather than to some one or other of the forms we tend to rate so highly, it begins to become evident that Our Saviour's idea of prayer cannot have been that of certain of his followers. He seems, somehow, to take prayer for granted in life, and to value it neither more nor less highly than the life of which it is a part. It is not in saying " Lord, Lord," but in doing the will of Our Father Who is in heaven, that we are true to our character as citizens of the Kingdom.

There is another reason, too, why prayer was not singled out for altogether special mention, and it is that men commonly do admit the need of prayer of some kind in life. Indeed, it is perhaps correct to say that there is a certain kind of piety, by no means rare in these our days, which is more willing to admit the need of prayer than that of anything else—than that of mortification, or humility, or obedience, or love of one's neighbour, or any other of the necessary and irksome virtues. There is a reason why this should be so. The moment a person is at all convinced of the existence of God he sees that he should submit to Him. And of all forms of submission the easiest is to shut one's eyes and to say "Lord, Lord." Believing oneself thus acquitted of all obligations one feels free to live the rest of the day in self-seeking, provided only that what is evidently sinful be avoided. It is well to mention in this context that there are two desires to learn about prayer, and that only one of them is good. There is the desire springing up in the soul under the influence of the Holy Spirit, conscious that a deeper knowledge of the nature of prayer is also a deeper knowledge of God's demands upon service, and willing to know more, only so as to know thereby how to give more. This desire is good. It comes from God and leads to Him. There is however, as well, a desire springing from curiosity. Prayer is thought to be an experience devised for our peculiar benefit. Find out all about it so as to exploit its possibilities to the full. Above all else concentrate on speculative questions. Be very sure of the precise moment at which the mystical element enters in, and become so familiarized with the thoughts, aspirations, and transports of the greatest of the saints that they at length seem to be your own. Is not all this a refined form of the Kingdom of self? Prayer is being treated really as an amusement, or as an intellectual problem, the solution of which will yield no small measure of natural satisfaction. Souls of this kind need a little of the divine sanity of the attitude of the Sermon on the Mount. God has given us a life to live. What is of importance is that we live it. Prayer has its importance solely and simply because it has its organic part in life.

To understand this last statement, which will be the theme of the present chapter, it is necessary to depart a moment from the consideration of prayer itself and turn to that of life. In this way we shall see it in its true perspective. And with regard to life, there is no reason why we should devote much time to its complete analysis. There is no need to go back as far as the philosophical concept of self-movement, which is life's manifestation reduced to its ultimate constituent, and work our way by laborious and scientifically exhaustive stages up to the form of movement which is prayer—that movement in which the mind strides Godwards. We may begin more than half-way down the problem with the idea of life in the kingdom of God, and take as starting-point the thesis that such a life may be summed up in the one word : devotion.

Devotion is a word that has almost succeeded in losing its original meaning and has quite succeeded in acquiring not a few misleading connotations. When we speak of a devout man we usually mean somebody who recites many prayers and has a general air of recollection. Religious functions are termed devotions ; we speak of going to evening devotions. A person who is given to some particular pious practice is said to have a devotion. It would be easy to add to this list. But no matter how it might be lengthened it would hardly help much towards bringing out the sense of the word which is relevant here, that namely of binding by vow, or consecrating. Devotion consists in vowing oneself to God, consecrating oneself to God, binding oneself to God. The devout person is he who has given himself entirely to God. St. Thomas tells us that he is devout who has the will to perform with promptitude whatever pertains to the service of God. And when we grasp this idea we see that the word devotion is still used in this, its more proper sense, in spheres other than that of religion. Whereas devotion to Our Lady is usually taken to consist in praying to her, devotion to one's mother or to one's wife means living for them, as does devotion to one's country or to any cause. Devotion to God—that is to say devotion in the spiritual order—really means just the same thing. Devotion to God means living for God as one would live for a father. It means entire and ready donation of self to God. It means spending self in the service of God. It means making God the goal, and, as it were, the principal beneficiary of one's striving and straining. Devotion is a noble thing. Only a man, and a great one at that, can be truly devout. It is the element of devotion in a Christian life that raises it from mediocrity to perfection.

Holiness and devotion are therefore one and the same thing. But, considered as devotion, that one thing is made to appear in a light which illumines it but too infrequently. What we see in that light is that human holiness consists not only in love but in love and service. Say, if you will, that all true love does issue in service ; that is but an apparent correction which leaves the main point intact. To be holy is to serve God ; to be holy is to love God. To love without serving is neither to be holy nor to love ; to serve without loving is not to serve as one ought. Let us expand this idea of holiness as love and service and we shall understand the kingdom of God all the better.

There is a virtue called religion which impels a man to render to God the debt due to Him in justice as Master and Lord of all things. It is not a theological virtue, for God is not its object but its end : it is concerned with the submission of man and all that is in man to God. Adoration and sacrifice are two of the acts in which it issues. By such acts man recognizes God's ownership and authority, and submits himself to Him. But the life of man belongs to God just as much as the being or existence of man do. All man's actions, all his thoughts, all his possessions, in short everything that he has, depends on God as ultimate Source, and should therefore be directed to Him as ultimate End. God is the Master Who is also a King, and Who has the right to rule in all that He has made. From this it follows that the virtue of religion is not confined to acts of adoration and sacrifice. It extends to the whole of life. It has rights over all that is man's and over all that has been given him by God—that is, to absolutely everything. Its function is to gather up, as it were, the stray fragments of human life, to bind them together in the unity of their divine provenance and destination, and to offer them to God as being held by man in subordination to and dependence on Him. Religion is in some way the peculiar virtue of the subject of the Heavenly King. It sees that God's so absolute rights are respected, allowing nothing of what He gave to man to be diverted from the supreme end of His great glory.

Suggested by this metaphor of gathering up and offering to God, the question might now arise : but why offer Him what we have so gathered up ? Why not gather up and offer to self ? Religion can give its answer : because to offer is just, to withhold is unjust, is robbery ; God has a right in justice to our complete and unstinted service. And had God never willed to rule in man otherwise than through His rights over human nature as such this would be the ultimate answer. But God has given man grace. He has raised us from nature to supernature. He has made us His friends. There arises therefore a second and deeper reason why we should offer God all we have to give : because we love Him. God is our Friend ; our whole life must therefore centre on Him. Every detail of life must be gathered up and turned Godwards. By charity we have received the power of centring life on God in loving friendship. All that life has must therefore be directed towards Him. We must only act so as to serve Him, even in what is necessary for our own existence. Love, then, uses religion. Religion gathers up our life as belonging to God and love offers it to Him. Love or charity is, as St. Thomas tells us, the principle of religion. It is love that brings religion its final complement.

It is now possible to see what devotion is : it is the result of the union of religion and love in a soul. By religion we recognize that all things belong to God and that we are obliged in justice to render them to Him ; by love we desire ardently to give them to Him as our greatest Friend. The result is devotion, promptitude in giving, promptitude in serving. Devotion, or holiness, is service in love and love in service. It is the essential characteristic of the true member of the Kingdom of Heaven : to serve the Kingdom because one loves the King.

Devotion, being so all-embracing, will imply prayer. This may be seen first of all if we consider prayer under its most generic aspect as approach to God in spirit. The human mind belongs to God, as does also the human will. When the will, captivated by the divine Goodness, bends the intellect to the consideration of God, one is said to pray. Prayer itself is therefore service. It is the use of intellect and will in the service of God. It is therefore in its essence one of the manifestations of the life of God's subject, not something standing altogether apart from life taken as a whole. To use our minds by concentrating them on the thought of God is to serve Him with our minds. To use our wills by getting them to concentrate the intellect on God and by rejoicing in the thought of Him, is to serve Him with our wills. And prayer being thus seen to be a part of life, it is not too hard to see as well how life may be a prayer. Life is a prayer if it be one of love and service, for it is these two that make prayer itself pleasing to God. To take an intellect and will that could be allowed to indulge in the contemplation and admiration of self and to turn them Godwards is to pray. Prayer therefore is not a relaxation, not even a spiritual relaxation ; it is not a safe position to which we withdraw from time to time from the struggle of life. True, it gives us rest and safety in the nearness of our King. But it is, before everything else, a part of life's struggle. It is service, active service we may say, for to offer a human spirit to God in prayer is to tame a rebel self.

Prayer is love as well as service. In prayer we bend intellect and will to the acceptance of the divine law ; but we draw near to God to do this, and it is charity which brings us near to Him. Religion, service, regards God as an End to be served : love turns to God as an End to be possessed and enjoyed. At the very core of our prayer there is therefore that amazing and essential spiritual paradox, the creature who is a friend and the friend who is a creature. What equality can there be between God and His handiwork ? Yet friendship is based on equality, and grace making us the friends of God must make us in some way like to Him, almost to the unattainable limit of pure equality. Try to explain all this as we may, our adoption by grace to the state of divine sonship will remain a mystery of faith. Our minds simply cannot see clear in the matter, no more than we can see how Three Divine Persons are one God. There is consequently but little to be gained in the spiritual life by endeavouring to construct a mental synthesis of submission and love in our relations with

God. There is only one synthesis which counts for us wayfarers, and it is that God has told us that we are both creatures
and friends. The two concepts are united in the revealed
truth of God. That is enough for the faithful soul. Any
attempt to reduce the spiritual life to love alone is harmful.
No less harmful is any attempt to reduce it to nothing more
than service. It is both; and both will be in our prayer.
The soul moved by the Holy Spirit in spontaneous prayer will
never hesitate, doubting whether to give voice to love or to
submission. It obeys quite simply whenever it feels drawn to
the one rather than the other; for it knows that God alone
sees what should be their exact proportion. All it can be
sure of is that there is need for both. And God Who sees
how they should be blended into the harmony of acceptable
prayer will come to the aid of those who trust in Him, and
give them that only synthesis of love and service which is
possible to man : the practical one, of living them better than
he can talk about them.

So much for the general connection between holiness or
devotion and prayer. What, however, of the different paths
of prayer and the different ways in which they lead to or
follow from devotion to Our King? If in answering this
question we keep to the consideration of the common paths
of prayer, this is not to discourage souls from aiming at
something higher, but because the fundamental principles of
all prayer are the same, and the surest way to progress is
docility to the Holy Spirit's first inspirations.

Among the means which man may use to foster devotion
a prayerful consideration of the goodness and mercy of God
takes the first place. The prayer of contemplation is therefore
the great fount of devotion. We shall experience no great
desire to give ourselves enthusiastically to the divine service
till we come to know God. The first germ of enthusiasm
will be planted in us when we know what God has done for
us in His Mercy : how He has created us, redeemed us, guided
and cared for us from the first moment of our earthly existence.
These are benefits that deserve some return. God has given
us many talents. Gratitude demands that we use them as He
would wish. But greater than the enthusiasm of gratitude is

that of love. Devotion reaches its peak point when we love God; and we come to love Him by gazing at Him with those eyes of desire whose appeal He cannot resist. One cannot reason oneself into the love of God any more than one can reason oneself into true friendship with a fellow-man. One is never truly a friend of another, no matter how convinced one may be of the value of his friendship and no matter what the efforts made to act towards him in a friendly way, until he comes to be known. Once he is known, friendship with him becomes spontaneous and ceases to be a matter of doing and thinking in a certain way merely because it is seen to be the one that will probably please him. Love of God grows in just the same way. To love God one needs to know Him; and knowledge is the reward of patient, humble, and trustful meditation on Him. It is a reward; that is to say, a gift. Its beginning, the infused virtue of faith, is a gift. Its continuation, the infused virtue of charity, is a further gift. Its perfection comes with the gifts of the Holy Ghost, most particularly with that of wisdom; and these, as their very name implies, are pre-eminently the gifts of God and are not of our making. But gift though this knowledge and love of God be, its donation follows a regular rhythm, for it is given to those who are faithful to the leadings of grace. Hence, fidelity in life and prayer will lead necessarily by the grace of God to love and devotion through prayer. We cannot argue ourselves into love or devotion; but we know how to win them from the mercy of God, and that is just as good. The first means therefore to devotion is meditation on God.

To recommend contemplation of the divine Goodness and Mercy is not however to dissuade from the contemplation of the Sacred Humanity of Christ, the King of our Kingdom. Though it is a fact that the Divinity, considered in Itself, is the Object most worthy of all love and most calculated to excite devotion, when we come to the particular case of man's love and devotion, we find that they are most connaturally fostered by something less exalted. God became Man that He might put Himself most fully within the reach of man, and it is through the veils of the Sacred Humanity of Jesus that God reveals Himself in normal course. We give voice to this belief in the preface of the Mass of Christmas, where we pray that, seeing God in visible form (in the Incarnate Word), we may be caught up by the love of what is invisible. The teaching of St. Teresa in this connection may be summed up in the statement that the most profitable path for beginners and proficients is that of the Sacred Humanity, and that even in the case of the most perfect, those namely who are favoured with the purest vision of the Divine Essence possible to a wayfarer, there may never be question of turning deliberately away from It. St. Paul said no less in his words to the Corinthians : "For God, Who commanded the light to shine out of darkness, hath shined in our hearts, to give the light of the knowledge of the glory of God, in the face of Christ Jesus" (2 Cor. 4, 6). It is in the face of our Saviour, with the possible exception of brief periods of high mystic prayer, that we see most clearly the lineaments of the face of God Himself. The same doctrine is repeated in a new form in the Epistle to the Hebrews : ". . . let us run by patience to the fight proposed to us : looking on Jesus the author and finisher of faith . . ." (12, 1-2). The eye of the soul should be fixed on Jesus : at least no soul is safe in banishing the thought of Him from its mind. Looking on Jesus we see in Him the light of the glory of the Goodness of God. Frail humans that we are, we come to know God better by seeing Him in a Man than in Himself. The blinding light of the Godhead needs to be toned down to the weakness of our eyes, and in the soft light of the Incarnation we see clearer than in the blinding brightness of pure Transcendence. We need never fear that the contemplation of Jesus will keep us from the simple and naked vision of the Divine Essence. To see the Divine Essence, in so far as it is at all possible for man, is a divine gift to which man cannot raise himself. He will obtain it, if at all, as from the divine bounty. And God cannot but be bountiful to those who approach Him through Him Who is the Way.

It is true as well, though in a lesser degree, that contemplation of Mary, the Mother of God, is a cause of devotion. Mary, like Jesus, is a revelation of God. She has nothing but what

God gave her. Seeing her we see the goodness and attractiveness of God expressing itself in a completely human way, so as to appeal to our human minds and hearts. For lack of very precise and universal teaching of theologians on the point, it is not possible to say exactly how necessary the contemplation of Mary is to perfect devotion. But it is quite certain from the practice of so many great saints that such contemplation does foster it, and that to a marked degree. It is hard to see how any soul would be justified in deliberately banishing Mary from all its prayers, even if no proof can be given for such a statement other than that such is the conviction of the ordinary faithful. Whatever, then, be the theological value of the propositions that might be drawn up on the subject of Mary's place in our prayer, it is certainly right to insist that prayer to her can be most fruitful, and that it is never wise to neglect it. One might without temerity be still more insistent on the importance of her place in prayer, but to say even what we have said just now is to give a grave warning which cannot be ignored without at least the possibility of serious spiritual loss.

After meditation on God and Jesus and Mary, devotion springs from meditation on one's own defects. A person who neglects the consideration of his sins and shortcomings may well come to adopt in God's presence an attitude rather of equality than of submission. To be conscious of one's true nothingness is an invaluable safeguard against pride and presumption. The result will be far from any crippling fear of inability to serve God. To know ourselves truly implies the knowledge of what God can do in us as well as of what we cannot do of ourselves ; and though we see very clearly that we cannot do anything of ourselves, that we never have done anything of ourselves except to prove unfaithful to grace and ungrateful to Him Who gave it, we see no less clearly that there is One always with us Who works in us both to will and to do good and to accomplish the good we will, and that with His assistance all things are possible. Knowledge of our own sin and weakness should lead nowhere more surely than to a more complete donation of self to God and to a more complete submission to the promptings of grace. It should make us more rather than less courageous in His service.

It is strange that the prayer of the kingdom of God should include thus a certain interest in self, the enemy of the kingdom, and the one, indeed, whose whole ambition is to attract favourable attention. There is no doubt that there is real danger in a too great preoccupation with self, even when the desire inspiring it seems on the surface to be that of learning its wiles and frustrating them at every turn. This is a danger against which we should arm ourselves. But in this matter it is difficult to give a more precise practical rule than that any preoccupation with self which turns the soul's eye rather towards self than to God is bad, and that whatever attention to self leads to a clearer knowledge of how to serve Him is good. This rule is evidently an elastic one, admitting of many degrees of adaptation to practical exigencies. And having done our duty by indicating it, we may proceed to insist on God's right to be the centre of life. For life is not a dethronement of self so much as an enthronement of God. We should wish to know God that we may love Him, and to know self that we may hate self. But there is a definite hierarchical order in our love and our hatred. Love comes first ; it is the reason of our hatred. The only way in which we can withdraw the powers of the soul from the service of self is by devoting them to the service of something else—of God, when it is question of the spiritual life. Normally then, self-knowledge, conviction of sinfulness and of committed but forgiven sin, will be rather in the margin of our soul's awareness than in its very centre. We shall serve God knowing what we are, and allowing that knowledge to give a very pronounced character of diffidence, humility, and gratitude to our service. If that character be totally absent we are at fault. If it transform itself from character of spirituality to content of spirituality we are also at fault—though far less than on the previous hypothesis. God demands of us both character and content. If either be absent our service in love is defective. If knowledge of self fail, our life may well cease to be service ; if knowledge of God—then will be an end to our love. We are not free to make a choice of the one or the other. There is just one degree of freedom allowed, and it is : to determine with the light of the grace of the Holy Spirit, the exact place that each will have. But each must have some place.

Knowledge of self, as we have just outlined it, is the subject matter of a prayer which leads to devotion. But this same knowledge is the fount of another kind of prayer as well—that, namely, which is known under the name of the Prayer of petition. If we are nothing and God is everything, we need His assistance to do no matter what good; and spontaneously we turn to God to ask Him to help us in our extreme need. What should we ask Him? To give us love and light and strength, certainly. But can we find no more precise formula; for to speak of love and light and strength is but to make a selection from among the quasi-infinity of graces and virtues of which we stand in need? St. Thomas gives us the answer in one of his most luminous phrases: *illud debemus orando petere quod debemus desiderare*—we should pray for that which it behoves us to long for. Could he have indicated more clearly the only worthy object of all petition, the spread of the kingdom of God? All our prayer, whether it be contemplation—of which we have just spoken—or petition, is the prayer of the Kingdom. Our prayer could not be anything else. As we have said, prayer belongs to life, and life is life in the Kingdom. There are two treasuries of the Kingdom, one of grace, placed in our hearts by God, the other of mercy, stored up for us as yet in heaven. Contemplation is the use of the treasure God has placed within us; petition is our knocking at the door of the treasury He has yet to open to us. But both treasures belong to the King and are for the support of His Kingdom. They are not for purely private uses; and this, not because there are no private uses, but because there are none that are purely so.

When the disciples asked Our Blessed Lord to teach them how to pray He answered in the words known now by the title of "Our Father." In this beautiful prayer we find a recommendation to both contemplation and petition: to contemplation in its exordium, where God, the Father reigning in heaven, is approached in love, confidence, and humility; to petition, in the body of the prayer, where our human needs are exposed. As we have already spoken of contemplation it is unnecessary to traverse the same ground anew in the examination of the " Our Father " which follows. We shall consider this prayer rather as the model of the prayer of petition, and the perfect illustration of how such prayer is also a prayer of the kingdom.

" Our Father, Who art in Heaven, hallowed be thy name, thy kingdom come, thy will be done on earth as it is in heaven "—this first part of the prayer is but one single petition that the kingdom of God be established on earth. " Hallowed be thy name " : may men recognize the holiness of thy name ; " Thy kingdom come " : may men accept thy rule ; " Thy will be done on earth as it is in heaven " : may men submit to thy law—all these are but slightly differing ways of praying for the growth, in depth and breadth, of the kingdom of God among men. The great preoccupation of the Christian soul should be the spread of God's rule on earth. If it be right to pray for whatever it is right to long for, then there should be no more constant subject of prayer than the acceptance of God's rights on earth. The truth of this statement is seen in most striking fashion in the lives of the saints. Where is the saint without interest in the spread of God's Kingdom ? Think of the Apostles, of the great missionary saints, of the Curé of Ars, of St. Thérèse of the Child Jesus, who in her Carmelite convent felt her unity of purpose with those who laboured on the mission fields. And if prayer in its widest sense be a kind of conversation with God, is it not reasonable to speak to Him of His Kingdom ? And if in its more narrow sense it be to ask what is becoming, what is more suitable than to ask that the purpose for which He created a universe be achieved ?

The idea of praying for the spread of the kingdom of God may well seem novel to many. To some it will seem so because they presume that the spread of the kingdom of God on earth is God's own affair and that He will provide for it Himself, leaving them free to ask for what touches themselves more personally. Abstracting from the selfishness and incomprehension which would account for the idea that the spread of the kingdom of God on earth does not affect us personally, even though we are supposed to love God, and to have therefore a very deep identity of interests with Him, it is worth while to recall that here we are in the realm of what is at once a mystery of mercy and of providence : a mystery, in that in spite of our weakness God allows us to share by our prayers in His rule of the world of souls and matter ; a mystery of providence, in that, to our way of thinking, His decision to act seems dependent on our petition. Even when we are told that God has not been dependent on our petition, that the only dependence is that between the event for which we prayed and our prayer, the most that can be said is that an apparent contradiction has been removed—that namely between the immutability of God, and the false implication that our prayers did really move Him in some physical way—but the mystery remains as dark as ever. And it is precisely because it is so great a mystery, and might therefore escape our feeble minds, that Our Saviour asserted its truth in His gospel. He tells us : " Pray ye therefore the Lord of the harvest, that He send forth labourers into His harvest " (Mt. 9, 38). The harvest of souls belongs to God Himself. It is His harvest, the produce of His fields. If it be lost, one might almost say it is His loss.

And yet, we are told to pray Him to send into His harvest those harvesters in the absence of whom it would certainly suffer cruelly. Has God then no care for His Kingdom ? Does He need to be reminded daily of its most elementary needs ? No ; but He wishes us to have the merit of being interested in it. He wishes to give our love of Himself some outlet. We are called to be about Our Father's business, to work for and to pray for it. Far from thinking that God's apparent waiting on our prayers is something to accept in puzzled suspicion, we should see in it the answer to the great longing of every generous soul to be an apostle. If God awaits our prayers before acting, there is another side to the picture as well : it is that, when and because we pray, God acts ; in other words, we by our prayers can act through God. Were any one soul to set out in love of God to reform the world, how little could it do, unless it were to be accorded one of these graces, such as that given to St. Francis Xavier, which are so very rare ? Left to itself its desire of spreading God's kingdom would be unrealizable. But it knows now, in virtue of what Our Saviour has said, that it can be realized by prayer. Is not this an amazing manifestation of God's mercy ? What we cannot do by our activity we can do by simply praying with sincerity. By prayer we can do those wonderful things for God which rise to the mind when love of Him is deep and true.

There is one restriction however to the efficacy of our prayer for the growth of the kingdom of God : we can never be certain that prayer offered for people other than ourselves will bear the fruit we desire, because they are always free to oppose the grace God will offer them. This, however, is no reason why we should not pray for others. Our prayers *may* be efficacious ; to say that they are not necessarily so is not to rob them of all value. In any case a person who has God's interests at heart will not need much argument to lead him to pray for their successful issue. But it is important to note that there is such a restriction in the case mentioned, because to do so points to a case in which there is no restriction whatever, that namely in which a person prays for himself : persevering and humble prayer for the growth of the kingdom of God in oneself is always heard. Our Saviour had that prayer in mind when He said : " Ask, and it shall be given you : seek, and you shall find : knock, and it shall be opened to you. . . . If you then being evil, know how to give good gifts to your children : how much more will your Father Who is in heaven, give good things to them that ask Him ? " (Mt. 7, 7 & 11). He has given us in these words a very definite promise that our request for what is really good for us will certainly be granted. But all the good of the soul is summed up in membership of His Kingdom. We should pray therefore for its perfection within us—and for that most of all. But let us note what is the meaning of praying that the kingdom of God may come in oneself. It means praying that one may accept more fully the law of God ; it means praying for the grace to submit more unreservedly to Him. That should be the first object of the prayers we offer to God for ourselves. And by first we do not mean first on the list of things sought, but first in the sense of being the underlying meaning of everything else we ask. No matter what be the object of our request, even if it be some grace or some virtue or the extirpation of some vice, we should ask it only as a means to more perfect submission to the divine will. " Nevertheless not as I will, but as thou wilt " (Mt. 26, 39). It can happen that we look all unconsciously on a certain grace or virtue as a fitting adornment to our souls, and ask for it in prayer without realizing that we seek it in self love. It may be, too, that a certain failing which is irksome to us has the salutary effect of keeping us humble, and that when we pray to be delivered from it, though we think that our prayer is motivated by the desire to make our souls fully pleasing in God's eyes, the real reason is that it displeases our æsthetic sense in our moments of self-contemplation. " Not as I will but as thou wilt " is not, therefore, a saving clause inserted at the end of a prayer ; it is the very texture of prayer. Whatever we may pray for should be desired as making us more fully submissive to the yoke of God. The very elements which go to make up our prayer are all in some way variations on this central theme of submission to God. Love is submission to the attractiveness of God ; Hope is confident submission to the power of God ; Faith is submissive acceptance of the truth of God. There is no such thing as a prayer of faith, of hope, of love, which is not at the same time, and of necessity, a prayer of submission as well. Man reaches his perfection by submitting himself to God in his proper place under Him. His prayer should be either the prayer of one who is in his place or that of one who wishes to find his place and keep it. Prayer of pure equality with God is prayer of pure delusion.

But if membership of the Kingdom in submission to the Divine King should be the theme of all our prayer, it is not necessary that it be also its sole elaboration. We may pray for a great variety of things if only they embody the theme in some way. It is not even necessary that the things for which we pray should be substantially spiritual. It is allowable to pray for material things as well as for supernatural graces. But it is so natural to some to make mistaken efforts to spiritualize every object of their prayer without exception—forgetting of course to spiritualize the motive, which is usually self-love—that it is almost necessary to invoke the authority of Our Blessed Lord to prove to them that human bodily needs may be the object of prayer too. "Give us this day our daily bread" are the words He taught us to say. It is true that this petition refers in its mystical sense to the Bread of the Blessed Eucharist. But this is not its only sense. It has a literal sense as well : we might almost say it has first of all a literal sense. And the literal sense is that which asks for the bread needed for our bodies. Material things are therefore an object of prayer. As we have said, all objects of prayer are properly such only in so far as they are needed for life in the Kingdom of God. It follows therefore that we should pray for our earthly needs only in the spirit of the "Not as I will but as thou wilt." God alone knows how far the satisfaction of such needs is compatible with holiness. But still they are needs about which we should pray. To exclude them totally from prayer is to risk spiritual harm.

The reason why we should pray for earthly needs is the same as that for every other "should" in the kingdom of heaven : man should submit his whole self to God, and his whole self includes a body with bodily needs. Spiritual people sometimes exaggerate in preoccupying themselves exclusively with their souls. It is possible for people such as religious, who as individuals have no part in the administration of earthly goods, and whose material needs are met by their community, to fall insensibly into the error of even restricting God's influence to the things of the soul. When the time will come later on for them to face some emergency of the material order, they never think of God at all—or think of Him but little—in their efforts to meet it. There is however no reason for suspecting that this mistake is confined to the ranks of religious : it is common to all who try to serve God as if they had no body and did not live in the middle of a very real world—both world and body needing to be subjected to God's authority. A few examples will make this clear. It can happen that people who pass for pious, look on illness as an unpleasant interlude in a life spent better in tranquil prayer. They forget to pray to be cured of their illness. They forget to pray for the grace to bear it with patience, and to derive some benefit from it. In their eyes the whole thing is a sheer waste of time, and nothing can be done of any worth till they are up again and at their usual work, whatever it may be. It happens too that in times, say, of famine, or epidemic, certain individuals will think well to manifest a certain distaste for the idea of turning to God to ask Him to avert His wrath from His people. They will find excellent reasons for their attitude. They will say that those who ask to be saved have no intention of ever becoming any better—in which they are possibly correct for most cases. They will say, too, that what has happened was well deserved—and who would venture to question that either? But it is nevertheless true that their attitude may be fundamentally wrong. Their idea can really be that famines and plagues are all very well for those who need them, but that they themselves have nothing to gain from such merely material aids to sanctity.

It would be easy to multiply examples of this apparent exaltation of mind, but the two given are sufficient to make the point clear. What is wrong in these and all such cases is that they exclude God from a part of His creation. There is no fault in trying to establish spiritual contact with God. What is a fault is to refuse to see Him in what is not purely spiritual. Man's pride leads him to ape the angel. Now the angel is pure spirit, and to be pure spirit is better than to be spirit just barely raised above matter, as man is by nature. To ape the angel consists therefore in acting as if we had no bodies ; and that is wrong. God does not want man to act as if he had no body. He wishes him to act with his body, though so to use it as if he used it not. The position is exactly the same with regard to being in the material world. We are not asked to pretend we are not in the world. What is expected of us is that we be in it and that we use it, but that we be not of it, and that we use it as if we used it not. We being what we are, God has placed our possibilities of holiness in the material as well as in the spiritual. Prayer will do us good. But so too will a plague, or famine, or health, or a good dinner. If we were to pray a little more about these things we should be more attuned to their spiritual significance. Prayer is made for life, and for the whole of life. Whatever is a part of life is a fit subject for prayer. That is the sum total of the matter. And a wonderfully balanced total it is.

There are certain other cases too in which we omit to pray for material things, due to an incorrect grasp of the nature of Divine Providence. It is far from uncommon to consider the world as ruled by two great principles. The one is the laws of nature, ruling the weather, and illness and such things. The other is God, the Father of men, Who occasionally intervenes to upset the laws of nature in our favour, and Whose rule is far more gentle than that of the blind chemical and physical forces which are the ministers of nature and of its Lawgiver. Prayer for no matter what temporal favour resolves itself, therefore, into an appeal to the Merciful Father against the blind workings of nature—and incidentally against God Who works through nature. And in cases in which a problem will seem to have worked itself out in accordance with the usual rules of life, we are even tempted to feel that no special thanks are due to God our Father however favourable the result will have been to ourselves.

What is of first-rate importance in this connection is to understand that in everything which has any bearing at all on our salvation—and St. Paul tells us that all things without exception work together unto good to them that love God— the distinction between a natural and a supernatural providence ceases to have any practical importance in our lives. What I mean to say is that even those events which fall out exactly as natural causes would have them, fall out no less exactly as Our Father in heaven wills in view of our eternal good. God is so supremely wise that He created a universe in which He allows natural causes to work in accordance with their own natures, and, notwithstanding, makes them conspire to bring about the good of the elect. Were we to endeavour to form some image of the divine deliberation before the creation of the world—and being a sense-image what we should form would be only very roughly correct—we should do so more correctly by representing to ourselves God the Father of the elect as drawing up first the plan of our salvation, and then as Author of Nature seeing how He should make a world in which the elect would be saved, than by thinking of God as first planning the material phenomena of the world, and then seeing what little changes He must needs make from time to time in answer to the prayers of men when they find it hard to fit in with His rigid and mechanical scheme of things. I do not mean to imply by this that miracles do not happen. They do happen : that we know by our faith. But an event can be a genuine answer to prayer without being a miracle : the laws of nature themselves were drawn up in answer to the needs and the prayers of men. There is no exaggeration then in thanking God for fine weather, or good health, or in praying to Him for such things, since it is anything but true that the event would be the same whether we prayed or not. The event is certainly predetermined from all eternity ; but our prayers may have had everything to do with its being predetermined. That is what we forget. And, to forget it is just another example of the way in which, all unconsciously, we keep God out of as much of life as possible. The laws of nature are made serve as pretext to allow us to separate Him in thought from our daily bread : a right attitude to prayer will restore Him the place that is His due.

In the next petition of the " Our Father " we pray to be forgiven our sins by God just as we on our side forgive men who offend us. The importance of a deep conviction that we stand in constant need of God's forbearing mercy has been stressed in the preceding chapter in connection with the beatitude of the merciful. The reader must be referred back to what is said there for all explanations. It is hardly necessary to do more here than to add that it is a good thing to ask for mercy as well as to be convinced that we need it. It is possible to know that you need mercy and still to take for granted, in a very presumptuous way, that there is not the slightest doubt but that you will get it. This presumption is banished by the practice of constant and humble petition. If we ask repeatedly for something we imply that there is no obligation whatever to give it, and that we feel it incumbent on us to keep up an attitude of actual supplication—an attitude which is very galling to human pride. It is easy to say that God does not wish us to be continually whining to Him for mercy; but this is less than half true. We should not whine; our prayer should be loving and confident, not servile and doubting. But we assuredly do need His mercy; and however you may cavil at whatever be the word chosen to describe the prayer that asks Him for it, the prayer itself is not a thing to be cavilled at. To ask God for mercy is noble. It is to recognize that you are not much.

The last petition of the Lord's Prayer is: "And lead us not into temptation. But deliver us from evil." This petition is not inspired by the belief that God could possibly be the provoking cause of the sins of His people. Its meaning is made clear by St. Paul: "God is faithful, Who will not suffer you to be tempted above that which you are able: but will make also with temptation issue, that you may be able to bear it" (1 Cor. 10, 13). It is rather a petition that God be at our side, as He has promised, in the time of testing. Conscious of our own weakness and of the strength of the forces arrayed against us, we know that our sole hope of victory is God's merciful assistance. From the very fact that He has told us to ask for His help we know that He is willing to give it. Prayer is not a means for wringing certain things from God when He is really unwilling to grant them. It is rather a condition of our being properly disposed to receive what He already wishes to give. He wishes to help; but we on our side are not fit to profit by His help unless we are turned towards Him in trustful humility. God has made man free and respects his freedom. If we except a few rare cases of miraculous conversions—such as that of St. Paul is believed to have been—He never forces a soul to accept His yoke. In this same way He does not force Himself upon us in time of temptation. If we are quite determined to throw off His yoke, He will permit us to do so. He comes to our aid in the measure in which we wish Him to assist us: that is what is meant by speaking of being disposed to receive His aid. Hence the need of prayer. Without it in some form we are impervious to the dew of grace.

When we repeat this petition we should think occasionally of our great adversary Satan. We can overcome him with

God's help. It might almost have appeared from what was said of his cunning and his power that no mere man could ever escape the meshes of his net. This would be so were man to fight him unaided—if we can conceive of Satan as fighting with so mean an adversary as man, in any way other than to finish him off at one blow. But God holds Satan in check. He has no power over us except what God allows him and what we allow him. We need have no fear that God will allow him to tempt us above the measure of our grace if we on our side are faithful. Our real danger is the opportunities which we ourselves offer him unceasingly. We open the gates of our own souls to him time after time by our pointless and protracted intercourse with danger. Though he on his side covers the world as a raging lion seeking whom he may devour, he is unable to make an unwilling victim. God, Who wills not the death of sinners but that they be saved, at the same time strengthens us and holds Satan in check. Humble prayer will ensure that our strength fail not.

Such is prayer in the Kingdom of God. There are two founts of the devotion of its subjects, and prayer draws from both. The first is the grace of God. This is obtained by prayer of petition. The second is our inner conviction of God's rights. This comes from contemplation. Hence prayer totally divorced from devotion to God's Kingship is but illusion. There are no backwaters in life's stream ; there is no escape from the stress of life which is not either a form of life or else is death ; there is no pause from the service of God which is not either a new form of service or else is rebellion. Life is so simple a thing as all that. And prayer, being a part of life, shares necessarily in its simple and exclusive purpose.

CHAPTER VIII

THE CONQUEST OF THE KINGDOM

"*Regnavit a ligno Deus*" : God reigned from the Wood.

OUR first parents left, by their rebellion against the authority of God, a heritage of sin, which considered in itself involved the spiritual ruin of their descendants. But God did not desert men, even though they were children of the first human sinners. For He determined that the heritage of sin would be accompanied by a heritage of pain, and that they who would incur through the one heritage the danger of His enmity, might be forced by the other to take refuge in the harbour of His friendship. Human pain is the fruit of human sin ; it is also, in God's designs, the occasion of liberation from sin. Pain leads to questioning, for it is a mystery. And whoever questions his world in good faith and with sincerity will find that there is but one answer to all questions, and that that answer is God. Submission to the discipline of pain must, therefore, lead back to God. And when we speak of pain as a discipline, the word must be understood in its original sense of a teaching. Pain is not a discipline as a reins or a bit might be said to be the discipline of an unruly horse. Pain is a teacher ; pain is a revelation of God ; God has never been known fully by man until He is known in the experience of accepted pain.

What makes the mystery of pain so insistent in life, beyond the fact that in itself it is a frustration of desire of some kind, is that it admits of no evident theoretical solution. We know that pain is ; but we cannot say why it should be, otherwise than to assert that God has allowed it in punishment for sin ; and we cannot say why He has allowed it otherwise than to point to the beneficial action it can have on our souls. And if, at the end of this searching, we enquire why God allowed the benefits to be derived from pain to outweigh in His judgment the intrinsic horror of pain itself, we can give no better answer than that He knows why, but that we do not. At that point the mystery becomes insoluble ; and it is precisely at that point that its sharpest edge is felt. What really does hurt our minds is the thought that God did allow pain when He was free to dispense with it. It is but poor consolation to think of all the good that pain does and will do. It seems so often to miss its aim, to be pointless, to crush ; and yet, though not necessary, it was chosen—sought out, as it were, when it had better been shunned. In what thought can the tortured soul find rest ?

The whole difficulty in the solution of this problem is that rest from pain is to be found not so much in a thought as in an attitude, whereas men persist in seeking it in their minds rather than in their hearts. Rest will not be found in a blind unreasoned attitude. It is therefore necessary to learn as much as possible of the meaning that pain has for the human mind. But even when this has been done there is no escaping the necessity of an act of trust and love as the final element in a truly soul-satisfying solution. No reason can be found why pain must be ; and a reason of that kind is the only one which will satisfy the mind. But there is a completely satisfying reason why pain should be accepted. It is that it comes from the hand of a Father Whom we love and trust, and that the path of pain was trodden before us by Our Divine Saviour. It is impossible to gainsay the cogency of these reasons. They at once capture the heart, even though they do not give full light to the mind. Some light they do give, for we know that what comes from a Father's hand must be good for His children, and that what was selected freely by the Son of God for His portion must have a surpassing worth, even if we can detect nothing more of that worth than the fact of its existence. Even so little light as this is enough to justify us in following our heart's leading. We love God, and embrace pain as a test and proof of love which surpasses our understanding of the fitness of a test of such a kind. We love Our Saviour and suffer with Him in order to be like Him, even though we can see no inner reason why He should have decided to come as a suffering Model rather than One all joyous. That is the ultimate Christian solution to the problem. And what makes it so difficult to accept is that it is unintelligible except to one who loves.

The mystery of pain is in a very essential respect the mystery of the Kingdom of God. God, Who could have selected for the redemption of mankind and the establishment of the Kingdom any means whatever consonant with the Divine Wisdom and Justice, decided freely upon the way of the Incarnation, and, within this way, selected further that of a suffering Redeemer and King. A single act of Our Saviour's would have sufficed to merit the redemption of all men. All His acts were of a divine worth in so far as they were necessarily the acts of a divine Person. They were therefore of infinite value, and could have been accepted as a more than adequate satisfaction in justice for the outrage of man's sin. But Jesus would not have meant quite the same thing to us had He redeemed us otherwise than He did. Had we been redeemed by some seemingly effortless act, the Redeemer would have remained in our memories rather as a Teacher and Lawgiver than as a Redeemer—even though in Himself He would have been Redeemer first of all. For, taking men for what they are, they tend naturally to be impressed most by what is most spectacular; and if they had been redeemed by an exteriorly simple and insignificant act they would almost necessarily have allowed it to be eclipsed in their minds by scenes of legislative splendour—such as the Sermon on the Mount—or of doctrinal brilliance—such as the conversation by night with Nicodemus. The divine plan was, however, that the price of our redemption would include the death of Our Saviour on the Cross rather than be concentrated in any other of the many acts of His mortal life. This was a free choice. But once made it becomes momentous. It implies that the existing Kingdom of God is unintelligible except in the light of the Cross. The Kingdom of God, as God selected it, has its origin in the Cross and is ruled from the Cross. Other kingdoms were possible. A Kingdom could have been established by a new legislation, given as was that of Sinai. One could have been established by a simple restatement of the Old legislation. But these were not the alternatives adopted. One kingdom only was established, the Kingdom of the Cross, and it is utterly impossible to understand it in the isolated light of any principle, however true, which is not the Cross—even in the light of the body of principles that go to make up the incomparable Sermon on the Mount. " Blessed are they that suffer persecution " is, after all, but the shadow of the reality of Calvary.

When we come to the consideration of the Sacrifice Our Lord offered in the pain of the Cross, the important question is not why He suffered pain, but what He expressed in the pain He suffered. That is a simple corollary from what we have just said of the mystery of pain. And the first answer we shall find to our question is that His acceptation of pain was an expression of His obedience : that is to say, of His submission to His Father. " He humbled Himself, becoming obedient unto death, even to the death of the Cross," says St. Paul (Phil. 2, 8). After St. Paul, Our Holy Mother the Church makes these same words the great theme of her contemplation of the mystery of Calvary in her offices of Holy Week. Grace had been lost through the pride and revolt of Adam. The redemption of Adam's posterity was to be a complete undoing of the essential guilt and consequences of their father's sin. His pride and revolt would be undone by submission and obedience ; and the grace of God's friendship lost in punishment of pride would be restored in reward of submission : " For as by the disobedience of one man, many were made sinners ; so also by the obedience of one, many shall be made just . . . . if by one man's offence death reigned through one : much more they who receive abundance of grace, and of the gift, and of justice, shall reign in life through one, Jesus Christ " (Rom. 5, 19 & 17). Adam had received a command from God that he should not eat of the fruit of a certain tree. He disobeyed. Christ, too, received a command from His Father, that He should offer His life for the salvation of mankind. He obeyed ; and thereby undid Adam's disobedience. " Therefore doth the Father love me : because I lay down my life. . . . No man taketh it away from me : but I lay it down of myself, and I have power to lay it down. . . . This commandment have I received of my Father " (Jo. 10, 17-18). Christ recognized that the Father's rights over Himself as man were absolute. He laid down His sinless life in recognition of them, since that it was that the

Father asked of Him. He laid down His life freely. He, Who was all-powerful, allowed Himself to be led as a lamb to the slaughter because His Father had decreed that it was by His death that we should be saved. It was this unquestioning and devoted acceptance of His Father's will which constituted the obedience of Christ.

The obedience of Christ converted what would have been otherwise a shameful crime into an acceptable sacrifice and the price of our redemption. For the central point in Calvary is not what the Jews did, nor what the Romans did, nor even the sufferings of Our Saviour considered under their aspect of pain. What is central is His attitude to what happened. " He was offered because it was his own will," says Isaias (Is. 53, 7). As Our Saviour Himself reminded His Apostles, He could have prayed to His Father and obtained from Him the help of more than twelve legions of angels. What was done to Him, was done with His own permission. He obeyed His Father's command when He could have prayed to the Father and so obtained release from the pain and ignominy which its fulfilment entailed. He preferred to submit in simple obedience to the will of the Almighty, and through His obedience His death became sacrifice. All obedience is sacrifice in the wide sense of the term, for both obedience and sacrifice spring from the one fount of acceptance of the right of God to command and of man's entire dependence upon Him. In fact, obedience pure and simple, is superior to a sacrifice in which there is no interior spirit of submission. That is why we read in the Old Testament that obedience is better than sacrifices (cf. 1 Kings, 15, 22). But the obedience of Christ was not merely a sacrifice in the wide sense. It was a sacrifice strictly so called. In His obedience He offered His life to His Father. His action included therefore the two elements required for a true sacrifice : interior attitude and exterior sign. Interiorly He was filled with reverence and submission, and this He expressed by allowing His life to be taken away from Him in obedience to His Father's command.

The greatest offering that a man can make to God from among the things of this world is that of his life. Life is the completest expression of what one is. To live is to unfold the richness of one's being. To live is more than to be. It is to be fully and completely. It is possible to be, and yet to be unaware of the marvel of one's reality. Life in its highest is intellect and will tasting reality. From this it follows that a pure spirit can offer nothing more complete in token of submission to God than its adoration. For its whole life is summed up in the action of intellect and will, and adoration is nothing other than intellect and will submitted in their action to Him Who is their Fount. In adoration, therefore, the pure spirit offers its life to God, by a living act of submission to Him. But man has life of body as well as life of soul, and this in such wise that he has a keener appreciation of what the life of his body is, and means to him, than he can ever have in this world of the life of the body's more worthy partner. Interior adoration will not suffice, therefore, as an offering of all that he is to God. Even though it be an offering of what is highest in him—his soul namely—it is an offering which touches his feeble powers of mind less deeply than will an offering in which the body is associated. The great act of man's submission must therefore be one in which life of body is offered to God as well as life of soul. Such an act is termed a sacrifice.

In the sacrificial act a material object is set aside as belonging to God the Author and Lord of all being. Such an act expresses man's acceptance of God's dominion over all he is, since material objects are intended to subserve the bodily life of man in some way or other, and an act which recognises God's peculiar rights over them will consequently recognise by implication His rights over human life as well. An offering of bread, or wine, or some such thing will do. And by offering we mean, not that the object offered is given to God for His use, as it would be given to a mere man, but that it is withdrawn by the sacrificial act from the ordinary use of men in sign of the priority of God's rights over it and them. Thus, wine could be offered to God if, instead of being used for the support of human life, it were poured out at the foot of an altar ; flesh could be offered if it were burned instead of being cooked for daily use. All such sacrifices have their value from a double symbolism. In the first place the exterior act symbolises the interior one of submission. This is a symbolism which is altogether essential to the very notion of sacrifice, and if it were absent sacrifice would cease. But there is a second symbolism which is not essential, and it is that whereby a material object is offered as symbol of the offering of a whole human life. This symbol may be absent ; in fact must be absent when sacrifice is at its highest. For it is certainly more to offer life than to offer a symbol of life, and if the whole aim of sacrifice be to express the dependence of what is highest in man—his life namely—on God, that sacrifice will be the most complete and eloquent in which life itself is offered. Notice that the first symbolism will still remain. Bodily life can be offered totally by the acceptance of bodily death. But spiritual life cannot be offered in the same way. Hence bodily death will remain itself a symbol of the accepted dependence of our spiritual life on God. And it will be permitted to insist once more that were this spiritual element absent there would be no sacrifice at all. Now this most perfect kind of sacrifice is that which Jesus offered on Calvary. He allowed His life to be taken away, because He admitted the rights of the Father over all that was human and created in Him.

The Father had disposed of the mortal life of the Incarnate Word in His determination of the plan of our redemption. He acted towards that life as One having absolute rights in its regard. " He spared not even his own Son, but delivered him up for us all " (Rom. 8, 32). And even when the time came for the Son to suffer, the hand of the Father was in all that befell Him, for the Father allowed Him to be taken and put to death. Was not Christ's acceptation of His death therefore a sacrifice ? His offering of His life to His Father was something very real. First of all, it was a complete renunciation of His rights as man to its use. It is something to renounce the use of bread or wine or some other material object and set it apart as God's possession. But there is nothing that a man can renounce more intimate to himself than his own life. And to renounce one's life in God's favour is to leave it entirely in His hands that He may do with it as He wills. By this act it passes from the hands of the man who offers it. He gives up his right to its use. And thereby he offers it to God ; he gives it to God to use as He may decide. These two elements—renunciation by the offerer, and offering to God—were present in Jesus' offering of Himself on the Cross. He renounced His own personal claim to His life in favour of the claim of His Father. His sacrifice was not a mere symbol of His renunciation of life. It was life itself He offered to His Father and not something else in its place. He did this in obedience and submission. Thus, His offering was made acceptable by the spirit of religion in which it was made. It flowed from His exact understanding of the rights of the Father, of the total dependence of His Humanity on the Father, and on the unreserved adherence of His just will to the obligations that understanding revealed. He yielded up His life because His life was more truly His Father's than it was His as Man. There was nothing in His death therefore which was not the expression of complete submission to Divine authority and rights. It was, in other words, sacrifice in its simplest and purest.

And yet, when we consider the sacrifice of Calvary as motivated by obedience and reverence, we have seen but part of its deeper meaning. For it was inspired by love too—by love, we may say, even more than by any other motive. "That the world may know, that I love the Father : and as the Father hath given me commandment, so do I" (Jo. 14, 31). Our Lord went to His death because He loved the Father, and accepted it when it came in proof of His love. He even gives His love as the motive for obeying the Father's command—not, of course, that He did not obey in reverence, but because He obeyed even more in love. And in the fact that Jesus suffered and died in love St. Thomas finds a truly sublime reason for justifying the statement that the Father delivered His only-begotten Son to His passion. The Father delivered Him to His passion, he tells us, because the Father filled Him with that love which made His will embrace the passion. Christ suffered because He wished to suffer : "He was offered because it was His own will" : and that it was His own will was due to the overflowing love of God and men which filled His human heart. He offered Himself, as St. Paul tells us (Hebr. 9, 14) by the Holy Ghost, unspotted, unto God. The Holy Ghost is love. Christ offered Himself because He loved His Father and wished to re-establish the reign of His Father among men. He offered Himself because He loved men and wished to draw them into the haven of the Kingdom of His Father. It is wonderful to think of that sublime co-operation of justice and love in Jesus' heart as He died on the Cross. It was just that He should die, of Whom God asked death. It was becoming that He should die, Who loved to give what the Father desired. Justice added fuel to love ; love added fuel to justice. And in that death, rich in the treasures of immeasurable love and submission, was born the Kingdom of God.

It was its redemptive character that made the death of Our Saviour the birth of a kingdom, and added to His other titles to Kingship the final and definitive one of King by right of conquest. The death of Jesus was infinitely acceptable to the Father. Considered from the side of those who put Him to death it was a foul crime, a sin, and the archetype of all sin. But considered on Jesus' side, considered in the light of His acceptance and its motives, it was the most perfect realization of God as The All in human life. The Father ruled and reigned in the dying Christ. The dying Christ is the Kingdom of God on earth. For, in the first place, the reign of the Father in His dying Son is the most complete that will ever be ; it is the Kingdom of God in its highest and most perfect manifestation. And, in the second place, the Father reigned in the Victim of the Cross as in the Head of all mankind, as in Him through Whom He would reign in whomsoever of the sons of men would be His subjects. Reigning in Him, He reigned therefore in the whole kingdom as in its Source. We were all made subject to the Father in the submission of His Son. The death of Christ was therefore infinitely pleasing in the eyes of the Father. It was an act of outstanding and unique heroism, an act of singular worth and divine attractiveness. Such an act could not go without its reward. It was an act of homage and love more than a king's ransom—nothing less in truth than a kingdom's ransom. The courage and glory of that act won for themselves, conquered, the reward of a liberated mankind. The salvation of men had been, as it were, a prize, and none could gain it save He Who would be strong unto the sublime daring of a submissive God-man, loving and serving unto death. It was thus that Jesus conquered for Himself a Kingdom, and became a victor King, meriting for Himself a Name above every name, at which every knee must bend. He bought us with a great price, bought us in pain, bought us in love and suffering, and made us thereby His. When we look on the Cross we see our King. We see there Him Whose we are. We see, too, the price of His Kingship, and the bleeding signs of His merciful power. He has won us, not by paying the devil a price—for he had no rights over us, even though we were under his power—but by the Father's acceptance of the sheer magnificence of what He did. We cannot but belong to One Who is all He is and Who has done what He has done. How far He is above us now—though still how human and how near—God, God-man, Victor. Can pride—even human pride—refuse to submit to One so great? Can selfishness—even human selfishness—refuse to love One Who has loved so much? We adore Thee, O Christ and praise Thee, because by Thy Holy Cross Thou hast redeemed the world, and made us to our God a kingdom and given us to reign upon the earth. We are Thine, and we will have Thee to rule over us.

Considering thus the Cross as the fount of the Kingdom of Heaven we see that there is room for suffering in our lives, more even than the Sermon on the Mount might have led us to believe. And for this we can give a certain number of reasons, of which the first is that God is not content to rule us through any code, no matter how perfect, but claims the right to take direction of every instant of our lives.

We find in the Sermon on the Mount a certain codification of the Law of God. To accept this in its entirety is already a great act of submission. But a greater is possible. A code is necessarily universal in its formulation. It states general principles which admit of latitude in their concrete applications. And when once a man has grasped the reasonableness of the code—in a merely intellectual act, be it noted—there is still much room left for self-will in his acceptance of it. Considering the question purely in the abstract, it is physically possible to accept the ethics of the Sermon on the Mount and remain in the kingdom of this world. One could see, as so many half-Christians do, that it is the best from the natural standpoint, and embrace it as being such from a merely natural motive, without any intention of making submission to it include a substantial submission to God the Lawgiver. It can in fact be embraced as the most perfect means to self-development. On the other hand, it is at least morally impossible for a man to allow Divine Providence a free hand in his life for any motive other than that of love and reverence for the divine Majesty. The workings of Providence, while not being irrational, baffle reason. They escape the directive control of man. They are not things that he can master in their principle as he can a code of legislation. Providence always treats a man as an inferior ; it disposes of him without asking his advice, at times while seeming not to consult his well-being. Providence demands nothing short of submission. Providence is truly the instrument of a King, and a great King, and an absolute King. Grant all that must be granted about the sublimity of Christian morality, but it remains that God deals with us most authoritatively when He speaks in the fortuitous events of daily life, and His accents are never more kingly than when they strike the note of pain. Let me repeat once more what has been said already, that we know for certain that God in sending pain has our good in view, and that pain is never pointless for those that love Him. The point now made is that pain is not served out to us in practice in a way our minds can comprehend ; it comes by way of an incomprehensible providence, and its appeal in the concrete instance is not to reason but to love and submission. Our Saviour's passion and death came to Him in that way. Ask the Church how He faced death, and you hear the answer : in obedience and love. Never a word of accepting it in mere logic. In obedience and love—that is how Christ faced the pain of establishing His kingdom. He has left us thereby an example how we should accept it in living in the same kingdom. Pain was at the birth of the kingdom ; it will grow and wax strong in pain. And where there is pain there is a call to submission ; and where there is submission God is truly King.

A second reason, which is ultimately but another form of the first, is that the offering of life in suffering can be intensely earnest. Once more let it be observed that this is not equivalent to saying that no offering other than one made in pain could have been equally so. Adam could have offered himself fully to God in the midst of unalloyed earthly bliss. Hence, to show that an offering can be made in pain is not to give a final reason why God should have chosen it as the one He asks from man. But it is still no small help to us in making our offering of pain, if we know that it has a deep worth, even though the ultimate choice to make it or refuse it will rest with our submissive or rebellious wills.

God has a right to the homage of our whole lives. But why, we may ask, should He not receive it by our living our lives fully in His service? The question cannot be answered completely. The most that can be done is to point to the pain of the Cross. The acceptance of pain from the hand of God can be an act of intense submission because pain is something that does not commend itself to man. Pain, considered in itself, is opposed to life. Pain results from the frustration of some vital urge. Hence, one single moment of pain strikes at the very core of life. Pain passes therefore in some way beyond the individual instant of suffering and the individual member that suffers, to become the bearer of a threat to life itself. When, therefore, we accept pain we accept something which embraces the whole of life in its implications. Whereas it is not so evidently felt that we submit all life to God when we submit to Him in some isolated pain-free action. It is possible to accept His rights, say in our words, while still holding back in other matters much more than we can give. It is possible to submit part of lived life without submitting its totality. And then, besides, what is the totality of the human life which we say we submit to God? Not one act but a life-long series of acts. And how can all this be submitted to Him better than in some act which embraces and includes the root of all others? And what act does this other than pain accepted in love and submission, which admits God's right to dispose of the very principle of our well-being— life itself?

There is room therefore in the Kingdom of God for pain. Pain does not run counter to its two great motives, love and submission ; rather does it afford them a unique opportunity of expression. But this is not all. Since Calvary, pain becomes more than a unique opportunity : it becomes for all men a necessary opportunity. Life in the Kingdom of God is union with Jesus in Calvary's act of submission and love. To suffer is not just the best way of serving God : suffering in some of its forms has become for every man the only way of true service. For all men there is but one way : that of death to self by life in Jesus. There is no life without the pain of death, just as there is no profitable death without the promise of life. Jesus on the Cross made His act of submission and love as Head of mankind. He was not, however, just One of us deputed to do something on our behalf to which we should adhere externally. He is a living Head, to Whom we are joined in oneness of life, and what He did as Head we must do in union with Him as members. Head and members must have unity of structure, for the mystical body is all-beautiful. There may be no opposition between Head and living member : there can be no true member which does not respond to the pulse of the life of the Head. If Jesus on the Cross is Our Head in the great moment of His headship, if at that moment He is our King on the day of His crowning, we His members and His subjects should conform ourselves to the life that then was His. Our whole lives should be a reliving, in all the varied circumstances of life, of His obedience and love. God must rule in us at all times in a way that is some share in that in which He reigned in the Crucified. Every act of acceptance of God's Kingship in the course of our day becomes therefore an entry into Calvary. It is Calvary which raises our service to the supernatural level. Calvary contained all that God sought on earth, and all that He can find pleasure in must be its echo.

Too seldom do Christians look on Calvary as a moment of triumph. Yet that is what it was. On Calvary the Crucified was Victor ; the crucifier (Satan and self—for Satan and self crucified Jesus) was the vanquished. Death made Jesus a victorious King. His acceptance of death was the most glorious of His acts. Everything about Calvary was a triumph, considered from the side of the Triumphant Saviour. The Church sings in Holy Week, and bids us sing in faith with her : *Regnavit a ligno Deus* ; God reigned from the wood of the Cross. The Cross is a throne ; pain is a crown of glory. And that, not because of what the cross of wood or the sting of suffering must be, but because of what the Son of God has made them to be. God reigned from the wood. And if God has chosen to reign from the wood of the Cross, dare we hope to find Him reign where live those who are clothed in fine garments ? Obedience made Jesus a King : sharing in His obedience will make us partakers in the glory of His Kingdom. Death made Him the Fount of Life : sharing in His death will make us draw from Him as Fount. Submit to God and God fills you with grace. Make yourself nothing, and God will exalt your humility. Grace and glory follow submission ; and they are even implied in it. To submit to God as we should is the fruit of grace. Submission to God is the act of a noble soul ; only a truly great man can be truly humble. There is more real life in an instant of submission than in an eternity of pride. Calvary was Jesus' triumph. Our Calvary will be our triumph also.

From all this it follows that Holy Mass is the central act of life in the Kingdom of God. It is the purest expression of the devotion which characterises a faithful subject of the Divine King, for it is nothing else than real entry into the love and service of the dying Man-God. But it is important to understand the way in which it is central. It is not central merely as that would be to which all things else converge—though it is undoubtedly central in that sense—but rather as that from which all things else radiate and receive direction. The whole day should be lived in the spirit of the morning Holy Mass. Attendance at Holy Mass tunes us in, as it were, to the divine in the daily. Holy Mass is a moment of retreat, a moment of contact with God in Christ, in which we come to learn the mind of God in Christ and are made sensitive to the law of God in Christ. A Holy Mass which ends at the " *Ite Missa Est* " has failed to achieve its purpose for the individual in question. We might say that Holy Mass had a beginning—it began on

Calvary—but has no ending, for it is for àll time and for all that fills time. Once a person understands Holy Mass he cannot conceive of It as ever being over and done with. He will be filled with the ideas of love and service. He will want to love God in daily life in union with Jesus, to serve Him in all things in union with Jesus. Holy Mass is one of those electrifying experiences after which life is never just what it was before. The external details of life may not change, but they will have a new meaning ; they will appear enveloped in deep mystery, and what was once trivial will appear peacefully momentous. Most of all, however, will he who lives have changed ; for to change life is after all a matter of changing living. Face the contact-worn and spiritually-exhausted minutiae of life's daily round in the warmth of a new conviction, and, in a second Cana, the drab becomes life-giving. Is there not more than a hint of this second Cana in the outer form of Mass ? Bread and wine are changed into the Body and Blood of Christ : in the power of God, what was of earth is transformed into Him Who is our Life. And by the spirit of Holy Mass what is of earth and what of pain is transformed into something life-giving. The law of God and the God of all law is seen in everything, and the guests of life's feast are replenished even when the wine of earth's gladness fails.

Calvary had the place in Jesus' life which we say should be given to Holy Mass in the life of the average Christian. Jesus lived for His hour. He did not will that the Jews should reject Him. Did He not Himself say that He would fain have gathered His chosen people to Himself as the hen does her chickens, but that they would not come to Him, that they rejected His earnest and reiterated advances ? But even when He endeavoured to draw the Jews to Himself He knew what the result would be. And He knew, too, that it would be by His death and by nothing else that mankind would be saved. On that account, in all that He did, one intention was supreme : to bring men gradually to an understanding of what His death would mean. To do so would take time ; but He never lost that purpose from view. All His attempts to win souls to light and grace aimed ultimately at bringing them, when the time would come, to an understanding of Calvary. And it is for that reason there is such intense pathos in the simple words which describe the attitude of the disciples to His crucifixion : "Then His disciples leaving Him, all fled away" (Mk. 14, 50). It is not so much that they deserted Him in a cowardly way, as that they showed by their flight that they never understood His teaching. All that He had ever said to them, all that He had ever done in their presence, was now to get its complete meaning, and their flight betrayed that the meaning had little or no signification for them. Jesus' whole life pointed to and was lived in the spirit of His Hour : our whole lives should proceed from and be animated by the same Hour relived in Holy Mass. Head and members are all of one piece. We must live as Jesus lived, not by doing what He did, but by doing what we do as He did what He did. That is the meaning of living our Mass. As we have seen, It persists in Its effects and in Its spirit. By so persisting, the whole day is made to become a simple pattern of love and service and devotion. Jesus lived for the Law of God because all that He did was directed to the fulfilment of the commandment He had received from His Father. Living the Mass converts all our actions too into an unbroken acceptance of the Divine Law.

Though it would not be possible to speak adequately here of Holy Communion and its place in the sacrifice of the Mass, it is nevertheless necessary to stress just one point : that the reception of Holy Communion at Mass—which is clearly the best time to receive, if at all possible—finds its deepest meaning in its juxtaposition to the act of sacrificial offering. In Holy Communion we receive Him Who has been both Priest and Victim in sacrifice. To receive Him means therefore to declare our internal adherence to Him in this dual rôle, and our will to grow ever more therein. Christ has offered sacrifice and now we receive Him into our souls. Could we express more clearly in sign that we agree fully with what He has done ? He has offered Himself, and still we receive Him, declaring thereby our belief that to offer oneself to God is a noble thing worthy of imitation. And, of course, Holy Communion is more than a sign. It is, as well, the reality of conformity with Christ as Priest and Victim : It makes us like Him under these two aspects. But whether we consider It as sign or as cause, Its import is the same : Holy Communion has no meaning apart from love and service in union with Jesus even at the price of pain, since It is essentially sign and cause of our conformity with His love and service as expressed in the great sacrifice of Calvary. To receive Holy Communion is not therefore an isolated incident in an otherwise-filled day, no more than Holy Mass is ; and for the same reason. It is the meaning of everything else. It quickens everything else. It fills us with reverence for the Law of the Kingdom, and makes us sensitive to its voice at every moment. Like prayer, Holy Communion is not one of life's recreations. It is, if you wish, one of life's oases ; not however in the sense of a temporary refuge, but in the sense of a refreshing fount which sustains in the thirsty toil of life. Bring your day's work with you to Holy Communion ; but as something to be set straight, not as a distraction. The work of the day must be ruled by the Law of God, and you will see how that can be by gazing at your work through the eyes of the Lawgiver. What is wrong with the world is not perhaps that there is little or no religion in it, but that what religion is in it is kept severely apart from the rest of life. Almost all men have their moments of religion. It is only the fool that can say in his heart that there is no God ; and even he cannot keep up the pretence of believing his folly without frequent interior warnings that he is not right. But there are men who pass for wise, and still reserve their conviction that there is a God, and that He has imposed a Law, for clearly circumscribed occasions. Their idea of God is never allowed to intrude itself into their idea of life. Christianity is something far different from this. "Therefore, whether you eat or drink, or whatever else you do, do all to the glory of God" (1 Cor. 10, 31). God's interests are involved in no matter what we do. Everything therefore has its place in Our Mass and Holy Communion. It may be that God will give us the light then to see in what we fail ; or it may be that He wishes us to ask Him for the grace to perform our duties in submission to His Holy Will ; it may be that Our Holy Communion

will result in nothing more concrete than a deeper understanding of the mind of Christ, and a clearer vision to detect
His interests and greater generosity to further them unselfishly—
but no matter how it happen, Holy Communion will change
life. That is the thing to be understood ; and that is the
thing to aim at.

We have spoken much in this chapter of submission to God,
and of obedience. And it will certainly appear to not a few
that life conceived in such terms is an intolerable burden, a
real slavery, and that God is nothing more than an Omnipotent
Being Whose pleasure it is to impose His Will. The truth
is very far from such a position. Speaking later of the peace
of the Kingdom of God we shall show how false it is to
imagine that our submission has no meaning other than to
make God an effective Master. Our peace could not be
achieved otherwise than through submission, because the
highest peace is the peace of God and there is no created peace
which is not a sharing therein. And it is equally false to
consider submission a form of abject slavery. Submission to
a Superior Being is in itself something reasonable, and therefore
good. It is felt to be bondage only when the superior and his
rule are hated. If he be loved submission becomes sweet.
To understand this we must go back to Calvary.

Jesus longed for His hour. He died that the world might
know that He loved the Father. And since He loved the
Father He laid down His life willingly : He was offered
because it was His own will. Indeed, to say willingly, is to
say too little. We must say that He died joyously. We do
not forget His cry of anguish ; we do not forget that moment
when He seemed to be abandoned by His Father. But we
believe, and St. Thomas guarantees our belief (3a, Q46, a7)
that even at the moments of greatest anguish the Man Jesus
rejoiced in the Father : God, he tells us, was at all times to
the soul of Christ a cause not of grief, but of joy and happiness.
And did not the Apostles rejoice in their trials, thinking it an
honour to be found worthy to suffer for the name of Jesus
(cf. Acts 5, 41) ? That service should be easy to one who
loves, is not something we are asked to believe as true of the
spiritual order while false otherwise. Our everyday experience

should convince us of its universal truth. Devoted children do not feel the strain of serving their aged parents. A husband does not dole out his services to his wife. It is a pleasure to serve those we love. The fact that we love them supernaturally does not make the pleasure experienced in their service anything the less real. It makes it rather more real, more genuine. The service of God is hard as long as we have not sufficient love to want to serve.

And that too must be our final answer to the problem of pain. Pain is a possibility of loving service ; and he who loves will accept it without questioning. If there be no love, pain is mere torment. If there be love, it is accepted even if it be not understood. Pain was the lot of Jesus ; it was the completest expression of His devotion. Therefore we, who wish to model ourselves on Him, will accept pain as something He has comprehended and found to be greater than all earthly sweetness. Pain is a mystery. Why should we strive to understand it rather than any other mystery ? We do not hope to fathom the mystery of the Blessed Trinity ; we simply accept it in faith. We do not hope to fathom the mystery of our own salvation ; we simply accept it in hope. Neither can we fathom the mystery of Pain. We must rest content to accept it. But God has given pain even here on earth a reward. For to accept it in life is neither Faith nor Hope, but what is greater than all virtues : Love.

The Kingdom of God was established by Christ the Conqueror in the pain of the Cross. Our life in the Kingdom must also be one of glorious conquest through accepted pain. He has left to each of us the exploit of a kingdom to be overthrown in His name. That kingdom is the kingdom of self. Its overthrow means pain ; and all pain can be a means to its downfall. For each of us there is therefore the possibility of a triumph. What if it costs ? The triumph of the Cross cost even Jesus' life.

CHAPTER IX

THE GOVERNMENT OF THE KINGDOM

" The Lord said to my Lord : Sit thou at my right hand"
(Ps. 109, 1).

THE conquest of the Kingdom was followed within three days by that Resurrection from the dead by which the truth of Jesus' conquest was made indisputable. After His Resurrection He remained still some time with His Apostles. For there were many things which He needed to say to them, things which nothing short of the shock of Calvary and Easter Sunday could prepare them to receive and understand. There were, too, things that remained to be done : there was, for example, the institution of His sacraments to be completed and explained, the organization of His Church to be exposed in clear outline. But this period of Jesus' risen life on earth was not to be of long duration. For He had already, during His mortal life, laid the foundations of His Church-Kingdom, and provided the materials out of which it would be made. Its perfection He would leave to His Holy Spirit. When therefore the purpose of His earthly risen life had been attained, He went with His disciples to the appointed mount of Galilee ; " And the Lord Jesus, after He had spoken to them, was taken up into Heaven, and sitteth on the right hand of God " (Mk. 16, 19).

Jesus' Resurrection, Risen Life, and Ascension are the key to the inner beauty of Calvary. If the life of Jesus be concentrated, as it were, in Calvary, we need for our understanding of all that Calvary contains to recall that He Who rose and ascended into Heaven in glory remained the Same Who had been crucified, and that He Who, walking this earth, offered Himself to the adoration of doubting Thomas, offered no greater proof of identity than that of open wounds. The whole of Jesus is on Calvary's hill, but our eyes are not strong enough to see more there than the depth of His submission and the shame of His chastisement. To restore the balance of our judgment it seemed well in the mind of God that the same Jesus should appear after death in a form which

would seem all glorious. In this new form, however, Jesus
would still bear the impress of His wounds. There would still
be that much of frailty about Him. But now it is a frailty
so interfused with strength, a horror so transformed by divine
Beauty, that in contemplating it the mind is led to suspect
that Calvary, where frailty and horror seemed to reign alone,
must have been in its essence a triumph of the Order and
Power of God, and that the submission and pain which jar
so rudely on our sensitive souls must in all truth have been
nothing other than signs and bearers of a transcendent bliss
and exaltation. We may, it is true, approach the Crucified
with compassionate hearts. It is good for us that we should
do so, since God has been so merciful to our weakness as to
give us the opportunity of seeming to be merciful to His.
But to do so is not the only possible avenue of approach. It
is not even the most essential one. Calvary is, before all else,
an enthroning. Jesus dies on the Cross as a King, and shows
by the manner of his dying that death is something He is great
enough to conquer.

The triumph of Calvary is made evident by the Resurrection : the Ascension shows forth the lofty and unbroken peace
of the struggle between the Author of life and the forces of
death. The Crucified was all peace. He was even fount of
our peace. Of Him could be said—but with what greater
truth—what is applied in the Book of Wisdom to the just :
" The souls of the just are in the hand of God, ... in the
sight of the unwise they seemed to die : and their departure
was taken for misery : And their going away from us for
utter destruction : but they are in peace " (Wisdom 3, 1-3).
Jesus was never submerged in that struggle with sin and death,
He was never caught in their current, and borne away, even
for an instant, in despairing helplessness. What current there
was broke furiously against Him ; but He breasted it, and
threw it mightily aside, and tamed the waters of created
iniquity in the strength of His power and mercy. But that
we might see that this was the truth, rather than that
appearance of defeat which seemed so real to us, He ascended
to Heaven and sits at the right hand of His Father in unending
glory. He sits in Heaven, in peace, in the tranquil flush of

victory. Death never had dominion over Him ; and now it will not even have that counterfeit of dominion it flourished on the hill of shame. He is all glorious now. He is God ; He is God-man ; He is full of Grace ; He is King and Victor. The glory and beauty of our King have been lifted above the heavens ; He Who emptied Himself, taking the form of a servant, has of His plenitude filled even that servant-form with majesty ; He commands Who was obedient to sinners, and empires tremble at His word. But what appeals to us first of all in the ascended Jesus is the peace of Our King ; and it must be the same idea which was uppermost in the minds of the Apostles when they so far forgot their grief at His departure from them as to look upon His face and read its message. They had known Him so long in the days of His flesh and of His weakness. They had seen Him baited, seen Him taken, seen Him put to death. His Kingdom, in spite of their ardent messianic hopes, could hardly have failed to appear, in moments of doubt and dread, as one that would have to reckon and parley with this world. They can hardly have grasped the notion of a peace that no man can take away, no more than their idea of peace could have been that of something the world cannot give. But the Kingdom and its peace became something new that day upon the mount. It became a kingdom which rose above the world with its King, and its peace was one of a depth no man could search. And perhaps they came to some faint understanding of those words spoken on the road to Emmaus : " Ought not Christ to have suffered these things, and so to enter into His glory ? " (Lk. 24, 26). And perhaps they understood, too, that in the very suffering they in their turn would endure, was concealed a weight of glory that would draw them one day near to the glory of the throne of their heavenly King.

In the peace of the Victor King is power. He governs souls from His throne in heaven. For true peace is always power. Peace is not just the absence of conflict. It is the possession of that fulness of being which excludes conflict. The rule of Christ in heaven is the continuation of His rule from the wood of the Cross. He remains always the Lamb Who was slain ; He bears still in His glorified body the marks of the wounds

He received in His great combat. But His rule from the throne of wood was but for a time ; for He was taken from the Cross and laid in a tomb. It is continued and perpetuated in His rule from His throne in Heaven whence He pours forth the streams of grace which Calvary caused to overflow. His rule from the Cross and His rule from Heaven are not therefore two rules. They are but stages in one and the same rule. Neither are His peace on the Cross and His peace in Heaven two. They likewise are but two stages in the one reality. We are still ruled from the Cross ; it is still the peace of the Cross which fills our souls. We can never escape from Calvary except at the price of missing the Kingdom of God.

There are many terms used to designate Jesus as Ruler throned on the right hand of the Father. The first and most obvious one is that of King. But there are others also which differ from it by but the merest shade of meaning. There is for example that of Eternal Priest. As Eternal Priest Jesus mediates unceasingly between God and Man. But this is in some way the meaning of His Kingship also, for He rules men to bring them under God's sway and to fill them with fulness of the supernatural life of grace. Another title is that of Head of the Mystical Body. Jesus throned at the right hand of the Father is this Head. But the very notion of Head implies a certain eminent dignity, which in this case is Kingly. And, in fact, it may be said that the reason why Jesus is spoken of as Our Head is that His relations with us as King are so intimate as to transcend those which are commonly found between earthly kings and their subjects, and are therefore more aptly described to our minds by those between head and members of the same body. Whatever may be said, therefore, of Jesus as King, is true in some closely allied sense of Him as Priest and Head as well. On that account there is no reason why souls should be confused at the multiplicity of titles given Our Saviour. They are in no way opposed ; they are essentially complementary. One who feels drawn to Jesus as Priest will profit by hearing Him spoken of as King. His Kingship does not eclipse His Priesthood ; It merely emphasises the fact that It is kingly. The first point therefore to be borne in mind is the essential unity of all the titles of the Throned Christ.

The second is the unity of His Person. Christ is both God and Man ; but it is the one Person of Whom both Natures are predicated. Hence, certain distinctions which are of great importance in speculative theology are of but little importance as regulative of life. I refer to distinctions dealing with Jesus' rule as God and His rule as Man. As God He rules equally with the Father and the Holy Ghost. The totality of authority in the Kingdom of God must be referred to Him as God in union with the Two Other adorable Persons of the ever Blessed Trinity, without there being any question of greater authority in the One than in the Other. As Man, however, He is less than the Father, and authority belongs to Him only in dependence on the authority which is divine. His authority as Man is to be traced to the grace of union, and the grace of headship, and merit. And the titles of which we have just spoken—those of King[1] and Priest and Head—belong to Him as Man, not as God. But having made and acknowledged all these distinctions, it is none the less legitimate to take them for granted in a treatment of the question which is rather affective than scientific, because they are all distinctions in the One Person. If Jesus be God as well as Man, then, no matter what exercise of authority in the Kingdom of God be considered, it will be attributable to His Person in virtue of One or the Other of His Natures. And even if we were to consider Him in His Human Nature, it must never be forgotten that that Nature is joined in the Unity of His Person to the Divine, so that even when as Man He acts on us as instrument of the Divinity, He is never an instrument subsisting in itself outside of God, but is One Which has no subsistence whatever except That of the Second Person of the Blessed Trinity. For these reasons therefore it will be permissible to speak simply of the rule of Our King without pausing at each instant to make clear whether or not the reference is to His Divine Nature or to His Human Nature as Instrument of the Divine. And what is thus theologically permissible may even be devotionally advisable. For conscientious distinctions in the

---

[1] We abstract for the moment from the consideration of His Divine Kingship. For this, see Chap. III.

objects of our faith, while they have their proper and necessary place in theological science, are but a poor help to pious contemplation, and may even prove something of an obstacle.

Jesus rules the Kingdom of God in the Holy Ghost. On the night before He suffered He told His disciples that the purpose of His going from them was that He might send them the Paraclete in His Name Who would be with them and rule them in all things : " It is expedient to you that I go : for if I go not, the Paraclete will not come to you ; but if I go, I will send Him to you " (Jo. 16, 7). Jesus Himself had been led at all times by the Spirit of God. The Holy Ghost never departed from Him from the first instant of His Incarnation. This ruling presence of the Holy Ghost in His soul was made manifest at His Baptism, the beginning of His public life, by the Dove Which descended upon Him. And following upon the account of His Baptism, there come in the gospel narrative those revealing words which tell how He was driven by the Spirit into the desert. It would be false to think that this was an isolated case of the action of the Holy Ghost upon Him. At all times He was moved to what He did by the Spirit of God. His journey to the desert was singled out as being thus inspired, not because it was the only act of its kind, but because of its great significance as the march of the Divine Warrior to His encounter with the foe. Viewing Jesus' life in the light of this continual presence of the Holy Ghost within His soul we may say that the fruit of His Redemptive act was to merit that we, too, should be ruled in our lives by the Holy Ghost as He was ruled in His. But since the Holy Ghost takes control of us in the power of Jesus as God and through His merits as Man, it is true to say that it is no less Jesus than the Holy Ghost Who rules us. From His throne in Heaven then Jesus rules us. His merits become fruitful in us through the Holy Ghost. All that happens in the order of grace is His work because He is its Fount. And Christ the Man Who merited what is now realized in us, is one in Person with the Word from Whose Divine Power all our sanctification ultimately proceeds. It matters little then how we restrict the efficient action of the Sacred Humanity in our sanctification. The Man Christ is Hypostatically united to a Person in Whom is all the power of God, and Who sends the Holy Spirit from Heaven to fill the earth and rule it for God. The Man Christ is never a subject standing apart from the Source of the life of Grace. He is One as Subject with the Second Person of the Adorable Trinity from Whom all life proceeds. Christ's unity as Man with the Word is so full that it becomes irrelevant at times to insist on what differences there are. The Man Jesus is so identified with the Word that theology can find no reason to baulk at that daring "communicatio idiomatum," or sharing of attributions, by which it is possible to say that He, the Man Jesus—even if not as Man—is Source of all that proceeds from the Divinity of the Incarnate Word, just as the Word is termed Principle of all that was achieved in and by His mortal flesh. Let us then think boldly of our King as ruling by His Spirit, and tracing the action of the Holy Ghost in the Church let us recognize therein the royal power of the King Jesus, our glorious Redeemer.

The first and most general effect of the mission of the Holy Ghost to our souls is to make us sons of God. The Holy Ghost was the Spirit of Jesus, true and eternal Son of the Father, and He ruled the actions of His Sacred Humanity. Jesus as Man needed to be and to act in a way worthy of One Who was also Eternal Son. The capacity for such being and activity came from the Holy Spirit. It is the same Spirit Who is now sent to take possession of our souls, and He will do so by transforming them after the image of the transformation He achieved in Jesus' soul. The Holy Ghost is the Spirit of our adoption. He comes to make us sons of God, and that in the name and after the image of Him Who was the well-beloved Son of the Father. Than this there is no greater act of kingly power over souls. It is an act of dominion over them, an exercise of a right to shape and determine, a laying hold on, by One Who acts as absolute owner. Our invasion by the Spirit of Adoption is Jesus' modelling of the kingdom of souls to the likeness of His all-conquering excellence. He imprints Himself on souls by the Spirit, He stamps them with His image, dissolves them and pours them into the unyielding mould of His great grace. Is not this an unequalled act of Kingship? If the act by which God poured grace into the soul of the first man, making what was of nature into a being of god-like grace, was one of a Master in Whose hands all flesh and spirit are as but a little clay, greater still is the act by which the Holy Spirit renders what is sinful god-like. For sin is not just creaturehood : it is opposition to God. Hence it is more to make a friend and child of God of a sinner than of a mere creature, just as it is more to harness a wild and raging flood than a river which flows calmly between high banks. We pray to God in the well-known antiphon : " Send forth Thy Spirit . . . . and Thou shalt renew the face of the earth." This renewal is a kingly act. It is a real reconquest of the rebellious kingdom of souls. The sin of Adam had overthrown the machinery God had set up in the human soul for its government, and had introduced the most fearful anarchy in the place of the order of submission. The Holy Spirit comes to us as He Who is all-powerful to bring our rebel souls to heel—even if He be powerless to do so against our wills. He comes in might, even if He comes in love and mercy as well. The touch of the Holy Spirit is gentle, but how infinitely strong and compelling. The psalmist speaks (Ps. 41, 3) of the "strong living God"—a wonderful description of the vivifying and all-powerful Spirit. For the Spirit is life as well as strength ; and the strength of the Spirit is employed in giving life. And the life the Spirit gives is life in our King, Jesus. So that He, the King, is all in all to us, and we, being ruled by His Spirit, are gathered into the fold of His subjects.

The next way in which Jesus rules us by the Spirit is His communication of the truth to man. For all fully-lived life proceeds from a certain understanding of what life is, and the life of the subject in God's Kingdom depends in the first place on an understanding of the Kingdom's Law. Jesus promised before His death to send His Holy Spirit on earth to rule mankind by this way of instruction and illumination : "The Paraclete . . . . whom I will send you from the Father, the Spirit of truth . . . . will teach you all things, and bring all things to your mind, whatsoever I shall have said to you" (John 15, 26 and 14, 26). Throned now in Heaven Jesus sends Him as His own Spirit, not to add to the revelation of the truth He Himself made, but to explain it and to give it effective sway over the minds of men. He sends His Spirit first of all to His teaching Church. It is understood by all Catholics that the infallibility of the Church is due to the continued assistance of the Spirit of Truth, Who ever sustains her in her divinely-given task of proposing the truth of Christ to the world, of explaining it, and pointing out its application to the varying phases of life. By so assisting the Church the Holy Ghost assures the reign of the truth of Christ over minds. He makes that truth stand forth, clear and challenging, as a city built on a high mountain. He endows that truth with its royal certainty, its unhesitating and uncompromising oneness. Wherever the voice of the Church can reach, men are aware of its greatness and majesty, even when they are so far in error as to think its claims exaggerated. Jesus, sitting at the right hand of the Father, reigns over minds by the palpable majesty of the voice of His teaching Church. The Church makes Him, the King, present to men. Her worth and dignity as a teacher are not distinct from His : rather are they manifestations of what is so fully in Him. While His Church continues to speak—and that will be till the end of time—He will continue to be present to the world as its Teacher, Master, and King. *Rex mortuus regnat vivus !*

By His action in the teaching Church the Holy Spirit illumines the minds of men from outside, presenting the truth to them as something which of itself commands acceptance. But the action of the Holy Spirit is not confined to this knocking at the doors of our minds ; He illumines us, too, from within, and submits us to the spell of Christ's truth by what He effects in the inner core of our souls. First of all He gives us the gift of Faith. Faith in so far as it is a gratuitous gift, leading to our salvation, is appropriated, like every other gift of the same kind, to the Spirit of Love. By Faith we are given the power of adhering with interior assent to the truth of Christ as it stands revealed in His Church. But we should not become so absorbed in the thought of Faith as a power as to forget that it is an authoritative urge as well. He who has the faith tends, vitally, but nevertheless in real dependence upon the all-powerful impulse of the Spirit, to submit his mind to Christ in an act of assent to the truth of what He proposes for belief. Faith is therefore the capture from within of the stronghold of the mind. By faith Jesus makes us, as it were, impose His truth upon ourselves by accepting it freely. The teaching Church lays siege to our souls from without : by faith the victorious King is revealed in our very midst. He no longer hammers at the walls of our citadel of intellectual pride. The gates have been opened and the King of glory has entered in. He has made us captives of His truth, and His truth has made us free.

Our submission to the sweet yoke of faith is completed by our submission to the yoke of the gifts of Understanding, Knowledge, and Wisdom. By the gift of Understanding we are filled with a certain divine curiosity, a certain compelling thirst to know, which keeps the truth of Christ ever before our minds, and subjects us to an unending growth in ever-deepening and ever-widening convictions. Knowledge compels us, sweetly though firmly, to look at things from a supernatural angle. Under its direction we begin to lose that old, and once thought happy, power of picking and choosing our own standards of judgment, of illumining a world with the rosy or other light of a passing mood and whim. The gift of Wisdom completes the subjugation of our minds. It makes them captives of the idea of God in a knowledge which is at once intellectual and effective. It leads them to view and judge all things from God's angle. But, most of all, it fills them with the idea of God Himself. He is never far from the centre of their consciousness, even in the midst of the most mundane occupations ; and in prayer, when He is not the great object of their contemplation, He is at least the background to every act of intellect and the ultimate motive of every movement of will.

Entry into the Kingdom of God does not consist, however, in nothing more than the acceptance of a new revelation. Our Blessed Lord Himself described His purpose as a rebirth of mankind. Not only must we receive the truth coming from outside ourselves, but we must be interiorly transformed to the image of the truth we receive. Learning and believing that God is our Father, we must put on interior sonship by means of the gift of grace. Now the great channels of grace are the sacraments. The sacraments effect our interior transformation to sonship of God after the image of Him Who is Eternal Son. The sacraments are therefore the great instruments by which Our King moulds the souls of men after the pattern He Himself is. Each reception of a sacrament is an act of submission to Christ the King. The person who receives it comes to Him as to a Master and allows Him to work His will in his soul. By Baptism we are taken possession of as His subjects, and filled with a grace which demands to express itself in a life devoted to His service. By Confirmation He takes possession of us as His soldiers. The service which, in virtue of the sacrament of Baptism, needed as yet to be but interior, must, after Confirmation, be exterior. By Confirmation Christ the King commissions us to the active service of His Church in its external social life. By Holy Communion He transforms us entirely into Himself, dealing as Master with all in us that is selfishly our own, filling us with His divine charity, by which we are impelled to spend ourselves without reserve in His love and service. He receives back in Penance those who may have fallen from their allegiance. The reception of this sacrament is a most wonderful recognition of the ultimate nature of Jesus' authority, because it involves an explicit admission that there is no way of life outside Him. The sinner has tried to set up his own little kingdom, and comes now, penitent, to admit the ephemeral nature of its glory. Extreme Unction is admission of the Kingship of Christ made by one who stands on the threshold of a new life. To receive Extreme Unction in a spirit of faith is to confess that the power of Christ the King extends beyond the frontiers of this mortal world even to the kingdom of immortal souls. It is, as well, a profession of faith in likeness to Christ as the best commendation in the eyes of God, the eternal and all-powerful King. Holy Orders moulds the priest to the image of Christ the King by giving him the power to share in an active way in His priestly and Kingly functions, and by imposing the obligation to perform such functions worthily. There is finally the Sacrament of Matrimony by which the Kingship of Christ is so brought into the union of husband

and wife, that the union itself is transformed to the image of that between Christ and His Church, and its purpose becomes the more complete winning for Christ of both parents and children.

The sacraments win us for Christ and rule us for Him by the grace which they pour into our souls. Each sacrament is source of a grace peculiar to itself, but as the difference between sacramental grace and sacramental grace is accidental and not essential, it will be permissible to consider them all here under the simple aspect of the conferring of grace without reference to the differences in the graces conferred. We may therefore say, in the first place, that the sacraments subject our beings to the being of God, in Jesus the King. The supernatural image of God in the world had been destroyed by the sin of our first Parents. The world of souls presented a scene of frightful anarchy. All in them that harked back to God's reign in the first days of creation had been rooted out. It was as if, after a revolution, a band of rebels had gone round in a wild philistine rage, and burned or trampled underfoot everything that could in any way recall the rule of the king they had overthrown. Grace had been destroyed ; so also the infused virtues and gifts. Nothing was left in souls to testify to the rule God once exercised, beyond their state of anarchy ; and this testified only by being a refusal to submit. Then came Our Blessed Lord on earth, full of grace and truth, the complete expression of what God wished to see realized in souls. The kingdom of His soul was loyal to God in every fibre. One had only to see it as it really was to know Who ruled it. Now the grace which we receive in the sacraments is a share in the grace of Christ Himself. Hence, it reshapes our being in accordance with God's desires, just as Jesus' being was all the Father desired it to be. Through the grace of the sacraments the world of souls is, therefore, brought back to its allegiance. The insignia of its Divine King are restored to their rightful place. If any soul has received grace in a sacrament, then whoever can see that soul sees at the same time that God is its Ruler. Instead of remaining, as it was before it received grace, the expression of some purely natural idea, it becomes the expression of a supernatural idea of God Himself, and its being, which before was that of a thing of nature, subject to nature's laws, is now sharer in the inner Being of God Himself and is ruled by Him immediately. That is what we mean by saying that the sacraments are the instruments of the Kingship of Christ by which He moulds our being to the image of the being of God. He came to restore all things not in action alone but in being as well, so that the very structure of the world of souls might be a hymn to the great glory of His Father, even were every mind and heart to remain silent.

We may say, in the second place, that the sacraments subject our lives to God in Jesus. Action follows necessarily on being. A non-free agent is bound by physical necessity to act in a way which corresponds perfectly to the manner of its being. An animal, for example, cannot but act in an animal way. A free agent is also subject to necessity, but this time of the moral order. That is to say, a free being *should* act in a way worthy of its nature and powers. A man should act on a human level, even though it be physically possible for him to fall below it if he so wish. From this it follows that in moulding our beings by the graces of the sacraments Jesus imposes on us the necessity of acting in a certain kind of way. When He transforms us into children of God He at the same time imposes on us the obligation to live as children of God. Being made children of God we are bound to act as such in virtue of the obligation which binds every free agent to live and act according to its true nature. I do not mean to say that the obligation to be true to what we are is the most ultimate of the obligations in the spiritual order. The obligation to be true to God is deeper still. But what is to be noted is that there is such an obligation, and that, since that is so, the binding force of the sacraments does not cease with the moment when they are actually operative in our souls, but that they leave, through the grace they confer, a permanent source of obligation and a permanent command to submit life to the rule of Christ the King.

As example of Christ's rule of our lives by the sacraments, we have just mentioned the case of the sacrament of Baptism which makes us children of God. But what has been said of it holds with the necessary qualifications for any of the sacraments. By Confirmation we are obliged to live as soldiers of Christ. The reception of Holy Communion obliges us to a life of union with Him, and to a life of union with His members in charity. Penance obliges us to a certain interior compunction as spring of all our activity. Holy Orders and Matrimony clearly map out a plan of life for those who receive them. By the sacramental graces which Jesus has poured into our souls He acquires therefore right of entry into our whole lives and the right to rule them in their every manifestation. This He does by the vital movement He communicates to us as Head of the Mystical Body. He really moves us to all the good we do. And moving us always in accordance with the demands of the grace which we have received from Him in His sacraments, He assumes complete control of our spiritual lives under whatever aspect we may choose to consider them. If we consider them under the aspect of their principle in us, that is to say, the habitual grace from which they spring— that grace is ours in dependence on Him. If we consider the actual movement of life which wells up within us—that movement is ours, but it is given us by our King. His rule in us could not therefore be more complete. We belong entirely to Him, both for what we are and for what we do. He bought us with a great price, and bought us completely, so that we are no longer our own possession but are entirely His. How little men owe an earthly king and how slight is their dependence upon him compared with their dependence on Jesus, and yet how unreal do we feel the authority of Him Who is of Heaven ! Our faith presents Jesus to us as a King that we may gather up all the feelings of reverence and loyalty that that name excites when understood in its human sense, and transfer them to Him, intensified beyond measure. He has been given a human name that we who are humans may know how to act in His regard. And how, indeed, if not by submission of our lives ?

Submission of our lives to the enthroned Jesus is recalled once more by the doctrine of the inhabitation of the Holy Ghost in our souls by grace. There are certain aspects of this doctrine which need not be stressed here. There is, for example, the fact that the Holy Ghost is present in the souls of the just by grace as a Guest, with Whom they may converse freely, as does a friend with a friend. It does not follow immediately from this that God rules us in any new way : though it must never be forgotten that if the Holy Ghost be present in our souls as a Friend, there arises on our side at once the obligation in friendship of treating Him as such—a point much neglected by those who seem to regard inhabitation as something given them solely for their convenience. But the point which concerns us here and now is somewhat different : it is that the Holy Ghost inhabits our souls not only to be the Object of their consideration and love, but to rule and guide them as the Spirit of Jesus. This is a point which is at once evident from even a cursory reading of the Epistles of St. Paul. He reveals the action of the Holy Ghost within our souls as being anything but that of a merely contemplated Guest : inhabiting souls He leads them, prompts them to mortify their flesh, guides and inspires their prayers ; He is so near to all they do that any neglect of grace is a disregard of His promptings. Were we to sum up His action in one comprehensive formula we could hardly do better than to say that the Holy Ghost, inhabiting souls by grace, appears in revelation as the living Law of God. The Holy Ghost within us is the voice of the law of God and Christ within us ; a Voice, which because It is living, speaks not in purely general terms, but which indicates what should be done here and now : an Authority, that is to say, Whom nothing whatever escapes. This is a point worth further consideration.

As we have mentioned already, submission to a law couched in general terms is never necessarily complete on the side of the subject. It is always possible to withdraw a number of individual cases from the range of application of a general principle. And even in the cases which fall clearly under it, there will always be room for latitude in the manner of its application. Hence, freedom-loving man rejoices in being ruled by general principles—one of the reasons perhaps for his immoderate thirst for drawing up constitutions which leave little or nothing to the common sense and prudence of rulers. A ruler who intervenes in a concrete instance is felt to be burdensome. He can, of course, be burdensome in fact, if he be unduly meddlesome, but that is not the present supposition : what we have in mind here is fallen man's objection to any form of rule which is more intimate than an abstract piece of legislation, given in such a purely impersonal way as not to emphasise unduly the inferior status of him· who is subject to it. Now God asks from man the submission of acceptance of an ever present authority. God has the right to do this— a right which earthly rulers have not—for He is Lord of all actions, whereas kings of earth are lords only in view of the common good, and have no right to intervene except when it is at stake. Hence the Holy Ghost inhabits our souls to direct and rule us in all things. That is what is meant by saying that the Holy Ghost is the living Law of God. There is the Law of God which is given once and for all and which is expressed in general terms. But there is as well the Holy Ghost, Who, by the promptings of His grace, indicates what we should do in individual instances. A good inspiration is therefore a kind of law. It is true that we remain free to reject for any reasonable cause an inspiration which takes the form of counsel. But even in such a case as this, God counsels us, when He does condescend to give counsel and not simple command, as a King, and we may not dare to reject His counsel lightly and without due reverence. When the matter is not of counsel it is quite clear that the inspiration comes to us with authority. If, for example, we get the grace to see that a certain course of action is dangerous for our souls, then that grace is also a command, given us by Jesus through His Spirit. If we are given the grace to see that to act in a certain way is our duty, it is the Holy Ghost with us Who is imposing that duty upon us by His grace. The voice of conscience is the authoritative voice of God within us. And conscience, as we know, never forsakes us. Conscience is always within us to keep vigilant eye on every thought, word, and deed, to deter from evil and to prompt to good. It is well for us when thinking of conscience to regard it as the voice of the Divine Lawgiver within our souls. In this way our lives become more explicitly devoted to the service of our King, and life in His Kingdom becomes an ever-deepening reality.

There is no reason for thinking that this vigilant presence

of the Divine Lawgiver within our souls must lead necessarily to servility in the spiritual life. The fact is that the Holy Ghost rules us by love, and that the more we submit to His rule the more we become filled with love, and the more therefore we are freed from the servility of unwilling and grudging service. It is true that conscience makes slaves in some fashion of those who do not want to serve. It gives them no peace, disturbs them in their plans—though, even in so tormenting them, it does not enslave them in the strict sense, for its whole purpose is ultimately to free them from the bonds of sin. But in the case of those who love God, conscience is the safeguard of freedom. It speaks to them not so much by telling them what they are bound to do as by stating in precise terms what they unconsciously want to do. So also with the authoritative presence of the Holy Ghost in the soul. He impels us to action most of all by filling us with charity: ". . . . the charity of God is poured forth in our hearts, by the Holy Ghost, Who is given to us" (Rom. 5, 5). This, it will be recalled, was His action in the soul of Our Blessed Lord as He hung dying on the cross for the salvation of mankind. The Holy Ghost filled the human soul of Jesus with such an overflowing fulness of charity that He gave Himself up into the hands of His Father with a desire that no pain could diminish. When the Holy Ghost comes to us as the same Spirit of Love, He gives us the grace to will spontaneously whatever comes to us in the form of the will of the Eternal King. Love breaks down opposition of wills. Those who love are one in will. The test of love is identity of will: "If you love me, keep my commandments" (Jo. 14, 15). Identity of will is made easy by love: "For to me, to live is Christ: and to die is gain" (Phil. 1, 21). God cannot be present in our souls otherwise than as a King, seeing Who He is and who we are. But by making us love Him He makes His presence sweet as well as majestical. No king is a tyrant in the eyes of those of his subjects who love him. We should not fear therefore to regard the Holy Ghost within us in the light of the doctrine of our necessary submission to the divine rule. God's authority and His lovableness are not two utterly distinct notions which it behoves us to keep well separated in our thoughts. There is no reason why we should consider God outside us exclusively as King, or God within us exclusively as Friend. The two ideas are mutually complementary, not opposed. God the Lawgiver is a Friend, and God the Friend is a Lawgiver. If the two ideas are quite disparate in our minds, that is a clear indication that we do not grasp either of them fully, and that we should pray to the Spirit of truth to illumine the darkness of our narrow minds.

It is usual to consider the action of the Holy Ghost in souls as particularly associated with the seven gifts which bear His name. This is not the same as to believe that He never acts otherwise than through them. We know that whatever of our acts have any value at all for our salvation come ultimately from the Holy Ghost. There are cases, such as those of the first movements of grace in the sinner, which cannot be due to the gifts, seeing that these latter are not in the soul at all at the time when the acts in question are elicited. And yet, such movements are attributed to the Holy Ghost—not inhabiting the soul, it is true, but moving it, and, as it were, seeking to find a way of entry. But this much we may say about the action of the Holy Ghost through His gifts : that whatever at all there is of ease, generosity, and spontaneity in our supernatural activity comes to us from that source. It matters not whether the act be very elevated in its substance or not. It may be some very commonplace one, such as to give a drink of cold water in Jesus' Name. The fact that there is anything at all of an instinctive urge behind it points to the action of the gifts. From this it is clear that the work of perfecting our membership of the Kingdom of God is to be attributed to the Holy Ghost moving us by His seven gifts. The gifts then are the last and most intimate channels by which the living authority of God and Jesus is conveyed to the soul. They complete the work of subjecting us to God's rule. They so transform us that it becomes almost difficult for us to act from a motive of self-love. They place God in undisputed possession of the throne of our souls so far as that is possible while still leaving our souls free to turn at will to evil. They make the soul so sensitive to every indication of the divine will, and lead it so firmly along the path of complete allegiance, that nowhere outside them does the absolute character of God's rights over man appear so clearly, since nowhere outside them does He seem to demand so perfect a submission. For by the gifts we are moved not only to do God's Will, but to do It as if It were our own.

We discussed a few pages back the relation between certain of the gifts and faith. It remains now to say a few words about their connection with devotion. By impelling us to devotion the Holy Ghost moves us to complete submission to our King in the Kingdom of Heaven. Devotion, as we know, springs in a certain ultimate sense from charity. But it has more proximate founts as well, and it is these that we must consider just now.

Devotion springs from the contemplation of God. This contemplation is perfected by the gift of Wisdom. But little would be gained by a discussion of the question whether the contemplation to which the gift of Wisdom leads us is of the purely intellectual nature, or whether it is of God as known through some image of the sensible order. What matters is that we understand that the Holy Ghost fills our minds by this gift with a sense of the divine presence and with a knowledge of the nature of Him Who is present, of such vividness, and compellingness, and intimacy, that the soul is aware that what has happened to it was not of its own doing, but that the Spirit of the Lord must have brooded over the darkness of its mind. This simple glance at God will not however be always equally rich in conscious content. There will be times when it will be so full that everything else, thoughts of saints, thoughts of virtues and vices, distractions, will for the time cease to count. There will be times, more frequent still, when it will be more a deep and tranquil conviction of the presence of One Who lurks in the shadows cast by a thousand dancing thoughts, but Who is no whit the less felt to be present for the fact that His features cannot be descried. But however He may be present, God will be the great object of the contemplation of the soul which submits to the discipline of Wisdom. The Sacred Humanity will be seen as a revelation of the Godhead. God will be seen in Mary and in the Saints. No matter what be the immediate object under consideration, God will be the underlying theme. The idea of God will be master in the intellectual part of our membership of the Kingdom ; God's right to rule our minds will be enforced in its final and most complete form.

Devotion springs in the second place from knowledge of self—leading, it will be remembered, to the prayer of petition. Perfection is achieved here under the guidance of the Holy Ghost acting especially through the gift of the fear of the Lord. First of all, the gift of knowledge will enable the soul to see itself at its true worth. Then, by the gift of wisdom, it will see itself in its relation to God : will see how God is everything, and how weak is its allegiance to Him. From this knowledge of God and self the gift of fear springs. We see that we may prove faithless to God : that, being what we are, we shall certainly rebel against His authority unless His merciful hand restrains us. We become filled with a profound sense of our weakness, of our frailty and unreliability in God's service. Seeing that we cannot be depended upon for what we are, we turn in great trust to God Whom we know to be all-merciful, and we ask Him to supply by His grace what is needful for us of generosity and of constancy. That is prayer of petition. And it is worthy of note that the gift of fear being for all time, and not only—least of all at its highest— for the period of beginnings, there will never cease to be room in our lives for petition ; and that petition will become more intense and earnest as life is lived more perfectly, precisely because one of the necessary consequences of growth in perfection is growth in the gift of fear and in the conviction of personal nothingness and instability. It is easy to see how such fear increases devotion. Springing as it does from the knowledge of our innate selfishness and meanness with God, it cannot tolerate selfishness and meanness in our actions. The man who is convinced that he is ungenerous with a friend will be quick to note and correct any real lack of generosity. It is the same with the man who is convinced that he is ungenerous with God. He will be at pains to serve Him with scrupulous loyalty : and that is another way of saying that he will be devoted to Him.

In the last place, we pointed out that devotion springs from religion and love. That is but to say that it springs from the gift of piety. By this gift we are enabled to regard God as a Father and give ourselves up to His service as His loving children. Piety is a matter of service ; that is why it is so intimately connected with devotion. Piety is the most perfect form of service given to One we love. The moment we have that deep affective conviction, which the gift gives, that God is really our Father, we hesitate no longer to give Him anything He may ask. He still remains Someone entitled to service : but He is now loved so much that the idea that what we do is really a service almost disappears from our minds. And it is in this affective attitude to God as a Father that the Holy Ghost gathers up finally all our supernatural psychology, making of presence of a King the welcome nearness of a Father. There is no one word which can sum up all that God is to us. Even the word King falls short of the full reality. The word Father is the most complete of all that man can formulate. It was taught us by Jesus Himself when He taught us to address God as Father in prayer. Hence the perfection of our submission to God the Eternal King is realized only when, under the guidance of the Holy Ghost, we have begun to realize that submission to the King is still more love and service of a Father. The gift of Wisdom will teach us nothing more than the meaning of the Fatherhood of God. The gifts which regulate activity will do nothing more than enable us to act as children of a Father—truant, it may be, but children. And ultimately, the very Law of God will be seen most of all as a Father's will, and the Holy Ghost within us will be the Spirit of That most perfect of all sons, Who wills that we should love and serve even as He did.

Jesus, then, ruling all men from the right hand of the Father, ruling them by the Holy Ghost living in His Church, and in the souls of men, rules but for one thing only : that all men may be gathered into the family of the elect, in the love and service of their Father Who is in Heaven. There is a certain hardness in the thought of the spiritual life as a combat between two kings and two kingdoms. There is infinite tenderness in the thought of it as the effort of the First-born to win back His unworthy brothers to the joy and peace of the love and service of their Father. But both thoughts are true. One does not exclude the other. Whatever difficulty there may be in reconciling them does not extend beyond the speculative order : they are very clearly one to the soul that knows and loves God. There is a very certain profit to be derived from both considerations. Selfish souls find in the Fatherhood of God an excuse for further selfishness ; it is good for them therefore to recall that He is a King. Timid souls fear a King and prove more generous with a Father : by all means then let them consider God mainly from that viewpoint. But whatever be the point from which one starts, the goal is always the same : a God Who is Father and King and Creator and everything else that He is, all in an idea of supernatural oneness. To give this idea is the unique prerogative of the Holy Ghost. It is not man-made. All that man can do with the supernatural is to analyse it and build it up once more into a fictitious unity. And our task here has been more humble still : to analyse the notion of Jesus' government of His Kingdom, and make not even a pretence of re-piecing the scattered parts.

We have seen how Jesus, throned in Heaven as Our King, rules us in the Holy Ghost. His rule is one of infinite love and tenderness. Great though the Majesty of His Person may be, greater still in our eyes will appear the marvel of His mercy. We are citizens of no mean city and subjects of no mean King. And what words are eloquent enough to describe our emotions, when we realize that this King is also our Friend ?

CHAPTER X

THE PEACE OF THE KINGDOM

" Peace I leave with you, my peace I give unto you " (Jo. 14, 27).

FEW more pathetically human cries rise to heaven from earth than the cry of man for peace. There is deep pathos in the prayer of war-torn peoples ; deep not only by reason of what it asks, but also, and even more so, by reason of the pain and the despairing weakness which send it speeding on its frantic errand. But the pathos in the prayer for peace of the secluded soul is no less deep, if we but pause to consider it. For why should a soul pray for peace when the true object of its desire is rather the happiness of God's friendship ? Again, why should we say of souls who have gone before us into the unending bliss of complete beatitude that eternal rest and peace have been given to their souls ? Why, in fine, should we habitually regard what is so essentially positive as the absence of the corresponding evil of strife, if it be not that the little kingdom of man's soul reveals itself to his gaze first of all as the seat of a dire conflict, and that in his pain he turns longing eyes to a state where not only joy may be, but tears and conflict will have ceased ? Original sin has wrought a deep evil in man's soul, and that evil is manifest in its consequences even though it be hidden in its inner nature. We have no need of a divine revelation to tell us that our minds and wills turn and toss in the uneasy bed of passion. What revelation is needed for is but to tell us how we came by such a broken slumber ; that we were not always so afflicted, but that sin intervened to change the repose of God's friendship into the nightmare of His enmity. The law of the members, of which St. Paul complained, is written in man in letters big and bold enough for the blindest to read and understand. And its content is so much a thing of horror, that to be freed from its yoke can even seem to him who groans beneath it the greatest of all goods, and man looks towards his liberation not so much as an entry into the joy of His Lord as a passage to where grief and bondage will be no more.

When to this inner consciousness of strife there is added the trial of warfare of nation with nation, the yearning for happiness conceived as peace becomes still more powerfully insistent. This complex of inner and outer warfare influenced strongly the Jewish concept of the meaning of the messianic Kingdom, and contributed, under God, to make pious and god-fearing men see it as peace. Zachary for instance, in his wonderful canticle, turns to the Messias as to Him who will " direct our feet into the way of peace " (Lk. 1, 79). God Himself used man's consciousness of this double strife to justify

His using the same word in His own revelation of what the kingdom really was. The angels for instance are made to speak of the effect of the Incarnation as being " Peace on earth to men of good will." And Our Blessed Lord did not disdain to use the same term, as, for example, when leaving His disciples He promised that the effects of His coming would remain with them, in the words : " Peace I leave with you, my peace I give unto you " (Jo. 14, 27).

If then we were to say that the fruit of membership in the kingdom of God is aptly expressed as peace because peace conveys to the mind the idea of relief from the burden of self and Satan, we should indeed say what is true, but our words would fall short of the whole truth. For peace is more than negative ; it is a positive concept. And even though the most direct avenue of approach for a human mind to the concept of peace is that which leads from the opposed one of warfare, there remains another one, which opens on peace itself, and which all others must at some time join if they be ever to lead to their goal. Were peace not something positive God would hardly have used it as a description of the most positive of all created realities, the life of grace. What was negative in it He used as a key to what was positive. Bidding us look beyond warfare He at the same time indicated that there was a true and full life in which warfare had no place, because it was incompatible with warfare, and not merely because warfare happened to be momentarily absent from it. The peace of His Kingdom is a peace springing from harmony rather than from weariness or enforced quiet. It is a peace which is the full flowering of life, not a peace which simply bars the door against death. It is the tranquil rapture of realized desire, not the restless monotony of empty purposelessness. It is the young vigour of ever-new experience, not the tired calm of a long-awaited rest. Such is the peace God has laid up for them who serve Him. It is their reward. Our Saviour asked men to take upon them the yoke of His Kingdom, promising them in return the recompense of peace. Peace is therefore that aspect of the spiritual life which corresponds most perfectly to the notion of membership in the Kingdom of God. We serve God as Our King that He may give us His peace, just as we accept to be His children that we may be allowed to share in the riches of His house. His riches are very real and positive. So too is His peace. His peace is no empty slumber ; it is the steady wakefulness of a transcendent power.

The reason why we should speak of the peace of the Kingdom of God in this place rather than of its joy, or its beauty, or any other of its many excellences, is that peace is the end and purpose of every kingdom. A kingdom exists for the peace of its subjects : an earthly kingdom for earthly peace and, analogously, a spiritual kingdom for spiritual peace. It is easy to see how this is so in the case of the earthly kingdom. Such a kingdom is composed of a number of individuals, grouped first of all into families, and coming together in order to find, in mutual intercourse and aid, that fuller perfection of human life which is more than the isolated member or family can attain. But that even the larger social group should attain to it, it is necessary that the individual wills be reduced to some kind of harmony. All come together for the common good ; but each will work spontaneously for nothing more than his own private advantage, and where this clashes with the good of the many he will never hesitate in his choice of which must be sacrificed. Some authority must be found, therefore, the object of whose care will be the common good, not in its bearings upon private purpose but in itself. He in whom this authority is vested is the king. The end of his rule is, therefore, peace. He rules, and imposes his will upon the multitude, that unity may be introduced into their conflicting wills and that the common good may be attained by their united efforts. If there be no king—at any rate, if there be no ruler—the state becomes a mob, and life in society loses its value ; things finally reach such a pass that the mob becomes burdensome even to itself, and commits suicide as mob by voluntarily entering some kind of state organization—such, as history tells us, has been the course of all revolutions. To reduce the essential function of state authority, in this way, to ensuring the minimum of peace required that the component parts may be enabled to set themselves about the work of achieving their end—they do not ask the state to do that for them !— may be unwelcome in these days of ever-increasing state intervention. It is, however, the headline set us by St. Thomas in his fragment on princely rule. It is, besides, what ordinary common sense, appalled as much at the officiousness of rulers as at the back-sliding and lethargy of ruled, sees to be so necessary in these days. We do not say that the state has no function at all beyond that of ensuring a minimum of harmony. What we do say is that that is what is essential. It may intervene positively as well, but only to supply some want which exceeds the powers—or the good will—of private enterprise. The rule of an earthly king, therefore, hardly enters deeper than the surface ; and the peace he must himself procure is little more than that which results from harmonious intercourse of man with man in those matters where the one cannot successfully dispense with the assistance of the other.

Spiritual peace is deeper and more far-reaching than that which is earthly. " My peace I give unto you," said our King, " Not as the world giveth, do I give unto you " (Jo. 14, 27). The peace of this world is established in view of tranquil and uninterrupted utilization of material goods ; the peace of Christ paves the way, and is the way, to those that are of eternal value. The peace of this world is but a painted, surface-deep peace ; the peace of Christ is the deep reality of a transformation wrought in the very marrow of the soul. The peace of this world is imperfect, for it does no more than remove harm from without, leaving the inner kingdom of the soul a prey to trouble and anxiety ; but the peace of Christ is soothing and strengthening, the peace of secure possession of desire. What ultimately distinguishes the peace of this world from that of Christ is, therefore, the attitude of each to what is external and internal. The peace of this world regards mainly the removal of the disorder which is external, and leaves that which is internal as yet in possession of the soul ; the peace of Christ calms first the soul, and then, proceeding from within, spreads itself out over life, harmonizing relations with men, and making him who is peaceful, not peaceful merely, but what is greater still, a maker of peace.

Though there be these great differences between the two kinds of peace it is nevertheless no abuse of words to give them both the same name. For lived peace is a matter of unified appetition, upon which even the peace of this world is based in some way. The peace of this world is obtained by the union of the different wills of different men in the common desire, through common means, of the good which is common to all. The peace of Christ is also a certain unity of appetition ; but with this difference, that it is now first of all a question of union of different desires in one and the same man. A man is at peace when all the tendencies of his being are swept along in the same calm current of regulated desire. He is at war with himself, and a burden to himself, when he is torn by conflicting impulses and aims. When flesh fights against spirit, when pride strives with love, the soul of man is torn and gashed like some great catastrophic battlefield. Each blind urge sears and rends its way across its surface, and its passage remains marked by an open, jagged, tear. That is the horror of war raged on the living battle-field of the soul. And the calm of peace is the fruitful plain, that spreads itself beneath the ripening sun, and lifts itself, as it were, in one great spontaneous wave to meet its mellowing rays. There are no gashes, no gaping wounds, no parched earth, sterile and shrivelled ; but a unity, a living unity, that turns itself sunward and quickens to fruiting in the Sun's embrace.

Peace comes to the soul, therefore, when it turns Godwards with all its powers, and in its full capacity of desire. For the moment it is not necessary to specify the precise nature of this turning. There will be in it a great element of love ; because love is turning to God as a Friend. There will, as well, be an element of submission ; because submission is turning to God as the Fount of all that is real. Both love and submission will be found at the root of Christian peace, and to know so much is all we need for the moment. It will be found useful, however, to consider peace first of all as the fruit of love, and then to add in conclusion whatever may be required on the other side.

Peace reigns in the soul which turns itself Godwards in love. This love, as we saw in the last chapter, is the fruit of the reign of the Holy Ghost within us. Peace, therefore, even considered as the consequence of love, is the result of membership of the Kingdom of God. Love is not content with taking possession of the will for God. It lays hold on all the other powers as well. Issuing in service, it submits to itself all that there is in man which can in any way be the principle of a human tendency or activity. It gathers up the different powers, each straying along its own selfish path, and sets them firmly upon the royal road of the glorious cross. There is peace in the soul that loves, because in such a soul there is a master. Love will not tolerate a rival. Love will force its preferences upon every other appetite. It will leave them no longer the power to drag their owner in so many different and opposing ways, by the simple method of forcing them along its own way. And the way of love is found to be easy. Even though it imposes a yoke and a burden, the yoke is light and the burden sweet. So light and sweet are they, that the time eventually comes when to cease to be guided by love is to fall into the uneasy fear of having lost the way. Not only is peace found in love, but outside it there is no peace.

Human peace establishes a certain harmony of man with man. Spiritual peace does no less. The end of human peace is that man may contribute harmoniously to man that in which the one is the complement of the other. Men are grouped together in society that by their combined efforts they may achieve that fuller measure of perfection which is unattainable to them as individuals. Now, in the natural order, a man finds what is lacking to him in his fellow men. But in the supernatural order a man finds what is lacking to him in God. Hence all men who enter the supernatural order of things are united in that they all find their perfection in the One Being by the direction of their wills to the Supreme Good. Establishing therefore harmony *in* themselves by the reign of the love of God within their souls, they necessarily establish harmony of wills *among* themselves, by their common tendency to the same End. The supernatural realizes therefore that which is found only so inadequately in the natural : the union namely of the demands of interior peace with those of exterior concord. The love of God reduces each man to unity, and all men to one. There is no created object which all men can desire without mutual antagonism. All created objects are necessarily finite in their capacity to satisfy desire. They may even be such as to be the possible possession of only one individual ; for there are things, such as certain amounts of the goods of this world, or certain kinds of reputation and fame, which can belong to a man under the aspect which makes them so intensely desirable, only if they are possessed in the same measure by nobody else. They may alternatively be such that a limited number of men may possess them to a satisfying degree ; examples of these are positions of lesser importance, a moderate degree of wealth. But there is nothing at all in which all men can find complete satisfaction simultaneously ; and even if there were such a thing, there is no power on earth which could restrain some men, at least, from the inordinate desire to have a monopoly of it. Nothing is equally accessible to all men but the friendship of God. And here there is no danger of monopoly. For God, Who is infinite Knowledge and Love, can be a Friend to each as if there were no others ; and, what is more, to desire to love God beyond measure is necessarily to desire that all men be admitted to the same friendship with Him which we ourselves enjoy, seeing that this is His desire and that to love Him means to be conformed to Him in desire. The more we love God the more we will that others too be admitted to His love. For we see that it is a triumph for God to be loved on earth, since loving Him is submission to the supreme charm of His attractiveness. Love of God, therefore, expands hearts. Love of self in the things God has created, contracts them. He who loves self is already on the road to hating his fellowmen. His self, considered precisely as his, can find, due to the warp of original sin, no congenial natural reason for disinterested union with other selves. He who loves God, already loves all men in principle. To love them in effect and individually is but the logical consequence therefrom. Perfect peace of man with man is, therefore, achieved uniquely in the Kingdom of heaven.

Peace, though so ardently desired by all men, is understood by but few. A common error is to reduce Christian peace to insensibility. In the history of Christian asceticism this error raises its head from age to age, at times escaping the note of heresy, at times clearly meriting and incurring it. That such an error should make frequent appearances on the historical stage is in no way surprising. Man's awareness of inner conflict is so keen at all times that there results in him a perennial tendency to seek all good in conflict's mere antithesis. That is the simple psychological explanation of the historical fact. And as a fact it is no mere matter of past history. It is alive to-day ; in its milder forms it is, indeed, always alive. What other than a false concept of Christian peace, is the reason why so many souls fall off from their attempts to serve God generously when confronted by the problem of the persistence of trial and temptation even when the will of God is taken as the norm of life ? A soul tries to serve God and finds, after a brief period of great consolation in His service, that meditation becomes a struggle with distractions, that the old sinful urges are as vigorous as ever, that the old indifference to the spiritual has in nothing lost its braking power. If this be so, it asks, where is the peace of Christ ? That peace, it thinks, has certainly escaped it. And it feels, in an instinctive way, that the loss of peace is grave enough to engender doubts as to the reality of its membership of the Kingdom.

The most revealing gospel statement on the nature of true Christian peace is probably that contained in one of the brief parables related by St. Luke : " When a strong man armed keepeth his court, those things are in peace which he possesseth " (11, 21). That is the answer to the soul that asks the meaning of the peace of Christ. The peace essential to the Christian life is the peace of conquest ; and that, not fully achieved, but as yet in process of achievement. Christian peace follows from the assurance that we have the power to overcome all enemies. It in no way implies that we have no enemies, nor that those we have are so bound and weakened that they can no longer launch on us anything more than a toy, sham attack. The devil's arrows are very real ; their wounds are deep. Pride can smart and will smart ; the flesh will rebel, it will drag and tug and sulk. What we here describe is no make-believe. It is a make-fear, a make-pause if it is a make-anything. Never-theless we remain at peace, because we know that the essential aim of our life—the service of God—can be realized success-fully in spite of, and even through, the tumult and apparent indecision of battle. Our Blessed Lord promised no other peace than this of which we now speak. " These things I have spoken to you " He said " That in me you may have peace. In the world you shall have distress : but have confidence, I have overcome the world " (Jo. 16, 33). I give you a peace, He tells us, the meaning of which is to be found in the peace of my victory. All our peace is an entry into Jesus' Peace. Our peace on earth is a sharing in the peace of His earthly existence : and that was the peace of One, assailed on all sides, even put to death, but ever conscious of His power and superiority over the forces that lay in ambush for Him. Throned glorious in heaven, He has now the peace of complete triumph. That peace too, is ours to share in ; but not as yet —not till, having suffered with Christ and having passed in His Name the portals of death, we receive it from Him as the reward of our battle for His Kingdom. The peace of the wayfarer is that of the strong man armed. What though he suffer, though he be assailed ? He is fixed and immovable in hope. In hope he is already triumphant. In hope he possesses already the undisturbed peace of complete beatitude. And in hope he rests with confidence in the possession of God's friendship even here on earth.

It is in no way strange that the spiritual peace of earth should be so markedly peace of conquest. All peace of earth, even its false peace, is such. No man ever rises to the attainment of his ambition except by triumphing over difficulties, and his permanence therein depends on his power to keep these forces in check which from the first opposed him. If to become rich requires a struggle, to enjoy the phantom peace of riches depends on vigilance to maintain the struggle. To enjoy fame, power, or no matter what earthly good, and to have peace in its enjoyment, is ruled by the same law. And what makes these earthly phantoms of peace so utterly hollow is that continued victory over the obstacles to their possession is never a matter which lies within the power of man. Riches can be lost by an accident ; a slander will destroy fame ; power goes when a mightier arises. No stable peace may therefore be built upon such things as these. There is only one thing which by God's help is entirely within the power of man, no matter what be the accidents of health or fortune which time brings in its train, and that is membership of the kingdom of heaven by grace. Grace alone can support a lasting and unshakable peace. If peace on earth must be won in battle, wherever it may be that we choose to seek it, then, even in the name of common sense, let us seek it where we can be sure of a reward for our pains. It is natural for man to live for peace. All men look forward to a time of peace, even here on earth, at the end of their days. Hence all men feel, even in another, the tragedy of a life from which peace has been snatched by bad investments or some misfortune of the kind. For years there has been human toil and human sweat and even human tears directed—blindly it must be admitted, but how easy it is to excuse that blindness !—to a few declining years of rest from labour ; and now all is frustrated. But the toil and sweat and tears of the kingdom of heaven are never amiss. No earthly power can take away from us the peace of Christ. It is God's merciful answer to humanity's timid quest of peace. The struggle of the kingdom is the only one from which man can emerge always triumphant ; and therefore is the only price which will buy a peace that endures.

If we view our spiritual endowments in the light of the foregoing remarks on the nature of Christian peace, we are granted an insight into their nature which falls to our lot only too infrequently. For in that light the virtues which accompany sanctifying grace reveal themselves the weapons of our victory over the enemies of the Kingdom, just as clearly as they stood out before as the instruments of our submission to Our King. Faith is a power of triumphing over darkness. When, therefore, darkness assails us, we should confront it with the simple yes or no of faith, with a simple assent to what faith reveals as true or a simple dissent from what faith reveals as false. Faith is not vision. It cannot banish darkness completely. When therefore we received the gift of faith it carried with it no guarantee that we should never be tormented by doubt. Its one guarantee is that it is able to overcome doubt in combat. And thereby it brings peace to our minds. In the same way hope brings peace to our wills by strengthening them to fight successfully against fear. It does not immunize from fear ; what it does is to enable us to look fear in the face with a certain tranquillity. And that in its turn is peace of the only kind man has a right to expect here on earth. We have already seen how charity brings peace by unifying and triumphing over discordant desires. The soul that loves God will be drawn by other loves.. Charity does not make it invulnerable to the shafts of created beauty. But it does enable it to hold tight in any emergency. Once more peace ; not absolute and perfect, but real and very human.

If now we recall what we said in the last chapter of the virtues as the instruments of God's rule in our souls, we see the close connection that exists between the idea of the kingdom of God and that of spiritual peace. God rules us by the virtues and by the same virtues we enter into peace. By the submission of faith we achieve peace and light in darkness ; by the submission of hope we achieve peace and constancy in the midst of fear ; by the submission of love we achieve peace and harmony in the conflict of desire. It is never out of place to call attention to the pattern and design of God's works, and now is it less than ever so. Get any one item right in the supernatural order and everything else fits into place. It does not matter so very much what the item is. All that matters is that it be got right. Learn what submission is, and peace follows without further effort. Allow yourself to be ruled, and you enter necessarily into the peace of a kingdom. And if Christ be the Ruler you have chosen, your reward will be that peace of His which surpasseth understanding.

God rules us, as we have seen, in the workings of His divine Providence. By accepting His rule generously here as in all other things, peace will result to our souls. "For I know the thoughts that I think towards you, saith the Lord, thoughts of peace, and not of affliction . . ." (Jer. 29, 11). When Providence sends us pain we are inclined to grow restive and troubled. We should recall on such occasions that the mind of God in the pain He sent was not to cause us affliction as an end in itself, but to cause an affliction which could heal into peace. It is by no means necessary that we see clearly how the present trial will work to our good. It is sufficient that we believe it will do so, and that our belief be based upon the unquestionable fact of God's unchanging purpose of bringing all men to salvation. This belief is something in which peace may be found. It affords a sure and firm footing when everything else seems to crumble beneath us. While we cling to it, the depths of our souls will remain tranquil and untroubled, however great be the tempests that rage in our purely human faculties. Hope and charity work this peace in us as well as faith. It is, in fact, the work of charity more than of any other virtue, and is to be attributed to faith not as to that which gives it its ultimate perfection but as to that from whence it draws its first beginnings. For the living and tranquil belief in God's love for us is in the last analysis the work of our love for God. Faith without love will convince that He means us no harm. But to continue life in the full force of this belief is the work of love. One can commit oneself in entire peace to God only when one loves God. One's hope in Him, even, one's trust and confidence, is fully peaceful only when it is wedded to the abandonment of love.

We have stressed what might be termed the combative nature of Christian peace almost to the point of making it appear that there was none other to be obtained in this world. It was, however, at no time intended to imply that there was no other peace. The main point was always that peace in the midst of conflict was the essential peace, not that it was the only one. And that it is not the only one follows from the simple fact that even the combat itself is not altogether uninterrupted, but that there are days even here on earth when the faithful soul seems in some way to enter into the joy of the Lord.

The second stage in spiritual peace—that namely which marks a certain advance on the idea of peace in tribulation—is what may be termed acquired peace. The natural consequence of the control we exercise over passion is that its attacks grow less violent in time. This is the normal process of the acquisition of virtue. Our lower nature is at first undisciplined. It resists reason and grace at all times except the rare ones on which there is unanimity about the thing desired. And even when there is this unanimity, it is never more than accidental. Our lower nature may at times desire the thing to which grace prompts us, but it will always be unsympathetic to grace's motive. Both grace and nature could, for example, prompt a man to take care of his health. But whereas grace will do so because health is needful to God's service, nature will be motivated by self-love or some similar impulse. Hence a sincere beginning in the spiritual life will always be marked by a conflict between nature and grace, at least in what regards the springs and motives of action. If in this conflict the soul corresponds with grace, grace will always emerge triumphant. The power of nature to resist grows less, though it never dwindles away to nothing, and never loses its capacity of recuperation. But an unbroken series of defeats makes it cowardly, gives it, even, an acquired tendency to follow the leading of grace without doing much more than to display a certain unreadiness to obey which but rarely rises to the pitch of open rebellion. This marks a new stage in interior peace. The soul has now something more than the bare power to resist and overcome an enemy. The enemy with which it is in contact is already half-beaten. Nature is a sullen enemy, it is true ; an enemy with whom the soul will always have to reckon. But the time does come, with the help of God's grace, when nature's assaults become less frequent and less violent, when the desire of the soul to turn to God finds less frequent and violent opposition from nature's conflicting desire to turn earthwards and selfwards. And when it comes, something new, even if only accidentally so, has been added to the peace enjoyed from the first moment of the infusion of grace—the experimental assurance that the power of God, which we always believed capable of overcoming every obstacle and every fear, has really done so within us and will continue to do so up to the day of our entry into the complete possession of heaven's untroubled peace.

There is no doubt whatever that this second kind of peace of which we are speaking comes, in the normal course of the spiritual life, as the lot of every sincere Christian. Some might be inclined to question whether or not certain kinds of peace which are more mystical in character are destined for all without exception. But no one has any right to question the universality of acquired peace, if we may so term it. It is of importance in this connection to note that, even though destined for all, it is not merely negative ; that is to say, not just the peace of a cowed nature and nothing more. It is more correct to regard it as something positive, as the peace of a disciplined and harnessed nature, than as that of a nature which just refrains from being intractable. The acquired virtues are positive tendencies of our natural powers. A man who has acquired the virtue of temperance really tends in a positive way, and by a tendency of his natural being, to be temperate. The natural tendency to be intemperate remains of course. But it is overlaid with a new tendency to temperance. The temperance of the temperate man is not in his will only, with nature reduced to some kind of quiescence. This would be the case were acquired peace a merely negative matter. But it is more than that. It is in the faculty of sensitive desire as well. It makes sense tend in the right direction no less than will. It makes sense back up the tendency of the will. The result of acquired virtue is therefore to unify desire—and that, as we have seen, is the formula of peace. Man continues to desire, and to desire strongly, even when he has disciplined himself to virtue. But now all his desires find their goal in the same object. All tend in a relatively unbroken harmony and rhythm to the same good. And peace is born of this tranquil ordering of desire.

Over and above this peace of the acquired virtues there is a higher peace which the Holy Ghost gives us through His gifts.[1] This is a peace which approaches still more closely to mystical union than does that of which we have just spoken. Nevertheless, in so far as it is implied in the normal growth of the gifts it, too, is a matter for all men. That it should be given to them rather than they should acquire it is an irrelevant consideration. There are gifts of God which are given to man normally, just as there are human works which he normally achieves. And the peace of the gifts is something which God

[1]This passive peace belongs in some measure to the theological and infused moral virtues as well, since every virtue gives a genuine tendency to its object. But it is perfected by the gifts, and is attributed here to them as being the cause of its ultimate completion. It should be noted too that, in so far as the theological and infused moral virtues and the gifts are present in every justified soul, the various kinds of peace should be understood not as mutually exclusive, but rather as component elements in the totality of Christian peace.

gives to all men who dispose themselves for its acceptance. But one thing must be stressed : it is that the peace of the gifts comes to them who are disposed, and to them only. Passive peace does not come to him who waits and does nothing else. It comes to him who toils and groans in the work of acquiring peace in its first two forms. And ultimately we may say that it comes to him who by his submission to the Eternal King has merited to be led by Him into the inner cellars of divine peace. Passive peace must be merited. It is not given undeservedly—except in the sense that no man ever really deserves any gift of God's. It is not given to the lazy, to the selfish, to the speculatively curious. It is given to the faithful subject. And it consists in this : that God, working by the seven gifts, does normally reduce nature to a condition of submission to and co-operation with grace, which exceeds that which man, even aided by actual grace, could himself effect, so that it is possible to speak of a certain passive peace even in the ordinary Christian. This is a peace which wells up from the very centre of the soul, as contrasted with acquired peace, which endeavours, rather, to work its way in from the soul's perimeter. The method of arriving at acquired peace consists in regulating the acts of nature. Sinful acts are repressed ; good, acts are strengthened and linked up with grace. And by this attention to the acts it happens that we succeed in time in working a certain metamorphosis even in their principles, such as to make these latter tend henceforth to produce acts which harmonize with the supernatural. Passive peace, on the other hand, comes into being as result of a transformation wrought in the first place in the principles of our actions themselves. The gifts so transform our whole being that we become interiorly docile to grace. We act no longer as we did by the acquired virtues—that is to say, we no longer do with ease just whatever in the supernatural coincides in a material way, by identity of material object, with what sound reason would advise. What attracts our natural being now is the supernatural itself. Just as the acquired natural virtue gives the lower part of man's being a tendency to what is in accord with reason, so also the gift gives human nature a tendency to and an affinity with what is supernatural. The gifts establish therefore a still more complete harmony and unity of desire in the soul. They so supernaturalize what is natural in us that even it tends with a certain ease and spontaneity to God and to His service. Charity is not left to be alone in her task of bringing man Godwards ; for now the whole man tends thither. Charity ceases to be a master, and becomes rather *primus inter pares*. She is no longer sole minister of God in a rebellious kingdom. The whole kingdom of the soul is at peace, and all that is in it hasten to pay the homage of loving service.

In the order of action this passive peace is, most of all, the work of gifts of Counsel, Fortitude, and the Fear of the Lord. The gift of Counsel gives tranquillity of mind in the face of a decision to be made. It does away with hesitation and doubt. There remains no longer the old agitation of mind at the prospect of a move fraught with weighty spiritual consequences. Counsel sees clear in the muddle of circumstance, and decides in peace what should be done. And it is, in truth, far from strange that the soul which seeks God sincerely and seeks Him alone should never be in great doubt about where to find Him. The gift of Fortitude gives peace in the face of danger. It is bred of the consciousness that God is with us ; but a consciousness not intellectual merely, as was that of the beginner in the way of peace, but felt even. The fact that we can face danger ceases to be a conviction we have hammered home by repeated experiences and becomes something we take, as it were, for granted because we feel it to be so. That is peace radiated from the soul's inner core, not just attached from outside. Finally, the gift of Fear gives peace in the midst of desires. The soul that fears with the gift of Fear, no longer really wants to tempt God by running after idols. It is too deeply convinced of its inherent frailty to ambition such dangerous freedom. It is consequently at peace from the strain of headlong striving. From within there has been imposed a curb on its desires, a curb which is at the same time a new orientation. Fearing to lose God it desires Him with every faculty within it capable of desire. And that, too, is peace.

In the order of contemplation our passive peace should be attributed most of all to the gift of Wisdom. Peace is possessed on the intellectual level when the mind is in tranquil and secure possession of a master idea which answers the world's riddles. The idea of God obtained in the gift of Wisdom is of such a kind. It embraces every problem that has any bearing whatever on the work of our salvation. It reveals God in a light in which He is seen as the beginning and end of all joys and woe, of all permanence and of all change. It is true that the intellect would find it hard, would find it even impossible, to formulate with precision what it sees of God in Wisdom, and how what it sees is so complete an answer to life's questioning. But inability to formulate is no sure indication that there has been no vision. St. Paul, rapt to the third heavens, saw things—and did in very truth see them—to which his tongue was incapable of giving distinct utterance. The vision of Wisdom is in some distant way akin to that of St. Paul. It is a real intellectual act, in which one sees, even though darkly ; and what one sees, for all its sublime obscurity, brings peace and confidence where the clear-cut datum of reason leaves room for doubt. It is a consequence of this obscurity of the eye of wisdom that its message is incommunicable to others. We cannot share with them our intellectual peace. If they be without wisdom they will find our attitude unreasonable, naïve, unreflecting. It has been given us by the Holy Ghost Himself, and He communicates it to whomsoever He and He alone wills. Why this should be, why wisdom is so completely the possession of him in whom it is, even though it be a form of knowledge, results from its necessarily affective character. Wisdom is not knowledge alone ; it is knowledge in and through love. It is a form of knowledge which brings complete satisfaction precisely because love shows how far-reaching it is. Hence it is not satisfying to one who does not love. The few ideas we could reveal to him would appear inadequate to his needs, because that which alone makes them adequate, love namely, is lacking to him. This is quite analogous to what happens so often with little children. Some problem arises, and one child has an answer to give. And when pressed for reasons in support of the truth of its explanation, it can only say that that is what its father told it. No one else, clearly, will be satisfied with such an answer. But the child is satisfied with it, and very satisfied at that. It loves its father ; to the others he is a man like so many other men. And that simple difference between the affective attitudes in the child and its absence in the rest of mankind is the whole reason for the peace which one finds and the hesitation in which the others remain. The gift of Wisdom gives us answer like that of the child : God is my Father ; this is my Father's affair. If we love Him we shall find peace therein ; if our love is cold we shall continue to seek reasons. But of one thing we may be sure : we shall never find a better reason than the one which Wisdom gives. Far better for us than to ransack our poor minds for human light is it to enter on the path that leads to Wisdom—the path of service and fear of the Lord.

Even this passive peace of which we now speak is never so complete as to exclude the trial of temptation. For although peace establishes our essential harmony with God and with mankind, the type of peace which we can have here on earth is compatible with occasional troubles in our relations with both the One and the other. Our peace with God, considered as an habitual state of soul, will never, even at its highest, be more than a repose of the higher part of the soul in God, admitting of a certain repugnance to the divine in the lower faculties. There will, of course, be certain acts, enduring for a greater or a lesser length of time, in which our repose in God will become intense, and even seem to us to be complete. But this will never become a permanent state while we remain wayfarers. The element of conflict is too essential to the notion of the kingdom of heaven to admit of a permanent escape from it of any kind other than the illusionary.

But what is harder to bear, and what is less often noted in books which treat of spiritual peace, is that it is as impossible to have complete harmony and undisturbed harmony with all men, even with the good, as it is to have utterly undisturbed harmony in our relations with God. The perfection of earthly charity admits differences on matters of opinion—and accidentally on more fundamental matters when they appear erroneously to be no more than matters of opinion. Leaving aside the problem set by the rare cases of two men who appear to be, in all respects twin souls, the fact is that peace with one's neighbour involves two limitations of the complete notion of peace : the one, that we shall not see eye to eye with him in everything, and the other that we must be content to tolerate and respect his God-given freedom to differ from us. It is not a small thing that we can all agree on the glory of God and the good of our neighbour as the two great things to be achieved at all times. In that agreement we have a solid harmony of wills which means genuine social peace. It is a very slight matter after that that others should differ from us in their ideas of how these ends may be realized. We are at one with them in the matters that really count. St. Paul and St. Barnabas were at peace, in the way in which two men can be at peace, even though they decided to follow different ways in their work for the nascent Church. Each knew that the other had but the purest of motives in what he did, and that knowledge, combined with the love they bore one another in God, was sufficient to enable them to triumph in will over the sense of friction to which their differences of opinion in questions of detail gave birth. We may well believe that St. Paul was sufficiently big to admit that good could be done in ways which his limited understanding did not comprehend. He was at peace therefore with St. Barnabas. He knew that St. Barnabas was a good man, and that God would bless what he did even if he did it in a way Paul would never have selected. He did not make the mistake of trying to force St. Barnabas to see as he saw. It is a very narrow conception of peace which thinks that two men cannot be in harmony if there be any point at all on which they disagree. We might even say— provided it be properly understood—that it is even a very narrow view of what is right and what is wrong to hold that in matters of pure detail and efficiency there is always a way so clearly right that whoever takes any other is necessarily a knave or a fool. Narrow down your concept of peace and right in that way and you will never be at peace with your fellows—not even with the best of them. Provided a thing be intrinsically good, God is more interested in how you set about doing it than in how it works out. It can happen, therefore, that a person will do something in a way which considered objectively and in itself is not the best, and will still act with God's approval. How, then, could we dare to submit him to our less expert views?

An exaggerated desire to force others to accept one's own views is ultimately a form of pride. It is absurd to aim at bringing all men into conformity with all our views on the plea that such harmony is the ideal. Such harmony is by no means the Christian ideal on earth. To aim at it breeds dissension rather than peace. It is pride to be so convinced of the truth of all your views that it becomes intolerable to think of another doubting them or refusing to accept them or, worse still, finding credence for his own opinions. It is possible to pose before one's own eyes as a zealot for the truth, while really being nothing more noble than a zealot for self. There will undoubtedly be cases when another is in clear error on an important point. It is necessary then to correct him, and charity will ensure that the correction is both given and taken in such wise as to leave the bond of peace unbroken. But there is no supernatural justification for a crusade against every difference of opinion. Charity demands, in fact, that when there is nothing more than a mere difference of opinion at issue, you rest content with exposing your view quite simply—if it be necessary to expose it at all—and then that you leave everybody quite free to do as God will direct them. If God directs men in such a manner as to respect their temperaments and characters, how can we claim to be united to them by the same link which unites us to God Himself, if we insist on forcing them all into the mould which was made for us alone? Let us then recognize once and for all that peace with our fellows, just as peace with God, admits of a certain friction; demands, even, that we allow for the possibility of and tolerate such friction. Saints have had differences of opinion in the past. Being saints they knew they could afford to have them. If our idea of peace is to level all opinions down to our own way of thinking, we shall never equal the saints in their union, even though we shall certainly surpass them in their differences. Let us be noble enough to discipline ourselves to peace with those who dare to differ from us. The Holy Ghost will help us in this task; but not so as to submit all minds to the yoke of our narrow convictions.

We started this chapter by shelving the question of the virtues which were the founts of Christian peace. We are now in a position to give an answer. They are, principally, charity and justice. Peace has been well defined as the tranquillity of order ; and we may say that whereas the order results from justice, the tranquillity results from charity.

There is in the first place the order of justice towards God ; and that is the order of submission and obedience. Considered alone, submission gives a certain harmony ; it gives at any rate freedom from conflict. Combine however with submission love's desire to be subject, and what is bare and unproductive order, is invigorated with the life of peace. Peace is loved and accepted order, and nothing more. It is rest in grace, in the created participation of the harmony of God's own Being. When, in love, we submit sense to reason and reason to grace we are at peace ; for we have both order and its tranquil acceptance.

There is in the second place the order of justice towards our neighbour. We are at peace with him when, having given him what is his due, we confirm him therein by love. It is impossible to have peace with our neighbour without justice : and that is a point forgotten only too often. Listen to St. James : " And if a brother or a sister be naked, and want daily food : And one of you say to them : Go in peace, be you warmed and filled ; yet give them not those things that are necessary for the body, what shall it profit ? . . . . Go to now, ye rich men, weep and howl in your miseries, which shall come upon you. . . . Behold the hire of the labourers, who have reaped down your fields, which by fraud has been kept back by you, crieth : and the cry of them hath entered into the ears of the Lord of Sabaoth " (St. James 2, 15 and 16 ; 5, 1 and 4). Love, affability, are no substitutes for justice. Without it they are utterly empty. Without it they are nothing more than the opium of conscience. True peace will reign among men only when the rights of all are respected. Faith without good works is dead ; dead, too, is love without justice. Where there is no order there can be no tranquillity : where there is no justice there can be no peace. Whether it be peace with God or peace with man, all peace is built upon submission to the demands of justice. And the reason that there is so little peace of either kind is that men are more willing to soothe themselves with the rapture of love, than curb themselves with the bridle of justice.

St. Thomas quotes St. Augustine for an extremely beautiful definition of peace : *Serenitas mentis, tranquillitas animæ, simplicitas cordis, amoris vinculum, consortium caritatis* ; Serenity of spirit, calm of soul, oneness of purpose, union in the bond of love. In that definition all peace is described. Expressed so, the rare beauty of peace shines clearly forth. Who would have dared to think that such a peace might be our share on earth ? Who of the pagans conceived of such a peace even for his god ? Our souls are weary and storm-tossed. But we have hope in our King. If we take His yoke upon us we shall find rest to our weary souls : rest from the tumult of blind desires within us, and rest from the dull despair of frustrated aims without.

CHAPTER XI

MARY THE QUEEN

" Regina sanctorum omnium ; Queen of all the saints."

WE have spoken much of submission ; so much indeed as to make it likely that some will ask whether the whole of the spiritual life, as we have depicted it, be not submission to God and nothing more. And though it might be easy to force a soul, by weight of brute logic, into the admission that nothing really counted beyond its acceptance of God's rule, it would be far from easy to bring it from the stage of mere admission to that of enthusiastic assertion. In some instinctive way we feel it true that even though submission to the will of God be the most important thing—even though it be, in some way, the thing to which all else must be referred—there are yet other things, not wholly distinct from it, it is true, yet not lost entirely in it as in some pantheistic mass of voracious formlessness. We feel that we ourselves do count for something. Not that we are so foolish as to think that we count if weighed in the balance against God ; our belief, vague but insistent, is that we count for something under God. If God is the All, we are not mere nothings. Far from our being nothing, the very meaning of our creation is that we have been drawn out of nothingness, that we who before existed only in the mind of God, exist now in an existence which the Almighty Power and Wisdom of God have contrived to make our own. Subject though we be to God, we are still real units, independent units, in His creation. It can, therefore, be no true picture of the Kingdom of God which reduces us to mere automata, to beings whose only glory is to act as if they had within them no genuine power of initiation and no native purpose fraught with consequences for self as well as God. The Kingdom must mean something in our own lives ; it must change us in some way, realize in some way the undeveloped powers of our being. It cannot be mere altruism, mere service, even though it be service of God. God asks no creature to burn itself out for His glory, perishing in the performance of its allotted task. His glory demands no wasteful sacrifice. He wills to reign not a tyrant throned amid splendid desolation, but a Father-King Whose rule is peace and life.

We can find in the true nature of the great sacrifice of Calvary a supernatural justification for our belief that God's service must mean something positive. Our Blessed Lord gave, on Calvary, fullest expression to His spirit of service. Yet He was at that time King, and under a new and glorious title, that of conquest. His service seemed to the eye of reason to be an exhausting self-immolation. But in its real nature it was a triumph. It achieved the purpose of His coming, gave His life its full significance, and earned for Him a Name Which is above every name. If we consider our service of God from this angle, the problem of its reconciliation with self-perfection is no new one. It is ultimately the same as that of the reconciliation of mortification with life, of self-denial with self-expression. And its solution is the same : Jesus dead, but living ; Jesus meek, but drawing all things to Himself.

Our belief that membership in the Kingdom is not without fruit for us finds a more natural justification as well. It is that there is in each man an innate and natural desire to be in fact what he is in germ by nature, a king namely. We learned in the opening chapter of this book that kingship is based on the possession of intellect, and intellect's power to grasp the subordination of means to end. All men have intellect. Hence all men have the capacity to reign in some kingdom. And this capacity being inborn and natural, expresses itself in a natural desire which God does not intend to frustrate. Nor should we believe that our adoption into the supernatural has stifled it in any way. Grace does not destroy nature. It canalizes and perfects it. Grace has left us the power and desire to reign, even when it imposed upon us a new and far-reaching obligation to serve. How this can be is one of the mysteries of the Kingdom of God; a mystery real and deep, and yet not so utterly obscure that the mind, enlightened by faith cannot see some flashes of its bright sublimity.

There is a prayer in the Mass for peace which gives the key to all human understanding of the mystery of which we speak. It is the Postcommunion prayer, and the words which contain its message to us are : *Deus . . . . cui servire regnare est* ; God . . to serve Whom is to reign. To serve God is to reign ! To be called to serve in the Kingdom of God, is to be called to reign there. There is then no deep problem of the reconciliation of service of God with kingship of man, since man's kingship finds its truest expression in God's service. There are kings of earth we may elect to serve ; but their rule is to enslave. There are things of earth we may endeavour to subject to self, but our attempt is despotic and its outcome is our enslavement. Whether we desire to serve or to rule outside the Kingdom of God the result is always the same : we are enslaved. God alone is a King so mighty that He can give a share of His authority—a share even of His life—to those who serve Him, without becoming Himself thereby the poorer or the less worthy of homage. We, on our side, are beings so noble, that to submit to one less than God is an unworthy servitude. Reign we must, for we are kings. Serve we must, too, for we have not the power to win our kingdom alone and unaided. We are impelled by an imperious necessity of nature both to reign and to serve, and in God alone will these conflicting urges be reconciled.

It would be possible to develop this idea by showing that the supernatural organization of our soul, by which, as we have seen, God reigns in us, is at the same time our perfection and the instrument of our rule and victory over the world. To do so is, however, hardly necessary. For we have already given on different occasions the elements out of which this synthesis must be formed, and it would be little more than mere repetition to gather and re-order them here. What is of greater value is to take some living exemplification of the principle under discussion. To see a principle in live and sensitive embodiment is to understand it better than in any speculative scrutiny. We propose therefore to see it in Mary, Our Queen. Not that we intend thereby to subordinate her to the practical exigencies of the book's completeness. One does no violence to the character of Mary when one sees in her the realization of : *Deus cui servire regnare est.* It may even emerge from what we must say that it is in the light of that principle we must understand her, if we are ever to do more than guess at her true greatness. We consider Mary as an example of greatness in littleness because that is precisely what she is. Mary's holiness was necessarily the holiness of the Kingdom. She must consequently have served and reigned. What will distinguish her from all others who have served and reigned after her will be seen to be nothing more strange and foreign to the notion of the kingdom than the completeness of her service and the uniqueness of her reign.

The most outstanding feature of Our Blessed Lady's life as recounted to us in the Gospels is certainly her humble obscurity. We are told still less of St. Joseph than of her. But he was nothing more than a foster-father of the Incarnate Word whereas she was His mother according to the flesh ; so that it is not strange that her life should receive fuller treatment than his does. However this may be, it is really strange to human ways of thinking that the treatment given her life is so very slight when judged by absolute standards. With the exception of two chapters in the gospel of St. Luke and a few incidents scattered here and there in the rest of the gospel narrative, Mary finds no mention in the inspired writings of the New Testament. But what little is said of her, throws her submission and docility to God's rule into unmistakable relief.

We meet her first in Nazareth, on the morning of the Annunciation. The angel appears to her, a messenger from her God, to announce her choice as Mother of the Redeemer. She, being a virgin vowed to the Lord, asks how this may be ; not in incredulity, but that she may learn God's will and accept it. And when she is told that it will be by the power of the Holy Ghost, she bows her head in reverent submission, and utters those momentous words : Behold the handmaid of the Lord ; be it done unto me according to thy word. She considers herself the handmaid, the bondmaid, of the Lord ; His to dispose of as He might will. Let her but learn what it is He .desires of her, and she will be entirely His to carry out His wishes.

We meet her again—led there, we may be sure, by the Holy Ghost—at the house of her cousin Elizabeth. The Word Incarnate is within her womb ; and she, living in union with Him, has come to realize even more fully than she did on the Incarnation day, the reason why she of all the daughters of Israel has been chosen for her office of singular dignity. Elizabeth, filled with the Holy Ghost, at the approach of one so favoured, cries out : Blessed art thou amongst women, and blessed is the fruit of thy womb. But in Mary, who by now knows God so well, wonder has given place to understanding. Wonder at God's choice of her has given way to understanding of the reason of His choice. And she answers : My soul doth magnify the Lord : . . . . Because He hath regarded the humility of His handmaid.

Let us pass, with but a glance to give, over the other details of these first two chapters of St. Luke. Glance at the humble and reverent Mary in Bethlehem—all love for such a Child, and all abashed at being His Mother. Glance at Mary finding her Child in the temple, asking Him why He had left her, that she might know and accept the mystery of her maternal vocation. Glance at her, too, in the home of Nazareth, pondering all her Child did and said in her heart, that she might receive as softest wax the firm imprint of His Person and His grace. Turn then to the gospel of St. John and see her at the marriage feast of Cana. It is just before the dawn of the public life. Jesus is about to leave the seclusion of Mary's home. Mary, who knew so much of Him, who understood the prophets in all they had foretold of Him, must have known that the time was near at hand when He would go forth, from her as it were, to reveal Himself to the world. She had a message to convey to those to whom He would offer Himself. She wished them to know how she had acted in His regard, and how she, in her love, desired that all should respond to His presence. And at that humble feast she spoke. The moment of the occasion wrung words from her who loved the silence of humility. But her words were humble too ; no less humble than her silence. " Whatsoever He shall say to you, do ye " : that was her great message to men before she sent her Son forth to redeem them. It was addressed to the waiters ; it was intended for the world. She had nothing deeper, nothing more profound than that to say : Do what my Son will ask of you. Yet, in those simple words are all her wisdom and all her understanding of Who Jesus is. He is a King ; we His subjects. Our peace is in His rule and not elsewhere. If we do whatsoever He shall say to us all will be well. The wine-pots, failing already ere our life's feast has more than begun, will be replenished at the Saviour's founts. And we, tasting the sweetness of God's inebriating peace, will wonder that such a vintage can be pressed from the tardy grapes our soul's poor soil yields.

We meet Mary once more, before the end. She stands on the outskirts of the crowd waiting to see her Son. It is His turn now to tell the world in what her sublime worth consists. " And it was told to him : Thy mother and thy brethren stand without, desiring to see thee. Who answering, said to them : My mother and my brethren are they who hear the word of God, and do it " (Lk. 8, 20-21). Could He have said more clearly that what made Mary so dear in His eyes was her acceptance of the will of His Father ? When, on another occasion, the cry goes up : " Blessed is the womb that bore thee, and the paps that gave thee suck," He insists once more on Mary's real glory. It is not that she bore Him according to the flesh, nor even that she nourished Him and brought Him to manhood. It is, instead, that she was submissive to her King : " Yea rather, blessed are they who hear the word of God, and keep it " (Lk. 11, 27-28). Here is no rebuke of His Blessed Mother, but rather a revelation of her beauty to them who have eyes to see and ears to hear. Realizing as He did how easy it would be to mistake what was honorary in her for what was her real title to glory, He lays such marked emphasis on her loving obedience to God's word. That, He says, is the secret of her greatness : not so much to be His Mother as the spirit in which she filled her unique rôle. What makes Mary truly great is not being Mother, but being such a Mother. And the world being too blind to perceive the distinction, Jesus Himself was forced to make it, lest it pass altogether unnoticed.

Mary at the foot of the Cross is more than ever Mary the handmaid and subject of the King. Not for an instant did she refuse the sacrifice asked of her. Though God willed to rule her, to dispose of her and of the Son she held dear, in a way that appeared cruel and nothing more to eyes of flesh, she submitted in trust and love. Her submission rose even to the sublime height of devoted spontaneity, for she offered her Son to the Father, just as truly as He took Him from her. Just as the Holy Spirit moved Jesus to will in sacrifice the death which the Father allowed to be inflicted by men on Him, so too He moved Mary to offer as a free gift what the Father asked of her on Calvary's hill. She consented freely and with desire to her Son's oblation of Himself. And in doing this she too offered Him, and that in union with His own offering. It is wrong to think of Mary as crushed and helpless on Calvary. Far from being crushed, she was intensely active there, in submission to the Divine Will ; far from being helpless there, she was the Virgin most powerful. But whether active or powerful she was the handmaid of the Lord. It was in His service she was active and in His strength she was powerful. In her great act of submission she achieved her great act of co-redemption. Mary Our Queen is Queen on Calvary, because she remained then as ever, the Handmaid of the Lord.

Thus far we have considered Mary as subject in God's Kingdom. She is Queen there as well : Queen by birth, in virtue of her Immaculate Conception ; Queen too as Mother of and Co-operator with the Redeemer ; Victor-Queen as offerer with Jesus, and under Jesus, of the great sacrifice of Calvary. The meaning of these different titles to Queenship are sufficiently clear from what we have said of Jesus' different titles to the name of King. They correspond to Jesus' titles as God Incarnate, Head of the human race, and Victor. Jesus is King by reason of His character as God-man ; Mary is Queen by reason of her immaculate purity and sinlessness. Jesus is King, further, as Head of the human race ; Mary is Queen as Mother of and associate with Him Who is King. Finally, Jesus is King by His victory on the Cross ; Mary is Queen by her intimate participation in His victory. All these titles to Queenship in Mary are analogous to and understandable in terms of Jesus' different titles to Kingship. But though we may consider it permissible to treat thus summarily the question of Mary's right to the name of Queen, it would be unpardonable to neglect to speak in some detail of the majesty of her Queenship. When we considered Jesus as King we were careful to point out the different excellences by which He was raised above His subjects, as for example, His Divine Nature, His fulness of grace, His created wisdom. We intend to do the same thing now for Mary Our Queen, that contemplating her sublime worth we may be drawn to revere her more, to pay her more lowly homage and more devoted service. If worth has the power of wringing recognition from even the ill-disposed, Mary's worth need only be known to captivate all hearts. That so many think they know her and yet remain indifferent to her rights is because they know her with the mind only. She must be known with the heart as well. To know her in this way however is not the fruit of study alone, but of prayer and study. He who would know Mary must pray for the grace to know her. The most that can be done in a book is to provide matter for pious meditation. Conviction is a gift of God ; it comes with the gift of understanding. And the gifts of God are communicated not in the whirlwind of human reasoning, but in the calm of humble petition.

The dignity of Mary is, in the first place, that of a human who has been very near to the Blessed Trinity. If a person gains in importance in our eyes because he or she has known or shaken hands with a celebrity, how should we not revere one who has entered into relations of the greatest intimacy with God Himself? Mary has been associated with the Father as Mother of the Word. She has brought forth in her womb Him Whom the Father brings forth from all eternity. She is the human fount of the temporal generation of the Word, just as the Father is the Eternal. When the Incarnate Word came forth from Mary's womb in Bethlehem the Father could at the same time say: "Thou art my son; this day I have begotten thee." Both Mary and the Father were needed that the Word might come forth, not as Word only, but as Incarnate Word. The Nativity, which took place in time, and the eternal generation, were both terminated by the same Person of the Word, the one in so far as He became flesh, the other in so far as He remained true God of true God. The Father and Mary, therefore, united, as it were, to give Jesus to the world. Mary was in consequence of all this the Father's associate in the Incarnation, obtaining by her intimacy with Him the privilege of having consorted with God.

It is impossible to speak of Mary's intimacy with the Father without at the same time saying something of her intimacy with the Word. The Word, the Second Person of the Blessed Trinity, equal to the Father in all things, took flesh in Mary's womb. And for nine months there existed between Mary and the Word that unique fellowship of the mother and the unborn child. Her Child was within her womb, united to her, living by physical contact with her life—and that Child was the Word. Can we say then that Mary has not known God, that God has held Himself distant from Mary? If the nod of a king can thrill, what did not the presence of the Word in Mary's womb do for her? If a man is respected because a prince has lodged with him, what homage is not due to Mary within whose womb lodged the King of Kings?

And she was spouse of the Holy Ghost! That is the meaning of the words of the angel of the Annunciation: "The Holy Ghost shall come upon thee, and the power of the most High shall overshadow thee " (Lk. 1, 35). The Incarnate Word was conceived of Mary without the intervention of man ; for Mary was virgin at all times—before, and at, and after, the birth of her Son. But the power of the Holy Ghost supplied in a transcendent way what in a merely human birth is supplied by the human father. Mary is termed therefore Spouse of the Holy Ghost. A wonderful degree of intimacy, a nearness to God which the mind could never have imagined ! Yet it was really Mary's. She has been in so close a contact with God as that. She has been united in chaste union with the Holy Ghost, Who, by His power overshadowed her, and formed within her womb, of her pure blood, the body of Christ the Son of God. That is an honour which the heart alone can grasp, leaving the mind amazed and the tongue silent. There are no words we can use here save words of praise of God and Mary. Her dignity defeats our thoughts : our love alone may hope to grasp something of it.

Though wonderful be the dignity of Mary as revealed in the relations between her and the Three Persons of the ever Blessed Trinity, she appears greater still if we consider her in her place in the work of Redemption. It may at first sight seem strange to speak of a greater dignity than that of Mother of the Son of the Eternal Father, and Spouse of the Holy Ghost. But this is only because we have not reflected that there is nothing more in these relations, taken in themselves, than a merely extrinsic contact with the Godhead. A thief is no less a thief if he has happened to shake hands with a king, and it is logically conceivable that the Mother of God should have been as it were nothing more than an instrument of God's designs, to be laid aside, intrinsically unchanged, when she should have performed the task for which she had been selected : logically possible, and that alone I say, because such a course would conflict with the harmony found in God's usual way of working in His world. But Mary was chosen by God for something more than extrinsic association with the Three Divine Persons. She was chosen to be the associate of the Incarnate Word in the work for which He was made flesh, the work namely of our redemption. Mary, therefore, would not remain entirely outside the actual realization of

God's scheme. She would work with the Incarnate Word, and for the same end as He. It is true that Jesus and Mary can hardly be said to co-operate in the strictest sense of the term, for what she did was necessarily subordinated to and dependent on His power and merits. But, it is none the less true that the work of Redemption is the work of Both. The Incarnate Word came on earth to be engaged in, bound up with, implicated in a work which would be known for all time as Mary's work as well as being His. Now it is a matter of common sense to recognize that it is becoming to pick those with whom you intend to associate in any enterprise that will live in history as having been your doing. No man wishes to leave posterity the opportunity of besmearing his good name with the mud and pitch of his chosen helpers' defects. Conversely, it is a sign of confidence in another and a real honour paid him to allow his name to be for ever associated with yours in whatever work you hope will perpetuate your memory. In this you do nothing less than offer him a share in your own title to fame. You declare in the most public way possible that he is a man whom you are not ashamed to call a friend, and that you wish the memory of his friendship to be green wherever you yourself and what you have done are held in high esteem. Now that is the meaning of Mary's co-operation with Jesus in our redemption. The Redemption was Jesus' peculiar work. It was the work which He Who was God came to perform, the work which He Who was God willed should remain for ever written on the pages of human history as His Own contribution to the sum-total of what is worth while on earth. And in this work He found room for Mary, rather than to do it altogether alone. Here we have genuine intrinsic contact of some kind. The reputation of the Son of God is linked up with that of Mary. While it is possible, though far from easy, for a man to live down a mother's shame, how can any man dare to live down the shame of a deliberately bad choice in the partner of the work of an entire lifetime? No man can do it, because it is opposed to the nature of things that it be done. Mary is therefore bound up with God. God has, as it were, compromised Himself in the world's eyes by His choice of Mary as co-redemptrix.

All the holy ones of earth might fall away, and God would still be beyond the world's reproach. But by His holy Will Mary means so much to Him that her shame would redound to the shame of Him, the Almighty.

Being thus closely united to God it was becoming that Mary should be adorned with the richest gifts of grace. It is axiomatic in theology that the nearer one comes to the Author of grace the more one is filled with grace. Since therefore Mary was nearer to God in Three Divine Persons than any mere creature, she was in some way entitled to a fulness of grace exceeding that given even to the angels. However, it is most of all when we consider her participation in the work of Redemption that the appropriateness of her fulness of grace becomes apparent. For this participation made of her, as we have just seen, the partner of the Incarnate Word. But He redeemed us by His merits, and merits rest upon the holiness of the author of the meritorious act. What made Jesus' sacrifice so pleasing to the Father was ultimately that Jesus Himself, true God and true Man, full of all grace, was infinitely pleasing in His own being. If therefore Mary is called to redeem us under Jesus and in union with Him, it must be by way of her merits also, and therefore ultimately in virtue of her personal holiness. She would be Jesus' partner only in a very remote way were He to redeem us by merit and she by nothing more than a mere pact or legal fiction. She needed therefore in virtue of the present divine decree of our Redemption to be holy, and that in a measure proportionate to the exalted nature of the task allotted her.

It is sometimes felt that by exalting the holiness of Mary we take away from the uniqueness of that of Jesus. But more careful consideration will show that this cannot be the case. Mary, as God has willed her to be, is, after Jesus, the great witness to the power and meaning of the Redemption. It is fitting therefore that she be exalted in testimony to its greatness. The greater we make Mary the greater we make Jesus and His redemption. Her holiness is not independent of His and of His work ; rather is it a share in His, and the fruit of His sacrifice. By exalting her, who is as it were an effect, we exalt Him still more Who is the cause of all she is. It is almost superfluous to note that in speaking of exalting Mary we do not mean attributing perfections to her which revelation and sound theology will not guarantee. There are limits in this matter which must be observed. But within these limits there is no danger to be feared, as if what was given to the Mother was taken from the Son. Mary is the great sign-post to Jesus, the great Way. Make Mary stand out in clear evidence and mankind is led to Jesus. Mary is the great masterpiece of Jesus' hand. Reveal the full extent of her perfection and the marvel of His Redemption is thrown into relief. Jesus has in point of fact achieved nothing greater than the holiness He merited for His Mother. Is it becoming therefore that we should form a lowly estimate of Mary, thinking thereby to pay tribute to Him? Is it not more true that every grace we deny her reflects upon the success of His great work? By unduly diminishing the glory of Mary we would make her a witness not to the unequalled excellence of her Son, but to the comparative failure of His earthly achievement.

The extent of this perfection of Mary was indicated by the Angel Gabriel on the morning of the Incarnation when he addressed her as full of grace. She was truly full of grace, full of godliness, near to God, far from sin. If we consider her growth in grace as an event taking place in time, and following the laws of vital expansion, the first stage will be that marked by her Immaculate Conception. Mary, we believe on the authority of the Church, was conceived free from the stain of original sin. There was no single instant of time in which her soul was not the subject of sanctifying grace. Almighty God intervened in the first instant of her conception, through the merits of her divine Son, to pour grace into her soul, and thus preserve her from mankind's unhappy heritage of the guilt of Adam's fault. Being as she was a daughter of Adam, she was of herself subject to original sin and would in the ordinary course of providence have contracted its stain. Her freedom from it was not a native immunity, but rather a gratuitous preservation ; and the reason for it was her intimacy with the Blessed Trinity and the Incarnate Word, and that place which was hers in the economy of redemption whereby she, like her Son, would be in irreconcilable enmity with the prince of sin and darkness.

Now, Mary was not given grace in stinted measure, at the moment of her Immaculate Conception. Grace was poured into her soul then in such fulness that she was full of grace. Full in a relative sense, of course ; as full, that is to say, as it was becoming that her soul should be then, without at all excluding the possibility of a greater fulness when she would be still more perfectly disposed. Thus Mary's fulness neither at the moment of her Immaculate Conception nor at any other moment was equal to that of Jesus. His fulness was absolute : He had all that there was and all that there could be of the grace of the present order. Hers was relative : she had at all times all the grace it was fitting her soul should receive. There is an additional reason for the distinction between the grace of Jesus and Mary, in that His fulness of grace is the cause of the fulness of hers, and hence must surpass it as does the light of the sun that of the moon, or any other heavenly body which draws the totality of its brightness from it as source. But with these reservations and explanations it is true to say that Mary was full of grace from the instant of her conception. She was pure intrinsic godliness from the very beginning. She was never turned away from God, even to the slightest extent ; not even to the extent to which the unborn child, as yet incapable of a free act, is turned away from Him by the corruption of its nature. He reigned in her fully from the first instant of her existence, and she, by the completeness of His life in her, was from the same instant singled out from all mankind as greater in spiritual worth than all beside.

Besides sanctifying grace and its accompanying virtues and gifts, Mary received the additional purification of the complete destruction within her of the disorder which reigns in the sensitive part of the nature of every fallen son of Adam. She came into this world, therefore, a perfectly harmonious being. Grace ruled in her soul, and sense within her was entirely subject to elevated reason. She had nothing of our tendency to cling to earth, nothing of our tendency to shirk effort. Her dignity of person was not confined to her soul alone ; it overflowed from soul to sense, extinguishing by its deep pervasiveness sense's unmeasured striving after what appeals to its baser taste, and even communicating to it a genuine impulse towards the God of all purity. If restraint and good-breeding make a queen, Mary was one a thousand times. She was conceived with that restraint which we hope some day to touch with outstretched hands, knowing that we can never grasp it and make it fully our own. She was conceived with the good-breeding which is in us the fruit of effort, and even then it is never ours more than imperfectly. Her utter liberty from all that makes base and common would of itself make her a queen among men, even had she no other title to the name. It is good to think of this exquisite fineness of Mary's human nature. All that is best that we admire in man—nobility, culture—these are hers. We should reckon ourselves honoured to know her ; still more to be allowed to call her mother. Should we then hesitate to give her the title of our Queen ?

In addition to, and in some sense as a consequence of, her freedom from disorder in the sensitive part of her nature, Mary was strengthened against all actual sin, even the lightest. In virtue of the Hypostatic Union and of the fulness of created grace, mounting in Him even to the beatific vision, it was physically impossible that Our Blessed Lord should ever sin. Mary's fulness of grace, though, as we have seen, a true fulness, was nevertheless of a lower order than His. Hence the opposition between Mary and sin, though so complete as to exclude sin from her soul, was also of a lower order. With passion weakened to the vanishing point, and grace strengthened even to fulness, sin could never have over her the power to attract, and almost to compel, that it has over other mortals. But while she remained on earth, a pilgrim to eternity, her opposition to sin could never amount to complete physical incompatibility For her will was a human one, and a human will is never fixed immovably on the good until it sees It in the face to face vision of eternity. Mary's sinlessness was therefore rather of the factual kind, than of the completely necessary ; she was safeguarded against sin sufficiently to be able to resist all temptation which would come her way—and to resist it so fully as never to give it the slightest foot-hold within her—but not so radically as to make the opposition between her and sin that of two irreconcilables. And as a consequence, we may add that her sinlessness included in consequence of its not being altogether absolute, a special divine providence by which the grace of God was always at her disposal to make her victorious over sin on every occasion that it might raise its ugly head to challenge her. She was therefore sinless, altogether sinless. Actual sin never had dominion over her, and could not, seeing that she had been called by God to be victor over sin, not its victim. It matters but little therefore that she was sinless in a less complete way than was her Son, our King. She was sinless enough—and more than enough— to lift her far above the rest of men, with their half-hearted and intermittent resistance to temptation. She was always a victor where we are so often the vanquished, and by the grace of God her victories would know no end. If we look therefore for one, after Jesus, under whose standard we may fight victoriously against sin, must we not turn to Mary? And turning thus to her, we admit she is our Queen.

Though Mary's victory over sin was always assured, she did not on that account fail to advance in grace from moment to moment. That we should find it at a first glance difficult to reconcile the ideas of merit and of immunity from the need to struggle, is due to our insistence on what is a most prominent feature in our own lives, even though in them also it be not the most fundamental. We are inclined to measure merit by difficulties encountered and overcome, because we ourselves seem always to meet with difficulties, and feel that the extent of the sacrifices we make in facing up to them is what gives our virtue its true worth. The truth is, however, that the sacrifice we make is never more than a test of the worth of our actions; the worth itself lies elsewhere, in the love which inspired them. For what gives our actions their real value is their godwardness; and that is a matter of turning positively to God by love, not a mere matter of surmounting obstacles. Nevertheless it is not without reason that we attribute such great importance to sacrifice in our own case, because there is no surer way of testing the driving force of our tendency to God than to note the obstacles it enables us to hurl out of our way. If however there be a soul for whom there are no obstacles, its actions will be godward without being difficult, and there will be nothing by which to gauge their value except the love which inspired them, considered solely and simply in itself. Mary was such a soul. She merited not by the earnestness of her struggle but by the intensity of her love. She merited, we may believe, by every one of her acts, an increase of grace and glory. She was never static in the life of grace. Rather was her life one of continuous and uninterrupted growth. Her love bore her ever towards her God, for nearness to Him served but to increase the compelling force of His attractiveness.

When, in an earlier chapter, we spoke of the Kingship of Our Blessed Lord, we devoted a special section to those of His qualities which made Him fit to govern and placed it immediately after that treating of what went to constitute His personal dignity. It will be well to follow a similar course when speaking of Mary, and add at this present stage a few words on her knowledge, leaving it to the piety of the reader to supply what should be said of her other qualities.

Our Blessed Lord was enriched, even as Man, with the illumination of the Beatific vision. Not so Mary, if we have her habitual endowments in mind. But though it be correct to say that she did not enjoy the Beatific vision habitually while on earth, we should claim that privilege for certain passing occasions of outstanding importance in her spiritual development and work. It is probable that she was favoured with the act of the beatific vision at the moment of the Incarnation. Her consent to become the mother of God was fraught with such tremendous consequences that she may be said to have had need of seeing them in the Divine Essence to be enabled to estimate their true nature, and that of the act which she herself was called upon to perform. It would be no adequate preparation for an enlightened acceptance of her position to have known nothing more of man and the future Messias than what the prophets foretold. Neither would illumination by way of infused ideas be sufficient; for they, however perfect in themselves, would remain but faint representations of the Divine scheme of salvation. A work, so much God's own, could be grasped clearly only in God. And so He Who willed Mary to become His Mother with a clear and becoming awareness of what He asked of her, could never have refused her that passing glimpse of His Essence which the circumstances of the Annunciation seemed to demand. We may postulate the same act of beatific vision for at least two other instants in Mary's life, and that for the same reasons as those which hold for the Annunciation. They are the instant[1] of Our Lord's birth and that of His death on the Cross. It seems peculiarly fitting that she should have had it on Calvary. The immensity of the sacrifice demanded then of Mary, including as it did the anguish of knowing that He Who was crucified by men was truly God, rendered it most becoming that she should see through God's own eyes the reconciliation of the fact of God being Victim at man's hands with the transcendence of the Divine Majesty. We blind mortals can accept with a certain amount of complacency that God was put to death for us. But that is because we do not know Who God is. If we knew God in all His glory and all His power, how could we believe Him the victim of man's schemes and plottings? Mary knew God better than we ever shall. For her therefore the death of Jesus was truly a mystery—the mystery of God at the mercy of man. No created vision, however perfect, could have enabled her to grapple with it. She needed nothing less than the vision of its essential logic in the mind of God. We can believe therefore that that vision was granted her. God would never have asked her to stand by Jesus' cross, knowing that He had not given her the strength to stand erect under the burden of what she could see there. He had made her a queen, not a cowering slave; and He would therefore give her a queen's understanding of the King's plans. That was the purpose of the Beatific vision which was accorded her then : that the Mother of Sorrows might taste the triumph of her Son's mysterious entry into His Kingdom.

Mary was endowed with infused knowledge as well during

---

[1] The word instant is not to be understood necessarily in its philosophical sense of a part of time which has no duration whatever.

her life on earth. Almighty God gave her in an habitual way whatever knowledge was needed for the worthy filling of her exalted office and which she could not obtain by means of the limited opportunities which were hers in the ordinary course of life. It is probable that she obtained in this way a very clear understanding of the mystery of our redemption and of the Person and Natures of the Incarnate Word. What we acquire by the study of theology was given her without study, and given too in a degree which no theologian may hope to equal. There is no reason for believing that she was illuminated in this way about the mysteries of the physical world. Such matters had no immediate bearing on her office, and hence were not necessary to her in order that she fulfil God's designs in her regard. But all that was necessary in order that she act in a way worthy both of herself and of her Son was given. She was a queen, and God saw that she had the spiritual trappings of a true queen. Not least of these trappings was her knowledge, its depth and light making her unique among the daughters of men. Her knowledge had surely that calm penetration we associate with a royal nature. Next after her divine Son she was the most fit to sound the depths of man's need, and see the surest way to raise him gently heavenwards.

Her dignity as Mother of God, her fulness of grace, and her virtues made Mary a Queen in the days of her sojourn on earth. But the plenitude of her royal character would be revealed only in Heaven, and that by a mystery of her life akin to that of the enthroning of her Son. For as He ascended glorious and immortal to heaven and now sits as King on the right hand of the Father, so also Mary was taken up after death, body and soul, and placed on a throne of glory next to that of Christ the King. Throned like Jesus, she rules too as He does ; not by a rule which is purely honorary, but by one which is real and efficacious. Jesus, as we know, merited our salvation by His Passion and death. As King and Eternal Priest He now communicates that salvation to us from His royal throne. Similarly, Mary merited our salvation for us, under Jesus : not as He did, on grounds of justice, but in a lesser though real way. And like Him, she communicates to us now from her throne what she merited on earth ; not however by acts of a formally priestly nature, but by a mediation of prayer and intercession. In other words, just as Jesus rules all men by His Priesthood, so does Mary rule them by her intercession. They are moved by grace which comes efficiently from God and Jesus. But that grace is conferred only in answer to Mary's prayers. Hence she too rules, though not entirely in her own name and by her own power. This however does not take away from the reality of her queenly rank. A queen, as queen, never rules of herself, but only through the king. Her all-powerfulness consists in the assurance she has that the king will accede to her wishes. That is just how Mary is all-powerful as queen. Jesus will always hear her prayers, both because she has merited by her life on earth that they be heard, and because she only asks the things that please Him. It does not really matter therefore whether we submit ourselves to the rule of Jesus or of Mary. Both rule as one. Jesus rules for Mary and Mary for Jesus. Mary's fulness of grace merited for her that she now fill souls with grace ; her freedom from all stain of sin, that she now free souls from sin ; her humility, that we be led in imitation of her to submit to the rule of God. And it is this last point that I should wish to stress : that her humility leads her now to rule souls that God may rule in them. She who was, and is the handmaid of the Lord does not shrink from her greatness. She sees that it has been given her in order that God may be Master of souls through her dominion over them. Were she to withdraw herself, or to allow herself to be withdrawn by a man's mistaken piety towards God, from the full gaze of humanity, she would cease to be humble. She has been made what she was made, that men might see God in her and submit to God by accepting her place and rights. She has an integral place in the framework of the Kingdom. There could have been a Kingdom ruled by a King alone, but it is not one of that kind that God selected. His choice was a kingdom where there would be a Queen and need for a Queen. We are not free to decide to submit to the King alone. To do that is to submit to a rule which is other than that which Jesus actually exercises. We must accept the whole Kingdom of Heaven, and love and submit to all that it is. Mary is its

Queen. Our love and submission are therefore her due ; and she, being truly humble, will insist that she be paid the homage God has declared her right.

It will be remembered that this chapter commenced as an attempt to illustrate by reference to Our Lady the truth of the statement that to serve God is to reign. That such was the case with Mary should be clear by now. Her life, we have seen, expressed itself in the most entire submission to the divine Will, while at the same time we are amazed to learn of the eminence of grace and spiritual worth to which she had been raised from the very moment of her conception. Mary served God, and yet reigned in personal excellence. What is more : her growth in grace was the direct fruit of her loving submission to God in every act she elicited. The concurrence of submission and majesty in Mary's soul was not therefore accidental. She was so great precisely because she made herself so little, and being so great could not find adequate expression of her deepest convictions elsewhere than in acts of profound humility.

It will be the same in our lives. We shall never be truly great until by submission to God we have disposed ourselves to receive from Him the gift of true greatness. And once truly great, we shall by that very fact know God so clearly that His Majesty will draw us irresistibly to our knees. The greatness we achieve in submission will, moreover, be no chimera. We shall be spiritually great, and as kings we shall rule others. For the soul that is genuinely holy merits not only for itself but in a less perfect way for its fellow men as well. And in much the same way as Mary's merits determine the course of the whole world, the merits, satisfactions, and prayers of God's faithful subjects exercise a tremendous influence over the destinies of the souls to which God in His wisdom applies them. To the eyes of men, the kings and the mighty ones of the earth seem to be they who shape the future of the world. But God knows, and we know too, that history follows the road built by the prayers and sufferings of the saints. They are the true makers of history, the true framers of the world's destiny. Invent a new machine, and you will merit the title of maker in civilization's tedious process from created formlessness to uncreated beauty. But have you really moulded the universe, or have you but battered it still more completely out of its true shape ? There is but one way by which you can give the world a shape it will retain in the crucible of God's judgment, and that is to mould it by grace. He who has done this will have been in truth a king among men, though none there were to suspect his dignity or his power. On earth he will have had but one ambition : to serve his God. But God, Who seeks His glory, not for His gain, but for ours, will have made him a king.

CHAPTER XII

THE GLORY OF THE KINGDOM

" The earth is the Lord's and the fulness thereof: the world, and all they that dwell therein" (Ps. 23, 1).

FROM the earliest days of Christianity there have been two elements of the spiritual life which, though in no way irreconcilable, are sufficiently distinct in their outer manifestation to suggest something akin to conflict in the minds of those who lack that breadth of synthetic view in which their opposition may be seen to be complementary rather than exclusive. The two elements to which I refer are embodied to some extent in Mary and Martha, to a greater extent still in the concepts of the King's daughter whose beauty is within, and that of a city placed on a mountain top in the full view of mankind ; and most of all in Him, in Whom they are at the same time reconciled and shown to be one, in Jesus hidden at Nazareth and in Jesus set up as a sign to the gentiles. It is usual to speak of a certain opposition in the notions these examples embody. And if the word opposition be taken to mean strict irreconcilability, to do so is wrong. But while stressing their compatibility it serves no useful purpose to insist so much on the one as to make the other seem not secondary, merely, but even optional. It is good to stress the supreme intrinsic worth of the grace which is within ; but it is certainly not good to divert attention entirely from the glory which marks God's kingdom from without, in the mistaken belief that to do so is to make sure of what is more important. It is only in human minds that there is strife between the inner and outer glory of the Kingdom. The riches of the kingdom of God, as they revealed themselves in Jesus' life, are of both the inner and the outer kind. Within, He had all the treasures of the Divinity ; and without, though appearing in the form of a servant, He came as a sign that would be held up in the clear view of men, a sign so inescapable that from whomsoever the homage of acceptance would not be forthcoming at least there would be exacted the tribute of contradiction. And just as the divine perfections exist in God as all one with the divine essence, but are participated in the created universe in many distinct ways, so too, the glory of godliness, essentially one in God Himself, is split up by the prism of the created weakness of its participations, and shines on the earth as two related glories, that of inner grace and that of exterior impressiveness. But few of the members of the kingdom of God are called to realize these two glories in their single persons. Some are called to stand forth most of all as holy. Others, though called in the first place to be holy, are nevertheless so evidently called as well to bear witness in their lives to the triumph of the Church's truth over error, or of her virtue over vice, that their inner holiness is lost sight of in the splendour of their outer achievement. But both glories are essential to the Church taken as a whole. She must at all times be eminent in the holiness of her children, and no less so in the majesty of her testimony to the truth. It is not demanded of each individual Christian that he reflect the full character of His God and His Saviour. But the Church as Church must do so. If therefore God is both Holy and Lord, if Jesus was both hidden and revealed, the Church must bear a dual character of inner sanctity and outer glory, and the member of God's kingdom must triumph over Satan not only by the victory he gains in the spiritual battlefield of his soul, but by that also which is his on the material one of our historical world of earth and stones.

We have confined ourselves hitherto to the inner struggle

and to the success which crowns it. We have seen that it consists in an uncompromising war with self, the world, and Satan, and that the reward of effort is peace of soul, grace, and power to rule others by merit. This is an entirely adequate exposition of the nature of the kingdom of God in so far as it affects the individual. It sets forth the essentials of the struggle and of the reward and triumph. But if we consider it from the side of the Church, it is not yet complete. The Church too struggles. And though it be no small reward that the struggle should result in the sanctification of her children, something more is required as well. For she is a visible organization, and wages a war which eyes of earth can perceive. Is it possible then that there be no glory in this outer struggle? We shall not be so lacking in understanding as to look for the complete victory of the visible Church on earth. Our Head and King found death on earth; His enthronement took place in heaven. But there must be something majestic about even the material element in the Church's warfare. It will be true that this majesty will reveal itself fully only when we view the battlefield from the divine angle. But it will remain an earthly majesty, however splendidly it be lit up by the divine. We shall see the Church stand firm while empires totter and crash; we shall see her baited and mocked, only to survive in more serene confidence. She will be at all times, and under every trial, nothing less than a kingdom, and no less a kingdom than that of the most High God. She will be a city firm and immovable. To attack her will be to dash oneself to pieces against her mighty walls. The nations may rage, and the people may think vain thoughts of her destruction, but God Himself will be her foundation, and her battlements will be eloquent of the strength of Him upon Whom they are built.

The problem which we are at present discussing emerges at once from those words spoken by our King before His Ascension to Heaven, whereby He gave His subjects the command to work for the visible as well as the invisible extension of His Kingdom on earth: " Going therefore teach ye all nations: baptizing them in the name of the Father, and of the Son, and of the Holy Ghost " (Mt. 28, 19). In addition He promised them His continued assistance as guarantee of the success of their mission : " . . . and behold I am with you all days, even to the consummation of the world " (*ib.* 20). But has their mission been so conspicuously successful as one would expect from Jesus' promise ? That it has we shall endeavour to show ; and we shall show too, as a necessary introduction to the question, how we must regard the Church in order to be in a position to see the triumph of her struggle as Jesus saw it when He linked it with His own all-conquering power. But there is no reason to hide the fact that there have been times in the Church's history, and that such times may well repeat themselves, when the fearful child of God might be forgiven for asking did the King sleep once more in Peter's barque. Think of the infant church attacked from outside by Jews and Romans while torn within by false brethren. Think of any of the great upheavals of later centuries, of Manicheism, of Mahommedanism, of the Reformation with its alliance of doctrine and force in opposition to her. Where, we may ask, is the glory in all this ? And asking the question we see one reason for the early Christians' longing for the triumphant second coming of their Lord. They were experiencing only too fully the truth of the words that promised them sorrow in this world. They could see no prospect of ever meeting their enemies on equal terms. If, then, truth must be victorious —and they knew it must—that could, in their minds, be only through a speedy manifestation of their triumphant King, forcing the world to its knees, and vindicating the justice of those whom the world persecuted. In this belief, which was never that of the inspired writers, we know that they were in error. But we should know too that their error sprang from a grasp of truth keener than ours has ever been. We of to-day have grown almost indifferent to the Kingdom's right to triumph, provided only we save our souls. Not so with them. They understood more of the magnificence of God's scheme than we do. They saw that He wished a Kingdom, nothing less, and that even as a Kingdom it should be worthy of its King. We are satisfied that the commandments be kept in the secrecy of chambers, and preserve our calm whilst error claims more public allegiances than truth. If we attempt at all to formulate a philosophy of our attitude it amounts to the belief that the interior triumph of grace in a soul more than compensates for the public failure of God's Kingdom. A specious philosophy and nothing more ; specious because so nearly true, so superficially spiritual. The truth is that God does not want failure in either of His battles, nor has there ever been failure in them. And that truth is the content of the Apocalypse.[1]

The churches of Asia Minor had already in the lifetime of St. John experienced something of the malevolence of Jews and other local enemies. But a greater trial was at hand. The power of the Empire of Rome might soon be turned more fiercely to their destruction. St. John, standing on the sand of the sea, and turning his gaze westward, could see rising before him the beast "having seven heads and ten horns, and upon his horns ten diadems, and upon his heads names of blasphemy" (Apoc. 12, 18 and 13, 1). It was the Roman beast he saw ; and seeing it he wished to strengthen his little flock for what would ensue, by revealing to them the majesty of God throned in Heaven, before Whose eyes all that happens comes to pass, and in Whose hands are even those tyrants He allows a little while of show. Seeing the beast he thought too of generations as yet unborn, who in their turn would be called to live a faith in a Church tossed by the fury of political might. Other beasts would arise, no less in power than that of Rome. Of them too men would say "Who is like to the beast ? and who shall be able to fight with him ?" (13, 4). To them too would be given power to do and to act for many months, and they would open their mouths in blasphemies against God, and make war on the just and overcome them, and win power over every tribe and people and tongue and nation (13, 5 sqq.). Nor would beasts, mighty in political power, be the only ones to rise. There would be as well the beasts of false intellectual and religious might, the beasts that would lead men to their destruction by the path of spiced sophisms and attractive moralities, the beasts who would teach

---

[1] I am deeply indebted to Fr. Allo's masterpiece, *L'Apocalypse*, Paris, Gabalda, 1921, in this chapter. However, as I have selected, omitted, and enlarged at will, he cannot be held responsible for each and every point made here.

that sin is illusion, that men are naturally good, that there is no higher God than man. And in a piercing glance that swept even to the confines of time, the visionary saw that fell alliance of beast with beast, of state with false prophet, in which pseudo-teachers would seduce them that dwell on the earth, causing the earth and them that dwell thereon to adore the state, healing with the balm of deceit the wounds time inflicts on the state that will be a god (13, 12-14). The gaze of John pierced beyond the lifetime of his little flocks. If he saw reason to fear for them, the reasons to fear for those who would follow, for us too of the present day, were no less real and compelling in his eyes. He spoke therefore for a church universal in time, a church living and fighting in all ages, a church ever locked in deadly struggle with the beast. We of to-day need his message of hope, his solution of the riddle of evil's strength. And he gives the solution our faith should have led us to anticipate. For he turns his eyes fearlessly to God, and sees the King Immortal holding the threads of human lives, weaving the pattern of His Kingdom's strength and beauty. And in that vision of God the world is suffused with a light of soft peace, of tranquil majesty, that streams from the great white throne.

It is impossible for us to grasp the meaning of the Church's struggle otherwise than by directing our gaze Godwards in imitation of St. John. The struggle that occupies the world's arena is not a self-contained and isolated event. God has His part in it. So too has Satan. The men who are engaged in it are members of God's Kingdom. And we cannot understand it, nor see where, in the perpetual swaying of conflicting forces, the victory really does lie unless we keep our eye on Him Who is Master through the ebb and flow of local skirmishing. If then we gaze reverently heavenwards we shall see there One sitting upon a throne (Apoc. 4, 1 *sqq.*). He is of wonderful majesty. He shines with a brilliance exceeding that of the most precious of jewels. And this great majesty is tempered with mercy ; for there is, as it were, around the throne a rainbow, the sign of that covenant of God with man, whereby He determined that He would no more destroy man from the face of the earth. He is surrounded by a court worthy of so great a King. There are spirits there, clothed in white garments of unearthly purity, having upon their heads crowns of purest gold in sign of their dignity. Before this throne stretches the created universe, all open and exposed before the penetrating eye of God. The world pursues its headlong course mindless of Him Who sees all things, forgetting that He Who sees is also He Who is and He Who rules. But within the court of heaven itself there is no forgetting. There God is the accepted King. He is seen to rule both the visible and the invisible, both men and spirits. And there arises from the wakeful hearts of heaven's greatest courtiers that unending hymn of praise whose notes, though ever sounding, demand to be struck ever anew : "Holy, holy, holy, Lord God Almighty, who was and who is and who is to come." God is holy, endlessly holy. He is all-pure, all-strong. Holy in what He is, holy in His strength to remain unchangingly what He is. Holy, holy, holy . . . the hymn rolls on in steady rhythmic waves ; and, as its notes beat powerfully upon the ears of heaven's hosts, they who are kings among God's subjects fall down before Him in adoration, and cast their crowns in homage at His feet. Prostrate before Him, sensitive to the spell of His transcendent holiness, their adoration is quickened to song. From their lips, too, escapes a murmur—if that may be called a murmur which is more powerful, more intense, than the most heartwrung of human cries : Thou art worthy, O Lord our God, to receive glory, and honour, and power : because thou hast created all things ; and for thy will they were and have been created. Who is worthy of honour if not the Immortal King Who made all things, and Whose they remain even when once they are made ? The spirits of God confess these rights of His over man, which man is too blind to see. They can bend their gaze earthwards and see the world God made, and see its misery, and its blindness, and its cheap pride, and its stubborn thirst for suicide. And looking at it they see it is God's and that it can never escape His mighty arm. Man who struts below them is blind even to the tragedy of his strutting. He thinks his stage is all that is, forgetting that he has received a no more autonomous vocation than to play a part at Another's bidding. He cannot, for he will not, look beyond and look through the glare of pride's foot-lights, and see the majesty of the eyes that are turned upon him. He is all too happy to play his part, and pilfer whose lines he can, and parade before his spirit audience, all that is worst and meanest and most contemptible in his repertoire of varied infamy.

There is in God's hands a book : the book of human destinies. It is a sealed book. There is no spirit, not even the greatest of those that throng His court, who can open it (Apoc. 5, 1 sqq.). For God has given to none of them the power to guide the universe and the destinies it contains at will, since it is His and His only. But now there stands revealed near the throne of the Most High, a Lamb, as it were slain, bearing in His body the marks of the wounds that caused His death. The Lamb approaches nearer to the throne. He takes the book of our lives from out the right hand of Him Who sits upon the throne. He opens it. To Him has been given what belongs neither to man nor to angel : to open and close at will the book of human life. Therefore He, too, is Lord of the Universe, like Him Who sits upon the white throne, for He too is God, and He is Redeemer. He is Redeemer, One from among the race He redeemed, a Man. When therefore He takes the book and opens it, the voice of the angels who sing His power is succeeded by the voice of man, His brother ; a weak voice, the voice of a few and not of all, but none the less a human voice, a voice of praise rising from the earth and gathered by the angels into the harmony of their majestic choir : Thou art worthy, O Lord, to take the book, and to open the seals thereof ; because thou wast slain, and hast redeemed us to God, in thy blood, out of every tribe, and tongue, and people, and nation. And hast made us to our God a kingdom and priests, and we shall reign on the earth (Apoc. 5, 9-10). The voice of man has scarce ceased to be heard when once more that of the angels bursts forth triumphantly, this time alone, an angelic tribute to the Man Who redeemed His brothers : The Lamb that was slain is worthy to receive power, and divinity, and wisdom, and strength, and honour, and glory, and benediction. And then, once more, the voice of man is heard, now united with that of the angels, in praise of God and of the Lamb : To Him that sitteth on the throne, and to the Lamb, benediction, and honour, and glory, and power, for ever and ever (Apoc. 5, 13). Praise is God's for ever. For ever . . . the words are taken up in deepest heaven, and the peace of a great Amen reverberates. So it is ; so it was ; so will it ever be. The world and all things are God's and the Lamb's. No created power can filch their glory and honour and power. All things are Theirs. Amen, Amen, Amen for ever and for all eternity.

Let us turn once more in humble faith to heaven, and see what God will reveal to us. The Lamb Who has all power over the book of human life has opened it. He opens a seal with the authority of a master and bids us look now upon our earth. And we see a white horse, and one seated thereon. A horse of amazing strength and beauty, and a rider who guides it with the sureness of a master. The horse and the rider are the Lamb's. He has sent them in His name, and given the rider a bow and strength, that conquering he may conquer among the sons of men (Apoc. 6, 1 *sqq.*). This rider is the gospel of the Lamb, sent forth from the Throne to conquer and take possession of the earth. He bears on his head a royal crown, for he goes forth as a king. In his hand is a bow with which he will strike his enemies and bring them into subjection. And those whom he takes willing captive he makes free, free with the glorious freedom of the children of God. Through all the wide spaces of earth he follows his triumphant course. Other riders on other horses follow him, precede him, accompany and try to hinder him. But to none of them has been given the power to go forth as conqueror. They can destroy whomsoever refuses to rally to the cause of the gospel of the Lamb ; they can rage against Christ's kingdom, causing the bodily death of those whose souls escape the power of their wrath. But they are incapable of arresting the course of the majestic rider on the strong white horse, incapable too of snatching from the hands of Christ as much as one of those whom the Father has given Him.

Look once more heavenwards, and you will see the Lamb opening the second seal. A new rider and a new horse are seen on the earth. The horse is red, blood-coloured and blood-stained. He who rides him is War. The Lamb has released him on earth since men refuse to accept His kingdom ; yet, released him with power to do only what he will be allowed to do. All power has not been given to War. He has not received the commission to go forth and conquer. His commission is to win by fear those who refuse to be won by love. But to trembling man he looks a mighty king as he sweeps across earth's anxious face and crushes beneath his horse's hooves as many again as his hungry sword consumes. It has been given him to take peace from the earth (Apoc. 6, 4), to move brother to the death of brother in a frenzy of fear and hate. "And the rest of the men, who were not slain . . . did not do penance from the works of their hands . . ." (Apoc. 9, 20).

The Lamb breaks yet another seal, and behold a black horse comes forth on the earth, and his rider, Famine, bears a pair of scales in his hand (Apoc. 6, 5). "And there followed hail and fire . . . and it was cast upon the earth, and the third part of the earth was burnt up, and the third part of the trees was burnt up, and all green grass was burnt up" (Apoc. 8, 7). And a great cry went up from the earth, the cry of starving multitudes, the cry of the victims of man's abuse of the earth which God had given him as his portion, the cry of the little ones who turn to their parents and they have no bread to give them. Yet "the rest of the men did not do penance from the works of their hands."

The Lamb breaks the fourth seal and the last rider appears. He is death, and hell follows him (Apoc. 6, 8). And power was given to him "over the four parts of the earth, to kill with sword, with famine, and with death" (6, 8). He rides a pale horse, a horse that strikes the beholders with dismay. He follows the path of the two who have preceded him. Whither war and famine lead he comes after, silent, relentless, snatching his victim noiselessly from under the hooves of the horse of War or from the blighting shadow of Famine's scales. He has his own army, too ; Plague and Pestilence are their leaders. To them has been given the power to make the air fetid and the running waters foul (cf. Apoc. 8, 11), to conjure up vapours in which the pale horse may lurk and its rider exult. "And the rest of the men, who were not slain by these plagues did not do penance from the works of their hands. . . ."

In the midst of these trials the kingdom of God on earth remains, afflicted, questioning, trusting. It appears as it were a woman who brings forth a man-child, Jesus the Saviour, Who will rule all nations (Apoc. 12). But for the moment she is assailed by the dragon, who makes war against the rest of her seed, against them who keep the commandments of God. Or again it appears as two witnesses, testifying on earth to the Lamb and to the King Eternal, against whom the beast makes war, and over whom he even seems to triumph (Apoc. 11). And the anxious questioning of the members of God's kingdom on earth is balanced by the amazement in which the Kingdom glorious and triumphant in Heaven regards the patience and mercy with which the Almighty treats His puny foes. So that they cry with a loud voice "How long, O Lord (holy and true) dost thou not judge and revenge our blood on them that dwell on the earth ? . . . and it was said to them that they should rest for a little time, till their fellow servants, and their brethren, who are to be slain, even as they, should be filled up " (6, 10-11). The patient God bids them wait. Their hour will come, but there are many yet on earth who must serve in His kingdom and suffer from His enemies. He bids them wait, because He too can wait. He never ceases to be King ; no rider ever really conquers except He Whom He sent forth on the white horse. The earth is the Lord's and all the fulness thereof. The Lord therefore can never be anxious, never be moved to haste. Anxiety and haste are the characteristics of him who doubts his power. But the Lord is Omnipotent. His very enemies have the power to rage against Him only because He has, in His wisdom, thought well not to withdraw it from them. They can never escape the limits He has willed to impose to their seeming triumph. They have their day and their little while of dire pageantry ; but their rule and their kingship is never true. God has merely slackened the strings of their puppet show, leaving them free to gesticulate as their folly will inspire. He has reserved to Himself a day when He will tighten the strings and gather in His puppets, and the evil will be set apart for eternal pain.

Afflicted though God's Kingdom on earth may be, it is glorious beyond the power of man to conceive. Looking at it with the eyes of the visionary St. John we see it as " a great multitude which no man could number, of all nations, and tribes, and peoples, and tongues, standing before the throne, and in the sight of the Lamb " (7, 9). The just, more numerous than we would dare believe, stand, even while here on earth, in the sight of the Lamb their King. They always serve in the royal presence. The enemies of the Kingdom, too, stand in the sight of their impotent monarch, Satan. They serve beneath the eye of him who rebelled and is now lost. They serve in the fell presence of him who sees what they too cannot but believe from time to time—that the pale horse is already on their track, and that hell follows him. But they who serve in humility and love are drawn up beneath the eyes of a King Who has Himself been victorious and Whose power is theirs to call upon at will. They do not fear death. They can conquer death as He did ; make their acceptance of death's coming the coping stone of the structure of their lives. And if they can conquer death there is no foe they need fear, for death is the sharpest weapon in the whole armoury of their enemies. They pass through great tribulation ; but they pass as its masters. It is in the hands of God, no less than they, and its power over them is limited both by the mercy of God and by the efficacy of the prayers of the saints.

Looking now once more at God's kingdom on earth, we begin to see some ray of the brightness of its glory. Considered even as an earthly institution it is royal. It stands for ever, though sword and famine and death ravage nations. It stands while empires fall. It stands while false teachers come, and lead many astray, and then perish, themselves victims of the death over which they did not learn to triumph through the cross. Power of arm, power of steel, power of intellect, power of fanaticism—all have been ranged against the Church of God, but she remains unshaken. If to-day it be the lot of her children, on whatever part of the earth's surface, to suffer, they should suffer with the proud consciousness that they do so as members of a kingdom that has never been conquered and never will. They are not the champions of a wind-inflated state which awaits the inevitable and fatal prick. They are not the followers of a new-fangled school of folly which has no higher recommendation than that its worthlessness has not yet been demonstrated. They are not the highly-strung neurotics of our false mysticisms, who live in a ferment, and mistake fear of doing wrong for love of doing right. They are the representatives of what, judged even by earthly standards, is the greatest of earth's institutions. They enter every struggle as possessors of the proudest title to man's respect. Whoever assails them has first of all to prove that he is worthy to do so. No matter who he may be, he comes as a parvenu, as an upstart, as a hot-head, a philistine, an ignoramus. He may do the world a certain amount of harm ; he can never do it good while he opposes God's kingdom. He will last a while, may even outlive those members of the Kingdom who were most active in opposing him. But he will not outlive the Kingdom itself. He is no more than one of the barbarians of God's universe. He came from outer darkness, and the light blinding him, he hated it. He will be thrust back whence he came. And this time there will be no return.

See now that greatest of earthly struggles, Church persecuted by State, reach its conclusion. The Church has triumphed once more. The state that challenged her has fallen, though her fall, however terrible, will not be enough to dissuade others from attempting what she found impossible. " Babylon the great is fallen " (Apoc. 18, 2 *sqq.*). Her sins have at length reached unto heaven. At length has God remembered the countless list of her iniquities. She had seated herself on a throne as if she were truly a queen, and said she would never taste sorrow. Princes and people crowded to her, to rejoice in her strength and her riches. Merchants were made rich by ministering to her needs, forgetful of the poor, forgetful of justice, forgetful of God. But in one day have her plagues come upon her, and God who is strong has judged her. She is fallen, fallen. Her ruin has engulfed the mad ones who came uncalled to her courts, the rich merchants who lived on her pride and greed. " And the kings of the earth . . . who have lived in delicacies with her, shall weep, and bewail themselves over her, when they shall see the smoke of her burning : Standing afar off for fear of her torments. . . . And the merchants of the earth shall weep, and mourn over her : for no man shall buy their merchandise any more. . . . The merchants . . . who were made rich shall stand afar off from her, for fear of her torments, weeping and mourning, And saying : Alas ! alas ! that great city, which was clothed with fine linen, and purple, and scarlet, and was gilt with gold, and precious stones, and pearls. For in one hour are so great riches come to nought. . . . " (Apoc. 18, 9 *sqq.*). Babylon has fallen ; but the Church lives on. Babylon will be succeeded by Babylon. But they will all fall ; and their ruin will be the ruin also of all who trusted in them. The world will refuse obstinately to learn the lesson her fall should drive home. The hope of destroying the Church of God with her uncompromising opposition to the schemes of human pride, springs eternally in the breast of sinful man. Think of the moth that singes its wings first and then flies headlong into the flame, and you have a picture of the world's antagonism to God's kingdom. It matters little how many kingdoms have fallen in the past, it matters little how great the storms the Church has weathered, each new kingdom thinks that it will surely survive, and that the storm it is able to raise will sweep triumphantly over the barque of Peter. Mad hope ! The Lamb is with His Church. She is immortal. She was made catholic by her Founder, and catholic she will remain to the end of time. She will always cover earth's globe : at one time less in one place, at another less where before she was more powerful—that cannot be denied. But she cannot be rooted out. She is royally indifferent to what man may attempt. Her vocation is secure ; his is not. He cannot take from her what God has given into her hands. And by opposing her he will merely cut himself away from the one sure refuge in this passing vale of tears. The church is all powerful in the strength and patience of Christ. While there remain to her children who know how to suffer—and there will always be such— God will see that they also be not lacking her who know how to fight. Nail her to the cross and you make her victory sure. There is but one weapon she need fear ; the weapon of an alliance promoted by the world. Were the Church to meet the world half way she would be already defeated ; while she opposes the world she is by that very fact victorious. But she will never join forces with the world ; of that we need have no fear. Were she of but human origin she would certainly do so. She is however of God, and Jesus has prayed for her that she fail not. She will remain then, ever a city placed on a mountain-top, ever glorious and resplendent. Her beauty, doubtless, is within ; but it shines forth as well. She stands upon our earth, a queen alone among a rabble.

Let us look once more at the kingdom of God on earth. It embraces a countless multitude who serve in the sight of the throne and of the Lamb. They seemed at first sight to be at the mercy of the world, to be tossed and battered by its waves, to have no course of their own, but only that determined for them by the blind strength and fury of their enemies. But looking more intently we see that the Lamb is with them. He guides them. The fiercest storms never separate them from Him. They can be cast just as far as He sees will be to their eternal good, and no created power can force them an inch further from their path ; no created power, in fact, can force them from their path to any extent whatever, for their path is wherever the Lamb leads them and allows them to be driven and nowhere else—it is no mathematical line of material progress, but a spiritual one which cuts across the boundaries of more than one of life's vicissitudes. Along this path the Lamb leads them to the goal of the waters of life. There God shall wipe away all tears from their eyes " and death shall be no more, nor mourning, nor crying, nor sorrow shall be any more " (21, 4). God's Kingdom never deviates from the path leading to its great goal. The universe may or may not be chaotic, but the Kingdom of God within it is order. It threads its unwavering way through the maze of empires' rise and fall. It feels the touch of its King's hand, and it sees afar off the brightness of the court to which He leads it. It strives onward therefore, not as one beating the air, not as one left alone in a dark and trackless waste. But it strives for a crown of which it knows, and toils with a trust God has made to be founded.

God has determined that a day will come when to the whole world will be revealed the reality of His throne and the true nature of man's history. Then will the heavens, which hide Him from our view, depart as a book folded up (6, 14 *sqq.*) and the King of kings will appear in the full view of mankind, the joy of them who have served Him, the terror of His enemies. It will be the great and final vindication of His Kingdom. They who have opposed it will be gathered before Him, confused by the inner realization of their miserable failure and the clear vision of the triumph of the Church they thought to have conquered. " And the kings of the earth, and the princes, and the tribunes, and the rich, and the strong, and every bondman, and every freeman, hid themselves in the dens and in the rocks of the mountains : And they say to the mountains and the rocks : Fall upon us, and hide us from the face of him that sitteth upon the throne, and from the wrath of the Lamb : For the day of their wrath is come, and who shall be able to stand ? " (Apoc. 6, 15-17). They, certainly, shall not stand who are rich only in the treasures that the moth consumes, and that time, the greatest of all thieves, can break through and steal. God will be truly terrible in their eyes— terrible without being harsh. If it is ever possible to speak of a relentless inevitability in the fate of man it is in connection with that dread moment of his judgment. He will come before God, and his own soul will cry out to him what his judgment must necessarily be. There will be no escape from that judgment the soul will pass upon itself. Nothing defiled can enter heaven —that truth, so obscure to us now, will be as clear, as evident, then, as that the soul itself is clean or defiled. There will be no second hope, deluding oneself into the belief that God's judgment may be different from what we have reason to expect. We shall see what we are, and in that vision will be written the sentence of the great Judge. The Lamb will be seated on the right hand of the Father to bring to their eternal home the souls He guided through the storms of life. All will stand before Him : " And I saw the dead, great and small, standing in the presence of the throne . . . and the dead were judged by those things which were written in the books, according to their works. And the sea gave up the dead that were in it, and death and hell gave up their dead that were in them ; and they were judged everyone according to their works " (Apoc. 20, 12-13). He will know His subjects, and they will know Him. He is still their king. And now He has led them to the very threshold of the kingdom. Now for the first time do they see that the path of the Church was ever sure, that her feet never strayed from the narrow way that leads from death to life. All their doubts will be removed. Her defeats will be seen as victories. We shall see then in whom of her members she really lived. Some there were who fell away from her. But she lived on ; it was they who died. Others there were who proved faithful to the end. In them she continued to live ; in them she realized to the letter the promise of her indefectibility. And now they hear the words of their King : " Come, ye blessed of my Father, possess you the kingdom prepared for you from the foundation of the world " (Mt. 25, 34). The hour of the great triumph has drawn near. The souls of the just are now in the hands of God, and malice has no longer power to harm them. In the eyes of fools they had seemed to perish, and their end was, as it were, without honour. But now they are at rest. They have entered into their Kingdom. They have served a little while in the absence of their royal Master, and He on His return has invited them into the joy of their Lord. Death shall be no more for them, nor weeping, nor sadness. For the time of trial has passed away, and God has welcomed them to the gladness of His eternal peace.

The judgment is over. " And I John saw the holy city, the new Jerusalem, coming down out of heaven from God prepared as a bride adorned for her husband " (Apoc. 21, 2). The Church was always the spouse of Christ ; she was always His kingdom. But now, for the first time, is she truly adorned as befits her Divine King. She is now holy and immaculate, without spot or wrinkle ; she is all fair and there is no spot in her. She is the kingdom, the city of God. She is a city that has no need of sun or moon to shine upon her ; for the glory of the Lord God lights her up, and the Lamb is the lamp of her brightness (cf. Apoc. 21, 23 sqq.). Into her throng the nations of the earth, rejoicing in her splendour ; and they who were kings of the earth are proud to be counted among her citizens. There is no night in that city, but an eternal day ; there is no sorrow there, but eternal joy ; there is no strife there, but eternal peace.

She is a city built of living stones, that once were souls wending their way to eternity. They are chosen stones, hammered and polished on earth by suffering to fit them for their destined place. High that city rises above the very stars; but with a peaceful loftiness; not with the straining eminence of the cities of men. Her ways are wide, her gates are open; there is nothing narrow, nothing mean, nothing sparing or stinted in her. And along her ways, and out of her gates there streams the light of the Godhead. She is a city, it is true, a Kingdom—and in her midst there sit enthroned the Father and the Lamb—but she is no less a living and a loving spouse; a living mirror transformed into the Light that shines upon her; a living robe of glory to clothe her King; a living crown to place upon His head. She is, before all else, living: living as never before; living with the participated life of God Himself; living a life from which pain and death are forever excluded. She has been led by Jesus to the Fountain of the waters of life, and from It she may drink unceasingly. Life eternal is hers now, life ever young, ever undiminished. Pain and sorrow and the former things are all passed away. God Himself has wiped all tears from her eyes, and she is free to feast them on the beauty of His face.

*　　*　　*　　*

It is the final triumph of the Kingdom and of the King. Jesus has brought His people to the Father's throne and presents them there, holy and acceptable. They are His conquest. He has snatched them from the world, won them from the power of Satan. But not for Himself. All that He has suffered and done was inspired by His love of the Father and by His intense desire that that Father might receive from man that tribute of glory in which His supreme Kingship over His universe is accepted. Jesus has been a King and a Leader. But He was our King, not that we might have None other, but that by His rule in us we might be led to submission to the King of ages; He was our leader that He might bring us not to Himself only—for He is the Way, not the goal of life—but to the Father, at once the Fount from which our being flowed forth, and the deep Sea into which we fall and find our rest. That He is the Way and the only Way is now apparent. For they who have trodden paths other than His are lost ; they who have followed Him through life are now with God. He has been vindicated in His claim to be King and Way. All things and all men have been submitted to Him ; some as His debtors for the happiness they enjoy, some as terrible proofs of the folly of refusing to bear His mild yoke. And now that all things are made subject to Him " then the Son also Himself shall be subject unto him that put all things under him, that God may be all in all " (1 Cor. 15, 28). He has led us to the Father, and the Father's we now are. God Himself in Person wipes all tears from our eyes, and fills us with the vision of peace.

While we struggle with the Church on life's battlefield, we fight beneath God as a King we do not see. The face of God is hidden from us who serve Him on earth. He rules us by faith, and not by vision. Jesus alone can be seen by us ; seen in His Gospel ; seen in prayer ; seen in the doctrine and guidance of His Church. The reason for this is that while we live our mortal life we can see only what is communicated to us by the channels of the senses ; what is purely spiritual cannot be seen, but only believed. Now Jesus had a body of flesh and blood. He could therefore be seen ; His voice could be heard with the bodily sense of hearing. But not only could He be seen by those who were His contemporaries in the historical sense of the term ; what is more, He remains always in some way a Person Who can be known by way of the senses. We can picture to ourselves, on the basis of what the Gospels tell us, the kind His bodily presence must have been ; we can, by a slight effort of our imaginations, hear His voice commanding us. And, though it be faith which tells us that it is He Who speaks and commands in His Church to-day, the voice of the Church is itself also one that sounds in the ears of flesh ; the message may be spiritual but the words conveying it are material. Thus our human lives are ruled by Jesus revealed by faith in forms of sense, and we have no knowledge of the Father—except it be in rare moments of mystical prayer— other than that which is by way of His Incarnate Son. In heaven, however, we are ruled no longer by faith ; in heaven we are ruled by vision. God Himself is our King immediately. We see God as He is, and in that vision we are made the willing captives of His beauty. There is no need now to draw us to Him by the cords of Adam, by the winning grace of His beauty in human form. Hitherto we were incapable of appreciating His excellence. Now at length do we see Him without shadow, without incomprehension, without the dulling weight of an unresponsive body. We see Him and we fly to Him ; for that it is which being ruled by Him means. We are locked eternally in the embrace of our King and our Father. Jesus remains a King ; for it is He Who has brought us to the great white throne. But God rules us now, speaking in His own voice. No longer does He tell us that He will be found in His Beloved Son. He is revealed now in His own self. We have loved and served Him. Now is the time of reward. And our reward is worthy of Him we served. It is nothing less than the vision of our King's face, and the sound of His voice thrilling us to pride and love : " Well done, thou good and faithful servant."